TOWARDS FREEDOM

The African-Canadian Experience

Ken Alexander
and
Avis Glaze

UMBRELLA PRESS

Toronto

Dedication

To Sharyn and Marcus for their patience and devotions.

TOWARDS FREEDOM: *The African-Canadian Experience*

Publisher:	Kenneth H. Pearson
Editor:	Olive Koyama
Artist:	Julie LoTauro
Index:	Edna Barker
Design:	Ron & Ron Design and Photography
Cover Design and Production:	Ron & Ron Design and Photography
Consultants:	Dr. Sheldon Taylor, Rita Cox, Jennifer Walcott,
	Dr. Donald K. Gordon, Archie Alleyne

Grateful acknowledgement is made for the kind permission to reproduce the following: to Louise Bennett for her poem, "Colonization In Reverse," from *Selected Poems;* to R. Bruce Shepard for the material from *Deemed Unsuitable;* and to Frontier College for the Bradwin Address by Rubin "Hurricane" Carter.

The authors of *Towards Freedom* have been supported by a $5,000 writing grant from the Black Business and Professional Association. In return, the Publisher, Umbrella Press, has agreed to donate $1.00 from each and every trade sale made to the general public to the Association's excellent Harry Jerome Scholarship Program. This agreement has not altered the price of the book.

Canadian Catalguing in Publication Data

Alexander, Ken
Towards freedom: the African-Canadian experience
Includes bibliographical references and index.
ISBN 1-895642-20-5
1. Black Canadians - History.* I. Glaze, Avis. II.   Title.

FC106.B6A4 1996   971.004'96   C96-930157-X
F1035.N3A4 1996

The Publisher acknowledges the assistance of the Multicultural Program of the Department of Canadian Heritage.

A *kennyp* Publication

Manufactured in Canada

Publisher

UMBRELLA PRESS
56 Rivercourt Blvd.
Toronto, ON. M4J 3A4
Telephone: 416 696.6665
Fax 416 696.9189

Contents

Preface

> Isn't it fascinating to realize that no image, no form, not even a shade or color, "exists" on its own; that among everything that's visually observable we can refer only to relationships and to contrasts?

> – M. C. Escher, 1951.

Though sight is a primary human function, there are many ways of seeing. Among people, relationships and contrasts are viewed differently. How do non-blacks see black people? Do they contrast them with whites? How do blacks see themselves and others? Is there uniformity to these visions? To what degree do media (radio, television, movies, newspapers, magazines, music videos) influence perceptions? How do students look at their schools? Is there a difference, here, between black and white? Must readers "see themselves" in books for meaningful learning to occur?

On this last question, most educators agree that they must. They further agree, given the global village which is our world, that seeing positive curricula portrayals of others is equally important. We have written *Towards Freedom* partly for these reasons. It is intended both for high school students *and* the general reader.

Some people have asked, "Why, in this screen-addicted age, write a book?" They raise an interesting point. Everywhere, it seems, book reading is in retreat, and many are prophesying the end of "Gutenberg's galaxy." The traditional school, an outgrowth–as Neil Postman argues–of the printing press, is to some futurists an anachronism. What need have we of books, teachers, principals, classrooms, custodians, entire physical plants, and all other costly expenditures meted out simply to bring people together, when "students" can, on a typical Monday morning, have their week's work pop up, like breakfast toast, on a home computer screen? Of course, such schools, with "teachers" accessible via E-mail and other computer technology, already exist.

To write a book today, then, one must value book reading, delayed gratification, conception over perception, and slowing down. To write a book for schools, one must believe in institutions where people meet in mind *and* body. To write a history book one must appreciate the power of antecedent realities, the laws of cause and effect, and worry that the current de-contextualization of information–the "news from nowhere"–is leading to a psychological and social existence dominated by a perpetual present. If the end of history has arrived or is on the horizon, it is because our collective consciousness has become ahistorical. However, while we forget, the world itself, as events constantly remind us, remains rooted in history.

Indeed, the old adage is true: *those who do not know their history are doomed to repeat it.* Thus, we must engage in more history learning, not less. It is equally important that we read history from alternative perspectives; for by studying difference, we learn about ourselves. *Towards Freedom* attempts two things: one, as with "contribution history" (biographies, chronicles of great achievements, etc.), to shed light on great but largely forgotten people and their deeds; two, to tell the story of Canadian nation-building and the drive for a distinct democracy from a black perspective.

Though often victimized, blacks in Canada have rarely assumed a "victim status." *Towards Freedom* elucidates the story of the black struggle for fairness and justice in Canadian society. It is a quest which began four hundred years ago, and has played a significant role in shaping Canada's democracy. Finally, this book hopes to contribute to the development of historical consciousness in people young and old, black and non-black, and to "seeing black" in a positive light. Like all narratives, it has shortcomings, gaps, oversights, and opinions that should be argued. Like all narratives, it requires a response to its call, a jazz audience to make it grow.

Acknowledgements

Towards Freedom would not have been possible without the assistance and determination of many. It is part of a grass-roots tradition which has kept black issues and black concerns on the table and part of our national conversation. The following is a list of people and associations involved. It is by no means complete, but brevity necessitates a shortened version of the truth. In this, there is a true lesson of history, and especially of history writing.

These are difficult times. Budgets are being slashed, and people are being asked to do more with less. The Black Business and Professional Association stepped into the breach and provided us with a $5,000.00 writing grant. This money allowed the authors to pay bills directly related to writing *Towards Freedom*. In return, one dollar from each trade sale of the book to the general public is being donated to the Association's excellent Harry Jerome Scholarship Program. This represents the kind of partnership which often turn dreams into realities. For your support, initiative, and dedication to recognizing black achievement, thank you.

Many other associations helped make *Towards Freedom* a reality. The Ontario Black History Society, Black Cultural Centre of Nova Scotia, Congress of Black Women of Canada, Black Educators Working Group of Ontario, Robert Upshaw and the Black Learners Advisory Committee of Nova Scotia, Everton Cummings and the Jamaican-Canadian Association, Harambee Centres Canada, and the National Council of Black Educators of Canada, gave freely their time, energy, and support. Thank you all for your dedication and superb work. Also, for their resourcefulness, knowledge, and assistance in gathering information, we thank Leonard and Gwen Johnston of the Third World Bookstore, and Michael deGale of Perception II.

For their encouragement and invaluable comments, principal thanks go to Rita Cox, Vincent D'Oyley, Harold Brathwaite, Jonathan Graham, Bev Salmon, Gare Joyce, Helen Taylor, Norm Gollert, Heather Mitchell, Harriet Sachs and Clayton Ruby, Bob MacAulay, Doug Bell, Bruce and Jennifer Hutchison, Lloyd McKell, Amah Harris, Carl James, Isaac Saney, Don Rooke,

Archie Alleyne, Olive Koyama, Devon Hanson, Sheila Hoyte, Marllyn Chang, Erica Phillips, Mark Evans, Ron Rochon, Lloyd Scheirer, Hari Lalla, Jennifer Walcott, Austin Clarke, Mairuth Sarsfield and Sheldon Taylor. Also, to history consultants Allan Hux, Dennis Gerrard, Jose Fernandes, Carl Hogg, Dick Roberts, Frank Taylor, and the many others we have grown to know and admire, thank you.

For reviewing the manuscript and for exquisite, professional, and detailed suggestions, this book owes much to Professor Donald K. Gordon. At a time when we were at a low ebb, his final review lifted our spirits and gave us the direction necessary to fill in the missing pieces. To Sheldon Taylor, Almeta Speaks, Rubin "Hurricane" Carter, Rita Cox, Charles Alexander, Jonathan Graham, John O'Leary, Debbie Seed, Abe Langdon, Sharyn Langdon, Alex Shenfield, and Jerry Lazare, for your reading of the manuscript and critical comments which followed, we are eternally indebted. To Student Critics Michael Brown, Carolyn and Katie MacDonald, Wendy Davis, Thomas Seed, Trevor Lewis, Sandra Fulford, Michelle Khan, and Linda Pierre-Jerome, your insights on this and other projects have had a direct impact. Furthermore, your enthusiasm, idealism, and dedication to excellence serves as a vivid reminder of young people's potential.

To the students of Westwood Secondary School (Mississauga, Ontario) who "seized the moment" and compelled the school to offer a full-credit black history and culture course; to Michael Bascoe and others who ensured that the course remained focused, academically rigorous, and that it blend racial uplift with history; and, to the Westwood basketball program for reciprocating to positive reforms by raising $10,000 for the school's computer laboratory, thank you.

It would be wrong not to acknowledge here the work of black Canadian artists, past and present. Though not credited enough, the elevated resonances of your art, poetry, prose, storytelling, music, dance, and films have been with us throughout. Mostly, it is your determination to "put your stuff out there" and to establish your voice, which has provided inspiration. From south of the border, *Towards Freedom* owes much to Carter G. Woodson's brilliant essay *The Mis-Education of the Negro* and to the visionary educational theories of Neil Postman.

To my wife, Sharyn, "thank you" is not enough. To say that *Towards Freedom* would not have been possible without you is both obvious and too understated. Your love, patience, and resolve made this book possible. To my son, Marcus, in your own idiosyncratic way you too have helped bring *Towards Freedom* to fruition. Daddy will now have more time to spend with you.

To our publisher, Ken Pearson, "thank you" is also not enough. Ken's commitment to publishing books on black Canadian history is well-known and appreciated across the country. *Towards Freedom* owes much to his dedication and courage. Sadly, in March, 1996, Ken's daughter Tracey lost her battle with cancer. She is survived by her parents, husband, two young daughters, and our thoughts. Tracey knew how important this book was to Ken, who worked through the final critical stages in her memory.

Finally, to the readers of *Towards Freedom*, we thank you for supporting us in this endeavour, and hope that the book serves as a beginning, not an end.

Introduction

Freedom, justice, peace, and equality. To those engaged in the black struggle for human rights the meaning of these words is simple: there will be no freedom without justice, no justice without peace, and no peace without equality. They represent goals which historically blacks have fought to achieve. It has been an uphill fight.

There are signs that the battle is being won. Never before have so many black people occupied so many positions of responsibility. Black lawyers, doctors, scientists, and educators are increasingly making their mark. Examples of black achievement can now be found in every walk of life.

But the struggle continues. Canadian society is changing quickly. There is a growing movement away from support programs assisting marginalized groups, and towards American-style individualism and independence. Less and less will the state intervene to help those in need. Freedom, justice, peace, and equality can be taken away or re-defined in a manner which frustrates black aspiration. Many black youth, in particular, are not optimistic about the future.

Will Canada's black community split along the lines of its American counterpart? There, it seems, blacks are either part of an upwardly mobile middle class or a downwardly spiralling underclass. There, race relations have hardened. Many black Canadians point to recent events–the 1989 outbreak of racial violence at Cole Harbour District High School in Nova Scotia, the 1992 Yonge Street, Toronto demonstration turned riot, and numerous examples of blacks being shot by police–as indications that freedom, justice, peace, and equality are dreams, not realities. A close reading of black newspapers suggests that many recent immigrants are turning their backs on Canada and going home.

In 1989, at Cole Harbour District High School in Nova Scotia, a fight between one black and one white student escalated into a battle involving 50 black and white youths. The event attracted national media attention and numerous articles portrayed it as a race riot, a situation out of control. Canadians claimed to be shocked by the violence. For Nova Scotian black activists, however, it confirmed a long-held belief: blacks were not free from racism, and whites were not yet free of prejudice. Racial tensions simmered just beneath the surface.

Black Nova Scotians mobilized around the issue of unequal educational opportunities. The Black Learners Advisory Committee (BLAC), after thorough research, in-depth consultation with community groups, and analyses of programs around the world, produced a report which could serve as a blueprint for positive change for black students across Canada. Nova Scotia's Ministry of Education announced, in 1995, a $1 million fund to establish black history and culture courses, scholarships for black students to become teachers or scientists, an African-Canadian division in the Ministry, and strong anti-racist initiatives. Nova Scotia, which had segregated schools into the 1960s, is now on the vanguard of educational reform. The school system, which long contributed to the creation of a black underclass, is being reformulated to include, rather than exclude by means of inferior services for black students.

The Cole Harbour incident suggests that shock is sometimes a necessary condition for change. Do we, as a society, only respond to catastrophe? Do we ignore the slow ebb and flow of history and wait, with a feeling of impending doom, for moments of reactionary outrage which signal social collapse? If so, we wait at our peril. History rarely disappoints. It often fosters acts of chaos, violence, and hostility.

Another such moment occurred May 4, 1992, on Yonge Street in Toronto. What began as a peaceful march protesting the acquittal of Los Angeles police officers (LAPD) in the now infamous Rodney King case degenerated into rebellious looting and trashing of Yonge Street stores. A day-time demonstration devolved into a night-time riot. (The savage beating of King at the hands of Los Angeles police officers was captured on video. The scene was aired on television repeatedly, resulting in widespread condemnation and the ensuing trial.)

Press reports criticized the protest, but few provided thoughtful analyses. Lacking historical context, newspaper, radio, and television stories focused on black youth, particularly young black men, again describing the situation as out of control. A mixed-race crowd was portrayed as overwhelmingly black, and the reports decried this "American-style" violence north of the border.

As with Cole Harbour, the black press and black activists had long indicated that an understanding of black frustration

Yonge Street, Toronto–May 4, 1992
After this peaceful demonstration broke down into rebellious rioting and attacks against property, press reports overwhelmingly described a mixed-race crowd as "black."

would have suggested that this event was inevitable. To them, the Yonge Street riot was not an accident of history, a momentary aberration, or American in any way. Rather, it was consonant with Canadian history, and the role that blacks have played in it.

As with Cole Harbour, Canadian society awakened to the context for Yonge Street through after-the-fact reports. Chief among these was the *Report On Race Relations In Ontario, June 1992*, by Stephen Lewis, former Canadian ambassador to the United Nations. This report details the areas of discontent leading to the Yonge Street disturbance. While the LAPD trial verdict, and the May 2 Toronto police shooting death of a black suspected of drug trafficking, acted as catalysts, the root causes of black unrest were simmering frustration over perceived police mistreatment, discrimination in employment and housing, and a school system dominated by Eurocentric curricula.

Many black groups mobilized in response to Yonge Street. Activists like lawyer Charles Roach have made some progress weeding out racism in the justice system and in other areas. It is in education, perhaps, where the most tangible gains have been made. Ontario's Black Educators' Working Group (BEWG), in conjunction with local and national black organizations, intensified its lobbying efforts to bring about genuine change in the education system. As in Nova Scotia, those efforts have borne real fruit.

Early 1990s demonstrations in Nova Scotia challenged the notions of democracy and fairness.

Official government documents, such as the 1994 *For the Love of Learning: Report of the Royal Commission on Learning*, reflect many of the black community's recommendations vis-à-vis black educational needs. Strong anti-racist initiatives are being implemented. Courses in black history and culture are offered in a rapidly growing number of schools. "Demonstration schools" modelled on "best practices" for black students are being established. More black students are attending university, many on scholarships. However, a disproportionate number of black students are still falling through the cracks. Positive opportunities must be matched by positive outcomes.

The BEWG held its first meeting in 1990. At that time it focused on two issues: the "needs of those Black students of African heritage who are floundering in the education system;" and, "strategies to have institutions deal with problems identified up to 20 years ago." Indeed, for decades the essential issues have been the same. Over 20 years ago, black unrest over discrimination in education made headlines.

On January 10, 1968, six black West Indian students lodged a formal complaint of racism and incompetence against Sir George Williams University biology professor Perry Anderson. The students alleged that Anderson was consistently giving blacks poor marks on assignments and refused to address them by their first names, as he did white students. After receiving low marks on final examinations in Anderson's course, they complained again on April 29 and June 14. In December the university established a committee to investigate the charges and required Anderson to stop lecturing until their probe was completed.

Initially, the committee's composition was approved by both the students and the university. When two black professors resigned, the students requested that they be replaced by student-picked representatives. This request was rejected and the students, sensing a negative result and Anderson's reinstatement, boycotted the hearings.

On January 29, 1969, the protesters and roughly 200 supporters occupied the ninth-floor computer centre at the university's main building in downtown Montreal. Anticipating the university's reaction, they barricaded themselves in. Two weeks later, on February 11, under the threat of seizure by 150 riot-gear-equipped police, a 10–hour rampage of destruction broke out. Computers were smashed, thousands of university transcripts, registration forms, and computer tapes were thrown from the windows, and a fire was set. The police forced their way into the computer centre and arrested 97 students. Damage was estimated at $2 million. The February 12 *Globe and Mail* headline read, **"Students Destroy Computer."** In a 1995 interview, African-Canadian historian Dr. Sheldon Taylor said:

> The 1969 Sir George Williams incident was a response to the hegemony which served to thwart the interests and aspirations of black students. As such, it has its parallel with the 1992 Yonge Street riot in Toronto. Both events were watershed moments in Canadian history. Both exposed racism in Canada. Both engendered the fear that Canadian society was becoming Americanized. There is a

real difference, however. Whereas the 1969 incident was swept under the carpet, Yonge Street produced considerable soul searching on the part of both blacks and whites. Once the dust settled on Yonge Street, an imperative struck at the core of the Canadian soul: we must get our own house in order.

Many whites attributed the Sir George Williams uprising to the Black Power movement in the US. In the early 1970s the Royal Canadian Mounted Police (RCMP) launched investigations at universities across Canada to verify whether or not American Black Power advocates had crept north of the border. Black Canadians recognized this as a "blaming others" syndrome. To them the conditions for rebellion, at Sir George Williams and elsewhere, were made in Canada.

There was, nonetheless, considerable division among blacks over strategy. With this incident, the method of peaceful lobbying was questioned in the streets. To the dissident students, real change was not occurring fast enough. Breaking with a historical tradition of activism through coalition building, they took matters into their own hands. Some elders resented this 'immigrant-knows-best' attitude. The black community, engaged in a struggle for recognition and human rights, could ill-afford division within its ranks. Such division served the interests of the status quo.

Much can be learned about a society by how it responds to acts of protest. At Sir George Williams, Anderson was cleared of charges and reinstated. Disparate sentences were handed out to those involved; harsher ones for blacks. The "radicals" were barred from returning to classes in the fall of 1969. They were "out of line," and deserved to be treated harshly. The university felt vindicated. No real government action was taken and the incident has since faded from memory, given only footnote status in Canadian history books. The symptoms of black unrest, not the root causes, were dealt with.

Cole Harbour and Yonge Street have, arguably, produced a different result. Sensitive observers recognized in them the causes of black frustration, and that society must play an active role in breaking down the barriers of systemic discrimination. Evidence suggests that these events will not fade from memory.

They have served to unite black Canadians in common cause. Both incidents speak to the central issues: freedom, justice, peace, equality, and–increasingly–education. In our collective consciousness they expose cultural anxiety on two related fronts: loss of innocence, and the constant worry that Canada is becoming Americanized.

As a society we cherish our innocence, are relatively self-effacing, and celebrate our heroes and achievements in comparatively muted fashion. Not being America, with all its trials, tribulations, and disparities, has, until recently, been enough for the Canadian soul. Austin Clarke argues in *Public Enemies: Police Violence and Black Youth* (1992) that Canadian innocence is hollow, part of our well-crafted self-deception. Is there now a greater acceptance of this view and a stronger compulsion to act?

Black Canadians are facing a critical moment in their long history. Will the over-representation of blacks in jail and as school drop-outs be interpreted as the result of systemic racism and social inequity, or explained away as a black predisposition towards violence and intellectual mediocrity? How will, for instance, Ontario society react to the major conclusion of the Commission On Systemic Racism In The Ontario Justice System (1996) that the justice system is biased against blacks? The Sir George Williams uprising was a watershed moment for the black community. If Cole Harbour and Yonge Street go down in history as watershed moments, it will be due to the responses by Canadian society as a whole. History has given us a second chance. It might not give us a third.

Black Canadian leaders like Rosemary Brown, Sheldon Taylor, and Robert Upshaw maintain that blacks cannot know where they are going until they know where they have been. Like Malcolm X, past Trinidadian Prime Minister Dr. Eric Williams, and others, they are committed to the notion that knowing black history is a necessary condition for the achievement of freedom, justice, peace, and equality.

They are committed to another notion as well, that of cultural pluralism. In many respects the search for democracy represents the unifying theme in Canadian history. And, because of the determination to be different and to make this democracy distinctly Canadian, it is the theme around which Canada's most vital historical narrative is woven. Importantly, this quest has been, and continues to be, shared by all those who make Canada such a rich and diverse country. Indeed, much of Canada's strength lies in its capacity to invent and re-invent democratic institutions in a fashion which takes advantage of the evolving cultural diversity within its shores; its capacity to alter the course of history by redressing past wrongs and adapting to new realities; its capacity to complement a profound story from one group with a profound story from another. Recognizing, appreciating, and understanding the democracy and nation-building narratives of a plurality of peoples gives Canadians both a window into the past and a vision for the future.

Towards Freedom attempts to add to Canada's essential narrative the story of African Canadians. It is a remarkable story, and, like the quest for democracy itself, is replete with transcendent moments, triumphs, severe disappointments, hope, irony, gains, and losses. For centuries, in Canada and elsewhere, black skin was viewed as a badge of inferiority. Many maintain that it is still so considered, and that, as such, the historic drive for true democracy is yet to be realized. Overcoming this negative stigma has formed a large part of the African-Canadian narrative. If Canadians look closely at this narrative they will discover an important truth: the ingenuity, intelligence, talent, and determination of black people has, and continues, to help shape Canadian-style democracy.

How did black skin become a badge of inferiority? If, indeed, it continues to be so viewed, what must be done to overcome this prejudice? What answers can history provide? *Towards Freedom* hopes to contribute to the answering of these and other questions for all Canadians. In so doing, it hopes to add to the symphony of voices which make Canada what it is today, and what it could be in the future.

1
Critical Times

Not long ago "Coloured Town," "Cape Negro," and "Nigger Harbour" appeared as roadsigns on the Canadian landscape. The signs demarcated the "place" for blacks in Canada. There was nothing subtle about them. They were official signs, not unlike others indicating the entry point of towns and settlements. With the exception of Cape Negro, they have since been removed and are now part of a largely forgotten historical record.

Today, a growing number of unofficial markings are replacing the signs of old. The outside walls of black cultural associations, Jewish synagogues, Sikh temples, and Native Indian institutions are fertile places for hate-mongers to ply their trade. They are increasingly being desecrated with racist graffiti. There is nothing subtle about these hate messages either. Their intent is to intimidate, to drive out, and to create exclusion zones.

Such hate-motivated activity represents an angry backlash against the global village which our world has become, a preoccupation with race and notions of racial inferiority, and a belief that different people should remain distinct and apart. Historically, Canadians have been divided by religion, language, geography, income, and race. Has race or ethnicity now taken precedence as the greatest point of division? Is the shrinking of our world bringing racists out of the closet?

Racism is often situational. In the wrong place at the wrong time was Lawrence Martineau, the son of a Trinidadian cabinet-maker and his wife who came to Canada in 1970. In 1987, at Lakehead University in Thunder Bay, Ontario, he met Helen Mouskos. Helen and her parents had come to Canada in 1974 as refugees from Cyprus, Greece, and risen to respected upper-middle class status. Helen and Lawrence were both upwardly mobile students, typical of many first-generation immigrants.

Shortly after meeting, the young couple began dating, fell in love, and decided to marry. After school ended, they moved into Helen's family home in Hamilton, Ontario. Lawrence, introduced as a university friend looking for work, was warmly welcomed. However, when it became obvious that the relationship was much more than a simple friendship, he was forced to leave. Against her parents' protests, Helen continued seeing Lawrence. Eventually she moved into his apartment. "The union of his daughter with a black man threw Mouskos into a fury; a forbidden line had been crossed" (Peter Cheney, *Toronto Star*, "Pride and prejudice," Aug. 7, 1993).

Andreas Mouskos was so enraged by the prospect of his daughter marrying Martineau, he hired a hit man to kill him. Fortunately, local police uncovered the plan and Mouskos was arrested for conspiracy to commit first-degree murder. At his 1993 trial, he pleaded guilty and was sentenced to five years in prison.

Peter Cheney quotes Chris Diamantis, a fellow Greek and a man who had known Andreas Mouskos for years:

> He worked hard, he loved his family. A good, good man. It would be very, very hard for me to accept. I would say, "Honey, I do so much for you. I love you. But now you disappoint me. Here is your suitcase, you can no longer count on me." There's nothing wrong with an Italian guy, a black guy, or an English guy. They're all okay. But we're not supposed to live together.

Andreas Mouskos was not driven by hatred of black people. His neighbour and good friend, Vernon Flake, was a black man. Nonetheless, racism and the notion that people of different ethnic backgrounds are "not supposed to live together" were the principal causes of his criminal act. This notion is behind an alarming increase in race-based crime and anti-immigrant sentiment across Canada.

At a time when some Canadians are taking comfort in a general decrease in crime, Canadians of colour, gays and lesbians, and certain religious group members are under growing attack. As Rae Corelli (*Maclean's*, Aug. 14, 1995) states:

No one knows precisely how many Jews, blacks, Asians, native people, gays and lesbians are murdered, beaten, threatened or harassed–or have their homes, schools and places of worship vandalized–every year. But a confidential study commissioned by the federal justice department suggests that across a nation that has always prided itself on tolerance, there may be as many as 9,000 hate-inspired crimes annually–vastly more than are reported to police by fearful victims.

Hard data support reports of this upward trend. In 1993, 155 hate crimes were reported in Toronto. In 1994, this figure ballooned to 249. Similar increases have occurred in cities across Canada. According to University of Ottawa criminologist Julian Roberts, over sixty per cent of hate crimes are racially motivated, and it appears that black people are being disproportionately targetted.

In his seminal book *The Blacks in Canada: A History* (1971), Robin Winks describes the "moving targets" of

White supremacists gather in Alberta: tough economic times foster public resentment towards immigrants.

Canadian anti-black racism. Historically, Winks maintains, such racism assumed less obvious forms than in the US, especially in the South. Convention more than strictly upheld rules of law largely determined the black place north of the border. In most jurisdictions, certain shops, hotels, and restaurants refused to serve blacks; others, however, accepted their patronage.

Racism in Canada appeared to be site-specific, not the systemic form illustrated by, for instance, turn-of-the-century US Jim Crow segregation laws. These laws firmly prescribed where blacks in the South could and could not go, what they could and could not do. A strict colour line was encoded into law and supported by the white majority. While the impact of these laws was devastating, they served as stationary targets around which blacks, determined to re-define their place in America, could mobilize.

The absence of such total legal prescriptions made it more difficult for Canadian blacks to unite in common cause and to organize behind leaders with a national focus. Nonetheless, black Canadian activists recognized the difference as one of degree, not substance. After WW II, they began making a concerted effort to expose discrimination and, like their brethren south of the border, to fight for a colour-blind society.

Today, black leaders argue that police shootings, hate propaganda, the streaming of blacks into inferior educational programs, and differential treatment in all walks of life have brought anti-black discrimination out into the open. The job facing black activists has never been so clear, the challenge never so great.

Stories about "black crime" and underachievement in schools have become a constant in the popular press. Their sheer volume has led many to believe that blacks are inherently anti-social and/or that there is something inferior about the black intellect, especially that of males. Streaming black students into vocational programs is part of a long history of defining their place in Canada. The over-representation of blacks in sport and entertainment feeds the view that they are naturally inclined towards jumping and singing, and disinclined towards pursuits requiring higher-order thinking skills. Black achievement in business, politics, science, or education is too often credited to affirmative action, or considered an exception to the rule.

Examples of anti-black racism are constant reminders that there are still many rivers to cross. There is a danger that Canadians will become inured to negative stories involving blacks. To a large degree this has already happened in the US. There, the over-representation of blacks in federal and state penetentiaries and as school drop-outs is used by some ideologues as proof positive that blacks are inferior, predisposed to violence, that black underachievement is due to "pathologies" inherent in black culture, and that society can constructively do nothing to redress the situation. There, "black problems" are increasingly seen as a "black issue," not a wider societal concern.

"I am a Man" civil rights protest. This 1968 picture sums up the black civil rights movement in America. Is it equally representative of the black struggle in Canada?

The Doctrine of Racial Superiority

Discrimination based on race has existed since the beginning of human civilization. People of one kind have forever sought to differentiate themselves from others, and cultural chauvinism has usually walked in lockstep with a sense of superiority.

Feelings of supremacy led some peoples into battles, caused others to construct great civilizations, and still others to build institutions spreading their culture's influence. Hegemony, or the exercise of dominance by one state over others, has been, and still is, fundamental to human history.

Before the nineteenth century such dominance had rarely been justified on scientific grounds. Over one hundred years ago a dramatic shift occurred, and black people were its primary victims. The doctrine of race, widespread in Europe and the US in the mid-to-late nineteenth century, held that cultural differences were based on racial or biological characteristics. It attributed superiority to white races, somehow genetically programmed to be rulers; and inferiority to black or dark races, the darkest of whom were thought to be natural servants or followers.

Slavery and the era of European expansion around the world was explained, after the fact, as a natural process of evolution wherein the dominant and supposedly more intelligent white races ruled the darker and supposedly less intelligent. Intelligence was measured in terms of cranial capacity, with the northern European brain presented as the highest form. Science provided a rational justification for slavery, replacing the biblical curse of Ham and crude economics. Science proved the supremacy of northern European civilization.

The impact of this doctrine on blacks in Canada was immediate. Following the US Civil War (1861–1865), it provided a scientific justification for anti-black sentiments and restrictive immigration policies. Early race science buttressed the prejudice already existent in the colonies and gave credence to the view that if Canada, confederated in 1867, was to prosper, it must remain white.

In the 1850s blacks in British Columbia, Ontario, Quebec, and the Maritimes were making their mark, contributing directly to Canada's economic, social, and cultural well-being. This decade represents the pinnacle of black achievement in early Canada. In the following decade the pull to help their brethren in the Civil War caused some blacks to leave and fight on the side of the Union. The exodus continued after the Union victory, through Reconstruction (1865–1877), and beyond. Canadian history books list numerous external reasons for this mass

The Science of Race in a Nutshell

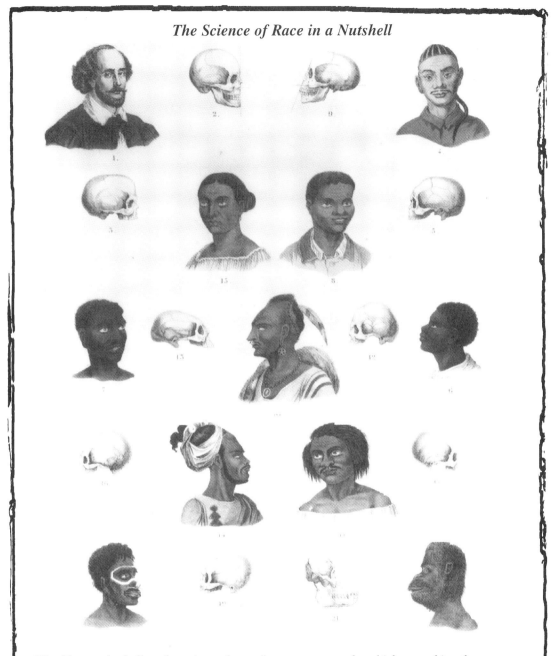

"Profiles and skulls of various "races" showing facial angles, from a European (top left) through various peoples to a "savage" African vis-à-vis an ape (bottom). A single plate suggesting evolution as well as hierarchy (1850)" (Pieterse, White on Black, 1992). Such racist portrayals were used as propaganda vehicles, reaching the person on the street through flyers, posters, and other advertisements. This practice continued through Hollywood's Tarzan depictions of the "dark continent" (and its peoples/animals) in need of taming and direction as provided by the white man.

migration south, the cold northern weather and reunification with family and friends being the most often cited explanations.

Certainly, the pull was important, but so too was the push.

Rather than building on pre-Confederation black success and achievement, through racist immigration policies Canada actively promoted black exclusion. After 1867, the Fathers of Confederation, facing the daunting challenge of settling the west and protecting the new nation from American encroachment, had a choice. Aware that immigration would create the future population, they chose white northern Europeans. Race science, holding that dark people could not integrate peacefully and on equal terms with whites, played no small part in their thinking.

At the Government House in Ottawa

His excellency in Council, in virtue of the provisions of Sub-section (c) of Section 38 of the Immigration Act, is pleased to Order and it is hereby Ordered as follows: For a period of one year from and after the date hereof the landing in Canada shall be and the same is prohibited of any immigrants belonging to the Negro race, which race is deemed unsuitable to the climate and requirements of Canada.

Prime Minister,
Sir Wilfrid Laurier,
Memorandum sent to the
Minister of the Interior,
August 15, 1911.

Race Versus Culture

Between 1900 and 1914 the Canadian economy grew at an unprecedented rate. It continued to steam ahead into the 1920s. Responding to the open-door immigration policy of 1896, white people from the US and Europe poured into Canada. They came in search of wealth and prosperity. By 1925, Canada's population had nearly doubled. Blacks from the Caribbean and the US, in contrast, were discouraged from entering. The campaign to keep them out was both vigorous and successful. The fact that all blacks were barred entry suggests that race and skin colour, not culture, was the determining factor. The same was not true for whites.

Most anthropologists reject race as a biological category. "There is no organizing principle by which you could put 5 billion people into so few categories in a way that would tell you anything important about humankind's diversity" (C. Loring Brace, University of Michigan, *Newsweek*, Feb. 13,

1995). The term "black," like the terms "white" or "Asian," is a misnomer. It casts a single identity over a plurality of people. It marks a marvellous diversity, a "mosaic" (to use a Canadian description), with a sameness that in reality does not exist. As Wolseley Anderson argues in *Caribbean Immigrants: A Socio-Demographic Profile (1993)*, it puts "Uncle Toms" and "Kunta Kintes" in the same category. In short, "black" is a leveller.

Given the fact that "black" is used to describe a range of skin colour from very light to very dark; physical features from short squat noses to long angular ones, thick lips to thin ones; and a sweep of behaviours too diverse to describe, one must conclude that it is born solely of convenience. But this convenient term is too often used as a synonym for backwardness and inferiority. It is tied to the history of black slavery common to New World countries.

The Myth Resurfaces

Race science has resurfaced and is gaining popular currency. So too, is the catch-all term "black" as a thinly veiled euphemism for "underachievement."

In the mid-twentieth century, especially after the dismantling of white supremacist Nazi Germany, race science became widely viewed as pseudo-science. It was exposed as based on prejudice and convenience. Historians successfully maintained that it was a sop to segregationists who could no longer rely on slavery to divide the races. However, though discredited, it did not perish. Today, politicians, culture critics, and talk-show hosts espouse the view that black underachievement is linked primarily to inherent genetic characteristics, and only secondarily to environmental conditions; and that, as a result, race-mixing should be curtailed.

This new version of an old theory holds or implies that there is something natural about the disproportionately high number of blacks in prison, among school drop-outs, and living in squalid ghettos. It is supported by University of Western Ontario professor Philipe Rushton and the authors of the controversial American text, *The Bell Curve*. These and other critics infer or directly proffer the view that blacks are not genetically predisposed towards tasks involving higher-order thinking skills. "Science" is once again attempting to prove that

"Black is…?"

The term "black" as it applies to people is a social construct, a product of history. As these pictures–taken of a group of students at Westwood Secondary School in Mississauga, Ontario–illustrate, among black people there is a variety of physical characteristics. In different regions of Africa many of these students would not be considered black. In other regions of the world (e.g. parts of India, Sri Lanka, Australia, Canada's north), many are considerably lighter than people of indigenous populations. "Black is…?" depends largely on historical and social circumstance.

hierarchical relationships are consonant with the laws of nature.

Most scientists agree that such a view is without foundation. They believe that the nineteenth-century use of Charles Darwin's theory of evolution to justify discriminatory practices against peoples of colour bastardized his key texts, *The Origin of Species* and *The Descent of Man*. They believe further that the high proportion of blacks in sports, entertainment, and prison has little to do with genetic predisposition, and much to do with environmental conditions. If blacks excel in sports and entertainment, it is because these are two areas into which they are streamed.

Nonetheless, the relatively muted voices of such scientists are not being heard, to the same degree, on North America's air-waves. Rather, with people clamouring for an easy explanation for black underachievement, the battle is being won by the per-petrators of racist stereotyping. The same argument used one hundred years ago to justify slavery, imperialism, segregation laws, and the rejection of all forms of inter-racial mixing, is now being used to justify discriminatory practices in present-day society.

Shattering the Myth in Black America

The word "underachievement" appears in quotation marks not because it is lifted from a scholarly text or government docu-ment, but because it is a loaded term not in accordance with the historical record.

In his excellent book *White on Black: Images of Africa and Blacks in Western Popular Culture (1992),* Jan Pieterse argues that "racial thinking developed not in spite of abolitionism but rather because of its success, and in response to the situation created by the questioning of the legal status of slavery." Indeed, after slavery's abolition there was a fear that black peo-ple would start to speak out and to succeed. A new rationaliza-tion to suppress their initiative became necessary.

There is a real possibility that the new science of race is gaining popular currency not because of black underachieve-ment, but rather because blacks have achieved too much. The backlash against affirmative action programs can be understood within this context. As one commentator said, "Goddamnit.

First, they take our jobs, and now they're moving into our neighbourhoods. Things have gone too far!"

On June 18, 1995, the *New York Times* printed an article entitled "Moving On Up: The Greening of America's Black Middle Class." The "green" refers not to the environment, but to money. In America money rules. It is the standard by which power, success, and intelligence are usually measured.

According to the article, in at least ten integrated American cities, the black median household income is greater than the white median household income. The comparison is based on data collected in 1989, a year in which black families in Carson, California, earned $53,424, and $50,385 in Southfield, Michigan. In the same year, white families earned $38,438 and $37,396 respectively.

America's black middle class buys significantly more books per capita than white middle class Americans. These blacks are committed life-long learners, and many return to university for upgrading or in pursuit of new degrees. Common threads bind black middle class Americans: most are married, roughly half have completed college, domestic responsibilities are shared, and both women and men work. This group shatters the myth that blacks underachieve in education and in other walks of life. The fact that so many of these families stay intact should also put to rest the notion that black men are biologically predisposed to polygyny and/or vagrancy.

There is a downside to the rise of the black middle class in America. As scores of blacks have launched headlong in pursuit of the American dream, others have fallen into deep poverty. The impoverished, ghettoized, and ill-educated black underclass

1. For young, college-educated two-earner married couples, income differentials between blacks and whites are negligible.
2. The number of black lawyers, doctors, and engineers has risen sharply as a result of increased access to education.
3. Almost as many black workers between the ages of 25 and 44 are college graduates as are high school dropouts. Just 20 years ago, there were five times as many high school dropouts as college graduates in the work force.
4. Just a generation ago, only 1 in 17 black families made the contemporary equivalent of $50,000 per year. In 1989, 1 in 7 did. From 1967 to 1989, this category expanded from 266,000 black families to over one million.
5. In 1970, only 1 in 20 of all young professionals was black; by 1990, the ratio was 1 in 12.

Source: *New York Times* (June 18, 1995).

has grown substantially in the last twenty years. Most of the victims are young black men, many of whom exhibit a psychological and social pathology of helplessness. This is the group most often documented in the popular press. This is the group that leads many to believe that blacks are inferior.

Good science recognizes data on both sides. That America's black community has bifurcated or split is the critical point. It suggests that environmental conditions (access to quality education, money, employment, equity, positive race relations, and housing) determine success. If American blacks fall into two distinct camps, the upwardly mobile and the downwardly spiralling, it must be due to opportunity and environment, and not genetic predisposition.

And What About Black Canada?

With some notable exceptions, for close to one hundred years (1860–1960) black Canadians lived in virtual exclusion from mainstream society. The depopulation of black Canada after 1865 and the restrictive immigration policies which followed, pushed the community to its lowest point. The heady days of the 1850s became a distant memory, overtaken by larger continental issues. No doubt, Canada would be a different country today had this "disappearance" not occurred.

Fortunately, black communities have since been rebuilt. This is as true in Canada as it is in the US or the West Indies. The rise of the Canadian black middle class has paralleled that of the US. Blacks from the West Indies, who began arriving here in large numbers after the immigration reforms of the 1960s, have contributed enormously to this burgeoning class. Professional blacks, both indigenous and Caribbean-born, can now be found in all walks of life. Black lawyers, doctors, engineers, architects, educators, writers, film directors, and business people, are all contributing to mainstream society. Black organizations, representing a myriad of interest groups, are established, activist, and lobby effectively for black communities.

Black people are sometimes described as North America's "metaphor." Their issues and concerns invariably lead to a questioning of society in general. Black intellectuals are keeping these questions on the front burner.

Interestingly, the rise of the Canadian black middle class has been accompanied by a dramatic growth in black scholarship. In the fall of 1994, the African Studies Association hosted a conference in Toronto. Attending were hundreds of black scholars from around the world. Canada was well represented. The growth of black scholarship will be accelerated by the Chair in Black Studies at Dalhousie University. As in the US, many Canadian black scholars use their positions on university campuses as platforms for social action and reform.

These positive developments have not exorcised old demons. Anti-black prejudice is alive and well in Canada, and popular press coverage concentrates overwhelmingly on the negative. But, arguably, whereas a large portion of the American black middle class has chosen to distance itself from black underprivilege by fleeing to the suburbs, Canadian counterparts remain committed to the struggle of freeing all of its people. This is a hotly debated issue, tied inextricably to our different histories and different notions as to the role of government in society, and the Canadian preoccupation with avoiding the worst of America.

History and the Colour Black in North America

For centuries the practice of divide and conquer as it applied to the trans-Atlantic slave trade achieved considerable results. Perhaps the most insidious of these results is the doctrine of racial inferiority. The stereotypical characterizations of black people as lacking initiative, dependent, unskilled, happy, sun-worshipping, and capable of work only in the service of others, is an outgrowth of slavery and viewing history through the filter of racism. That some young black people believe these stereotypes about themselves attests to the power of prejudice.

Today, in Canada and around the world, this prejudice is perpetuated by degrading and one-sided popular press imagery, too little meaningful contact between blacks and non-blacks, and institutionalized forms of anti-black discrimination. Nevertheless, as the history of slave resistance indicates, neither the whip nor the "softening" strategies used to suppress the black thirst for freedom and achievement ultimately succeeded.

If one considers the enslaved and penniless conditions under which blacks were brought to the New World, the segregation faced by "free blacks," and the obstacles facing contemporary black communities, the term "underachievement" is, at best, inappropriate. If one further considers the remarkable triumphs in overcoming externally imposed anti-black prejudices, the growing number of black people flourishing in all arenas, and the true black heroes of yesterday and today, "underachievement" can be relegated to the ash-can of history.

There is a popular belief that black history on this continent is *really an American thing*. The black fact in the US is a fundamental part of America's historical record, and sensitive contemporary critics describe current issues, problems, and accomplishments within the context of the total black experience in America. Analyses of the rise of the black middle class, black intellectualism, the black urban underclass, or black success in business, law, science, arts, sports and entertainment, invariably take readers back to slavery and/or the colour line of segregation. The history of these two phenomena reverberates in the American consciousness. The oft-repeated black sentiment that they *brought us here as slaves, but now, as free men and women, don't know what to do with us,* is one of America's most contentious and widely-debated issues.

Obscured under the US' dramatic history of slavery, slave revolts, the Great Negro Plot, David Walker, Sojourner Truth, Nat Turner, Frederick Douglass, Harriet Tubman, the Underground Railroad, the Civil War, the Emancipation Proclamation, Clara Brown, W.E.B. Du Bois, lynching, race riots, Jim Crow, NAACP, Marcus Garvey, Jesse Owens, Langston Hughes, Jackie Robinson, Rosa Parks, Martin Luther King, Jr., Selma, Thurgood Marshall, Brown vs. Board of Education, Black Power, Vietnam, Shirley Chisholm, Jesse Jackson, Clarence Thomas, Anita Hill, Rodney King, and O.J. Simpson, is the black fact in Canada. Blacks, too, have been in Canada since the beginning. But how much do we know about their struggle for equality, dignity, and respect? How much do we know about Canada's own colour line and what blacks have done and must do to overcome it?

While in the US the civil rights movement reached its apogee in the 1960s, its history dates back to the first slave rebellion. In a quieter and less dramatic manner, black Canadians of great distinction fought the same fight north of the border. Mattieu da Costa, Olivier Le Jeune, black Loyalists, Thomas Peters, Harriet Tubman, Josiah Henson, Samuel Ward, Mary Ann Shadd, the Victoria Rifle Corps, John Ware, Elijah McCoy, Black Oklahomans, the Jamaican Maroons, the Niagara Movement, George Dixon, Matthew A. Henson, Nova Scotia No. 2 Construction Battalion, the 93rd, 95th, and 97th black construction regiments, the Olivers, Sleeping Car Porters, Stanley Grizzle, Don Moore, Lenore Richardson, Harry Gairey, Dan Hill, Viola Desmond, Carrie Best, Howard McCurdy, Africvilleans, Kay Livingstone, Ferguson Jenkins, Leonard Brathwaite, Harry Jerome, Rosemary Brown, Emery Barnes, Rita Cox, Lincoln Alexander, Rella Braithwaite, Chief Justice Julius Alexander Isaac, Herb Carnegie, Rubin "Hurricane" Carter, Louise Bennett-Coverley, Bev Salmon, Carolyn Thomas, Clifton Joseph, Almeta Speaks, Burnley "Rocky" Jones, Abdi Mohamoud, Inez Elliston, Fil Fraser, Robert Upshaw, the Congress of Black Women of Canada, Sheldon Taylor, Lennox Farrell, Enid Lee, Alvin Curling, and others, all contributed, or contribute, to securing a free and democratic Canada for all its citizens.

History is of little use if it does not help us comprehend the present and enable us to project into the future. Why is it that, as a society, we seem so preoccupied with negative stories? Why is it that we know so little about the burgeoning black Canadian middle class? In *Racial Discrimination In Canada: The Black Experience* (1985), James Walker writes:

> Locked in poverty, denied the means of self-improvement the blacks suffered from an image of helplessness and lack of industry which in turn reinforced white stereotypes. Discrimination was fulfilling its own prescription. Traditions established in slavery, exacerbated by the haste and limited resources attending the Loyalist settlement, had resulted in a prescribed economic position for blacks which was reflected in their social status, and which fixed them at the lowest level of the class hierarchy. Their colour was a label announcing their inferior position.

He is describing how blacks were viewed in Ontario and the Maritimes over two hundred years ago. To what degree is this

Michael Conrad.

Male. Age 28.

Trafficking.

Armed Robbery.

Assault and Battery.

Extortion.

Rape.

Murder.

Apprehended

January 1994 by

Police Lieutenant

Joseph Cruthers,

shown here.

Urban Alliance
on Race Relations

Look again. Read again. *This Clio award-winning ad upsets conventional
beliefs through a powerful reversal of expectations.*

perception still true today? When white people see a black man driving a BMW or Mercedes Benz do they think, "Oh, he must be a lawyer or a doctor?"

If the Cole Harbour and Yonge Street incidents were decisive moments, they were such because Canadian society as a whole recognized that "black problems" were also its problems.

2
In on the Ground Floor

… just as the battle against slavery was being won by abolitionists, the war against racism was being lost. The Negro was legally freed by the Emancipation Act of 1833, but in the British mind he was still mentally, morally and physically a slave.

–Stepan, Nancy, Historian,
The idea of race in science:
Great Britain, 1800–1960.

The first black slave in Canada was a nameless six-year-old boy from Madagascar, Africa. He came in 1628 in the property of David Kirke, an English privateer conducting raids on the French colony of the St. Lawrence River. In 1632, he was baptized "Olivier LeJeune." At the age of sixteen he was set free. Olivier LeJeune died in 1654.

From this simple beginning black slavery in the French and English regimes of Canada-to-be grew into a vital social and economic institution. In New France slavery had been commonplace since the time of Champlain. Blacks from Caribbean plantations were bought and sold. Others came to New France during its period of active trade with Louisiana. By 1760, New France's black slave population totalled nearly 1,200.

Had early Canada developed a plantation-style economy thousands more slaves would have been imported. Climate and geography were unsuited to such a development, and thus slavery here took on a different form than in the US and the Caribbean. Canada's comparatively short growing season and harsh winters necessitated development of an indoor culture, and it was indoors that most slaves worked as free-labourers.

In well-to-do homes of Montreal and Quebec City black domestics washed clothes, cooked meals, ironed linen, and took care of children. Women and men toiled long hours doing jobs

*The first known black to set foot on Canadian soil was **Mattieu da Costa**. He arrived in 1605 with the French force of Pierre de Gua des Monts. Along with another black man, name unknown, who died of scurvy, da Costa helped found Port Royal in Nova Scotia. Given his membership in The Order of Good Cheer (Canada's first social club) and his job as a translator between French fur traders and Micmac Indians, it is unlikely that da Costa was a slave. His knowledge of the Micmac language and customs suggest that he may have been in Canada before 1605. The first black in Canada appears to have been a free nation-builder.*

about the house, though the lion's share fell to women. The total exclusion experienced by "field slaves" on the sugar and cotton plantations of the Caribbean and the southern US, was not inflicted on Canadian black domestic servants. On the surface their work seemed easier than picking cotton or working cane. However, they worked in isolation, without recourse to any community. They were alone, the lowest caste in an extremely hierarchical society. Loneliness drove some to madness, abuse drove others to flee. For slaves in New France the average age at death was 25. Though medical records were not kept, it can be safely assumed that most died from the combined forces of malnutrition and a lack of will to live.

A *de facto* colour line existed in early Canada. Black slaves were joined, as part of a servant class, by Indians. Many town-dwelling aristocrats and merchants preferred using Native Indians (called *panis*) captured in wars as domestics. By the standards of the day they were considered more exotic, and therefore preferable to have about the house. Also, in urban settings, separated from their tribes, they were believed to be more docile and less dangerous.

On the frontier the situation was quite different. Many French and English colonists preferred blacks to captured Indians for protecting fur-trading outposts and as heavy farm labourers. Blacks had nowhere to run to, no land or heritage in which to seek refuge.

Colonists from France, England, and the British colonies were certainly aware of the disastrous history of Indian slavery in the Caribbean and the US. Amerindians in both regions died by the millions in wars, from disease, and under slavery in the post-Columbus period. Blacks came to be preferred as slaves and American blacks came to know of no life outside slavery.

From 1628 to 1783 almost all black people in Canada were slaves. In 1685, the Code Noir became law in France. It established strict prohibitions against slaves marrying whites and carrying weapons. The Code gave guidance on the religious instruction of slaves, how they were to be treated in cases of theft or attempted escape, and allowed whites to take ownership of slave offspring. Though never officially proclaimed, slavery was legalized, under the spirit of the Code, in New France in 1705.

The celebrated case of Marie Joseph Angélique vividly depicts the degree of racial discrimination in New France. Angélique was a black slave who, after being informed that she was to be sold, was alleged to have set fire to her owner's house. The fire raged out of control, destroying nearly fifty Montreal houses. As Daniel Hill writes in *The Freedom Seekers* (1981):

> Angélique was arrested, convicted of arson, and sentenced to hang. A rope was tied around her neck, signs bearing the word "Incendiary" were fastened on her back and chest, and she was driven through the streets in a scavenger's cart. Worse was to come: she was tortured until she confessed her crime before a priest; then her hand was cut off and she was hanged in public.

Painting by François Beaucourt (1740-1794). As this painting illustrates, slavery was an accepted institution in New France. The model is said to have been Beaucourt's servant and, given the seductive nature of the painting, quite possibly his mistress.

This hideous event occurred in the spring of 1734. Would a non-black have suffered the same degree of humiliation and brutal violence for a crime against property? Only a person not accorded the status of human being could be so treated. The case against Angélique was never proven. The fire may have resulted from an accident. Clearly, her torture and hanging was intended as an object lesson. Blacks had to be taught their place.

Angélique's sacrifice was not in vain. Her case brought attention to the conditions under which most slaves lived. To some in the black community she was a martyr, and New France's ruling class displayed concern that her case could become a rallying point for black unrest. Many whites were outraged and, within a few short years, the torture of convicted slaves was outlawed.

Slavery and the British Regime

New France officially passed into British hands in 1763 as the Seven Years' War ended. For blacks, this change brought no perceptible change in conditions. Slaves continued to be nonpersons under the law. They were property and had no legal rights. Slaves were listed in wills and passed on to white sons and daughters, many of whom had established friendships with their servants. Under these conditions slaves could not be assured of kinder environments, the conventions of the time militating against such a result. They were sold and traded like any other piece of property.

Slave auctions were common, especially in Nova Scotia, and newspapers regularly advertised sales of skilled slaves. Some papers, like the *Montreal Gazette* and the *Nova Scotia Advertiser,* published notices of escaped slaves, offering sizable rewards for their recapture and return.

Absent from their condition of enslavement, however, was any racial justification. Colonists, being dependent on free-

Shackles (balls and chains) were used to prevent slaves from escaping when blacks were sold "down river," and as physical reminders of slaves' place in society.

labourers to work the fields, as tradesmen, and as house servants, recognized blacks as a servile economic class and accorded them access, albeit restricted, to services offered by church and state. Such access was deemed a privilege, not a right, and could be removed at the whim of slave owners. A slave's position was determined by economics and servitude, a legal category which held, at least on the surface, the promise of change and upward mobility.

Though early Canadian slavery had no official colour, most slaves were black. Some were directly imported from Africa, but the vast majority came, after "seasoning," from the southern colonies or the Caribbean. In these regions, slavery had long been an almost exclusively black condition. With the British conquest of New France in 1760 came a rapid increase in black slave importation to Canada and the gradual elimination of real distinctions between the rights of Canadian, American, or Caribbean slaves. In all three regions blacks were preferred to indentured European servants, who could fade into the general population. Black skin was a badge of slavery.

A dependency syndrome developed in the slave populations of all three regions. Whatever gains or advancements blacks made came within the context of the master/slave relationship. On a personal level, whether in the cane-field or the manor home, this relationship demanded "Yes Massa" responses. On a national level, colonies, especially single-crop ones, were equally dependent on the good graces of the motherland. No country more thoroughly and efficiently inculcated these forms of dependency than England, the overwhelming colonial power in North America.

Black Loyalists and Black Slaves in the Maritimes

Canada began to develop a reputation as a safe haven for blacks during the American War of Independence (1775–1783). To slaves or free blacks who joined their cause, the British promised land, freedom, and equal rights in exchange for services rendered. Some 3,500 black Loyalists arrived in Canada in 1783. Transported by ship, most settled in Nova Scotia and New Brunswick. Others moved into scattered communities in Ontario and Quebec. They came with great hope and promise.

In addition to the free blacks, roughly 1,500 slaves arrived in the company of white Loyalists. Again, most settled in the Maritimes. (In Nova Scotia, newcomers were listed in the *Book Of Negroes,* a special register of black Loyalists.) The largest concentration of blacks lived in Shelburne and Birchtown, Nova Scotia. The Black Pioneers, the only all-black regiment fighting for Britain in the War of Independence, helped design and build Shelburne. By 1784, Birchtown was home to 2,700 blacks.

Less dramatic examples of segregation soon appeared throughout the Canadian colonies. By 1785, Prince Edward Island had approximately 100 slaves, a sizable number given the island's total population. Across early Canada integrated places of work provided the only means of meaningful daily intermingling between blacks and whites. Still, in most workplaces blacks held the lowest paying jobs; and being relegated to jobs without responsibility accentuated their slave status.

The actual granting of lands was representative of a history of privilege, power, and racism. Whites generally settled on arable lands and established farms capable of providing crops within one or two years. Their commitment to England seemed clear. Blacks, on the other hand, were perceived as migrants. Without country of origin, it was thought by most that their stay in Canada would be temporary.

Only a small percentage of the black Loyalists received any land at all, even though many were proven farmers. The land they did receive was rocky, marginal farmland, given in small allotments and in segregated districts. While providing a sense of community, these segregated settlements rapidly became home to a distinct black underclass dependent on white charity. In *Blacks: Peoples of the Maritimes* (1993), Bridglal Pachai describes how land was distributed:

> ...those who had lost the most in the war were to be served first. The size of the grants in such cases was to be in keeping with the estates they had left behind in the US. Less prosperous refugees were to receive 100 acres for the head of the family, plus 50 acres for each family member, including slaves attached to the household. Disbanded military men received grants according to rank, ranging from 1,000 acres for a field officer to 100 for a private soldier,

plus allowances for family members. None of these provisions was helpful to the Blacks, who were placed at the end of a long bureaucratic line. Two-and-a-half years later, in 1786, almost all white Loyalists in Shelburne County had received their grants. The first Blacks had to wait till 1787, when grants were made to 184 of 649 black men in Birchtown. The average allocation for the whites was 74 acres; for the Blacks it was 34.

Black settlers Thomas Peters and Murphy Still initiated a protest against these delays. Both were members of the distinguished Black Pioneers. While these and other black activists were successful in petitioning for land grants for some black Loyalists, the majority remained landless and became dependent on employment offered by white farmers, tradesmen, or the government. Many of the blacks who received grants could not

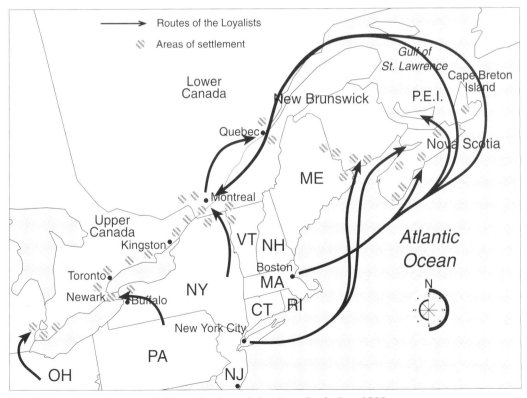

Black Loyalist settlements in Nova Scotia and the Canadas before 1800.

afford the surveyors' fees and/or initial costs, and abandoned their lands.

The use of blacks in low-paying manual labour jobs, at cheaper wages than others would accept, created discontent amongst marginalized whites. Acts of hostility, race riots, and the destruction of black property became commonplace as blacks and whites intermingled in the towns. Denied the vote, victimized by food and clothing shortages, and economically exploited, the black underclass grew. Worse still, sweeping segregation took root. Blacks, already relegated to separate housing districts, were barred entry into churches and schools. The distinction between free and enslaved was becoming one more of form than of substance.

The existence of both free and enslaved black populations posed real difficulties for pre-Confederation Canada. There was an uneasy coexistence between the two groups. What was to be done about this dangerous incompatibility? How willingly would slaves accept their lot when other blacks were free? This problem was exacerbated by world events.

The French and Haitian Revolutions

On July 14, 1789, a mob in Paris, France stormed and captured the infamous Bastille prison, marking the beginning of the French Revolution. Determined to oust an oppressive government, in the streets demonstrators shouted "Liberty! Equality! Fraternity!" The uprising sent tremors of revolution around the world. On the Caribbean island of St. Domingue, France's richest colony, black slaves set fire to the source of their oppression, the sugar cane plantations.

In October 1790, civil rights granted to the free mulattoes of St. Domingue were withdrawn. The authorities recognized that having free mulattoes intermingling with enslaved blacks was a dangerous mixture. This prompted a revolt led by Ogé, a Paris-educated student who returned to the island hoping to overthrow slavery. Ogé's attempt to spread revolution was crushed. He and his supporters were brutally tortured and executed.

But the seeds of insurrection had been sown. In August 1791, the slaves of northern St. Domingue rose in revolt, setting fire to plantations and murdering whites. The fires soon spread. Across the island, nearly 200 plantations were burned to the ground, and in savage fighting over 12,000 people were killed. Within months much of the white French population had been wiped out. Haiti, the first independent black republic in the Caribbean, was born in 1791. It was not recognized as an independent state until 1803. European colonists feared that this spirit of revolution would spread, domino-style, throughout the New World, leading to an end of slavery. The Caribbean islands, where mobility was restricted by geography, were considered relatively safe European holdings. They were treasured possessions and the British, especially, would go to great lengths to keep them.

In 1793, after the execution of the French king, Louis XVI, Britain went to war with France. Using its naval advantage, Britain attempted to claim St. Domingue. Slave revolts, however, had turned into a national uprising. Francois-Domingue Toussaint, a former slave, by 1795 commanded an army of more than 20,000. The British brought in black regiments from Jamaica to quell a rebellion that raged for five years. In 1798 the British left the island, defeated. Five years later the French evacuation was complete.

The years of international struggle did not end until 1815, by which time Britain had solidified its position in the Caribbean. It had gained much more than it had lost. Peace treaties awarded the French islands of Tobago and St. Lucia and the Dutch territories of present-day Guyana to the British, giving them greater control of the export trade. With a near monopoly on sugar and coffee, prices soared and Britain's national wealth increased dramatically.

English parliamentarians, cognizant of the effects of the French Revolution on St. Domingue, weary of Jamaican Maroon uprisings, and fearful of further slave rebellions on southern plantations, began listening to abolitionist voices. In 1807, an Act of Parliament made enslaving British subjects illegal. Slave resistance, though, would continue until

Toussaint L'Ouverture, *a former slave, led a revolution which resulted in the first independent state of the Caribbean.*

all blacks were emancipated. This resistance and enlightened self-interest dictated a change in thinking which led to the abolition of slavery in the British Empire in 1834.

Blacks and Native Peoples in Loyalist Canada

In Canada, evidence of the dangers involved in retaining both free and enslaved black populations came also from south of the border. Britain recognized the birth of the US in 1783, and was at peace with its former colonies. Nonetheless, certain parliamentarians argued that the existence of slavery amid freedom in the Thirteen Colonies was a contributing factor to the war and that Canada should chart a different course in terms of race relations. Black Loyalist populations were making similar demands. After all, these people, a full ten percent of the total Loyalist emigration, made critical contributions to Britain's war effort.

The British granted freedom to runaway slaves who joined the Loyalist cause. Most of these came on foot to Upper Canada and Lower Canada. Again, differentiating between free and enslaved blacks was difficult, and tensions arose. Opposition to slavery was growing throughout British North America as abolitionists were making inroads. Also, numerous black Loyalists gained a degree of respectability by proving themselves in various trades.

Britain's central preoccupations were that of settlement and commerce, not human rights. Settling Canada with farming and trapping colonists capable of feeding and clothing the mother country was the overriding concern. The colonial custom of granting land to "servants of the empire" was used extensively in Canada. That the settlers would use slaves as free-labourers was taken for granted, and was consistent with colonial expansion in the US, the Caribbean, and elsewhere. Preventing settlers from bringing slaves to the colonies was considered a recipe for economic disaster. So, this customary practice was encoded into law with the Imperial Statute of 1790.

Further indication of the lowly status accorded to blacks is evidenced by the contrasting treatment of Native peoples and blacks during the time of Loyalist settlement. Scarce land, resources, and employment in the Maritimes encouraged settlers to travel west. The laws of settlement and commerce in Canada necessitated a degree of cooperation between Native peoples and

European colonists. Mohawk and Iroquois Indian bands were part of the move west. They were given large tracts of land and allowed to enslave blacks.

The relationships between Native peoples and blacks were qualitatively different from those between white settlers and blacks. Often these relationships were based on a far superior sense of equality. Historically, both groups had suffered unremitting persecution. Some Indian bands provided safe haven for escaped slaves from the US. Though these blacks generally retained their slave status, with the blessing of leaders like Joseph Brant, many married Indians.

In the Caribbean, the virtual elimination of the peaceful Arawak and more warlike Carib Indian populations had left no room for such a relationship to develop. On the island of Hispaniola, Spanish settlers hunted Indians for sport. Throughout the Caribbean tens of thousands died of malnutrition, torture, and disease. Thousands of others committed suicide. When, in 1655, the English captured Jamaica from the Spanish, there was not a sole survivor of the Indian population. Trapped on islands, vulnerable to European diseases, and forced into bondage on European plantations, Arawak and Carib populations were driven to near extinction. With the advent of the trans-Atlantic slave trade from West Africa, European colonists had no use for the indigenes.

Such "ethnic cleansing" did not occur in Canada during the Loyalist period. In the hinterland of the

Joseph Brant

Native people, too, sometimes owned or traded in slaves. The Shawanabe and Potawatomis and other western tribes brought slaves from Ohio and Kentucky and sold them in the north...Settlers farther east bought slaves from the Mississaugas. Traders of the Six Nations sold slaves to settlers in the Niagara region...Another famous Native slave-holder was Thayendinaga, or Joseph Brant. This Mohawk chief, who fought as a British ally in the Indian and Revolutionary Wars, was granted land on both sides of the Grand River. Black slaves whom Brant had captured in war did much of the work in his home Brant House at Burlington Beach and in his more modest house at Oshweken near Brantford. Other slaves worked on his land and tended his horses. In all, Brant owned 30 to 40 blacks.

Daniel Hill, The Freedom Seekers *(1981).*

European torture of Caribbean Amerindian people. Disease, wars, torture, and slavery almost wiped out the first peoples of the Caribbean.

Canadian frontier the relationship between European and Indian traders was relatively harmonious. In the more economically diversified settlements of early Canada, Native Indian bands had bargaining and negotiation powers. As a result, they were not categorized as "non-persons," a title reserved for blacks.

After Confederation, in 1867, this relationship took a negative turn. With the fur trade in decline, agriculture became the central economic industry. The Indian Act of 1876 disenfranchised Aboriginal peoples, restricted them to living in secluded and segregated settlements, and legislated strict prohibitions against Indian land ownership. This racist Act stripped Aboriginal peoples of their civil rights and cut them off from the developing nation of Canada.

In 1787, British abolitionist Granville Sharp established a colony in Africa for 2,000 freed slaves from Britain and the New World. Called Sierra Leone, the colony stayed under British control until 1961, when it became independent. Liberia was founded in the 1820s as a colony for freed slaves by the white southern American Colonization Society. It too is located in West Africa.

Self-Help and the Exodus to Sierra Leone

Church leaders were instrumental in the black fight for dignity, respect, and opportunity. In 1785, John Marrant established the Huntingdonian congregation at Birchtown, Nova Scotia. Along with other congregations, it was supported by English (e.g., the Associates of Dr. Bray) and Canadian (e.g., the Anglican Society for the Propagation of the Gospel) white charities, who provided funds for building black churches and schools. Perhaps the most important early black reformer was David George. Using only black community money, he founded Baptist churches throughout Nova Scotia and initiated a self-help movement still in existence today.

Most Maritime blacks were first or second generation Africans, and many still had fond memories of their homeland. Even with viable communities in Nova Scotia and New Brunswick, the gradual elimination of slavery, and the hope of future progress, racism caused many to depart.

The exodus to Sierra Leone, West Africa, was initiated by Birchtown's Thomas Peters, who returned to Nova Scotia after delivering a petition of complaint to the British government in London. In England, he met with Sierra Leone Company representatives who needed black settlers for their colony. After lengthy negotiations a deal was struck. On January 15, 1792, nearly 1,200 blacks, many of them influential, set sail for Sierra Leone. They left in the hope of realizing Canada's promises–freedom, equality, and land–in a new country.

Traditional outdoor baptism in the black Baptist Church. David George is recognized as the "founding father" of the black Baptist Church in the Maritimes. He personally baptized white members of his congregation.

For Thomas Peters and other prominent leaders, this exodus represented the best hope for blacks. To them leaving was the ultimate form of self-help. Unfortunately, their departure left a leadership vacuum in the fledgling black community which remained. It also fuelled the notion that blacks were ill-suited to the Canadian climate and the tough realities of frontier life.

Jamaican Maroons in Canada

Given this exodus, it was somewhat ironic that, in 1796, the British government transported 600 Jamaican Maroons to

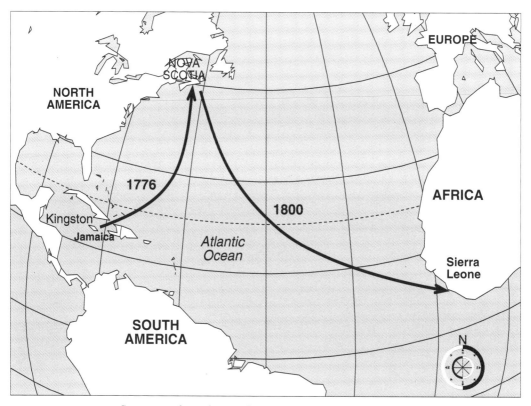

Sea routes from the Caribbean to the Maritimes to Sierra Leone.

Halifax. These Maroons, escaped slaves from Trelawney, had successfully fought the British since 1655. England feared Maroon resistance would lead to slave uprisings throughout the Caribbean. Despite their surrender in 1796, they were anything but loyal to Britain, and would be unlikely to assimilate with free or enslaved blacks in the Maritimes.

Though the Nova Scotia Maroons lived relatively peacefully for four years, and helped build the Citadel in Halifax, disputes arose between Jamaican and English authorities regarding financial support. In 1800, most of the Maroon population was removed to Freetown, Sierra Leone, where some of their descendants still live.

The Abolitionists

The movement to abolish slavery was international. In 1787, the young US passed a law, under the Articles of Confederation, prohibiting slavery in the Northwest Territory. Sovereignty over certain northern districts of this region was disputed, and when Upper Canada came into being in 1791 it claimed Detroit as its own. As Daniel Hill (1981) describes:

> This meant that the district was at the same time "free" American territory and "slave" British territory. After the Ordinance of 1787 abolished slavery in the American Northwest Territories, British subjects still living there ignored the new law, but some of the slaves living in Upper Canada did not. Several of them swam across the Detroit River to freedom.

In 1777, slaves escaping from New France had fled into free Vermont, a fact punching yet another hole in the popular misconception that Canada banned slavery before the US.

In the British House of Commons, reformer William Wilberforce tabled a bill to stop the importation of slaves in all British colonies. He was supported by John Graves Simcoe, back in England after serving with distinction in the American Revolutionary War. Though the Abolition Bill was defeated, Wilberforce doggedly pursued the issue. Meanwhile, the abolitionist movement was growing across Europe, leading Denmark to abolish slavery in 1804. Finally, Britain passed its Abolition Act in 1808. It stated that slavery was to be "utterly abolished, prohibited, and declared to be unlawful."

In 1791, Lieutenant-Colonel Simcoe became the first Lieutenant-Governor of Upper Canada. In 1793, he confronted a highly publicized case of brutality against Chloë Cooley, a slave girl from Queenstown. After being beaten and bound by her master, Cooley was transported, against her will, across the Niagara River and sold. Many were shocked by this mistreatment; but existing English law continued to view slaves as property, making prosecution impossible. Charges of human rights violations could only be levied if the alleged victim was human. Slaves were not considered human.

For abolitionists this case clearly illustrated that new legislation was necessary. In 1793, the government passed a law entitled An Act to Prevent the Further Introduction of Slaves and to Limit the Term of Enforced Servitude Within this Province. For Simcoe and Chief Justice William Osgoode, this legislation was a compromise. It did not ban slavery, left slave-owning opposition legislators unaffected, and freed the children of slaves only

TO BE SOLD,

A BLACK WOMAN, named PEGGY, aged about forty years ; and a Black boy her ſon, named JUPITER, aged about fifteen years, both of them the property of the Subſcriber.

The Woman is a tolerable Cook and waſher woman and perfectly underſtands making Soap and Candles.

The Boy is tall and ſtrong of his age, and has been employed in Country buſineſs, but brought up principally as a Houſe Servant—They are each of them Servants for life. The Price for the Wowan is one hundred and fifty Dollars—for the Boy two hundred Dollars, payable in three years with Intereſt from the day of Sale and to be properly ſecured by Bond &c.—But one fourth leſs will be taken in ready Money.

PETER RUSSELL.

York, Feb. 10th 1806.

Public slave auctions (this one in York, now Toronto) presented, in bold face, the degraded position of blacks in Canada.

after they attained 25 years of age. It did, however, prevent new settlers from bringing slaves into the province.

The importance of Simcoe's Act on the future of Canada is a subject of active debate. Though limited in scope, the Act is one of the earliest pieces of anti-discrimination legislation. It is questionable whether the Act would have passed had slavery not acquired a most definite colour. The dehumanizing treatment of Chloë Cooley and other black slaves provided much of the impetus.

Canadian colonists appeared to be following the example of southern plantation owners by reserving such ill-treatment for blacks. This situation was intolerable for the black and white abolitionists who, as witnesses, gave testimony before Simcoe's Executive Council. Also, second generation slave-owners, many of whom were brought up by slaves, were becoming (in private at least) more kindly disposed towards blacks. Some freed their slaves and became abolitionists.

Under English law slaves were still considered property. This precluded any possibility of prosecuting the perpetrators of mistreatment and/or violence. Perhaps the chief defect of Simcoe's Act was its absolute silence on this vital point. Slave owners continued to be protected by the over-reaching laws of property and commerce. In the pioneering development of Canada, slavery, in short, was deemed too important for outright abolishment. Black slaves helped build the country and were necessary for its continued prosperity.

Simcoe's Act predates Confederation by seventy-four years, and though the British North America Act (1867) does not mention human rights as such, victims of racial discrimination were protected under the common law provisions of the English Constitution. Simcoe argued strenuously that Christianity and the British Constitution opposed slavery.

In 1803, William Osgoode, then Chief Justice of Lower Canada, ruled that slavery was incompatible with British law. Simcoe and the abolitionists were vindicated. The hypocrisy of slavery "under the law" had been exposed. Though not officially abolishing slavery, the ruling set free the 300 slaves of Lower Canada. Of equal importance was the impact of Simcoe's Act and Osgoode's historic decision on American blacks, who soon began moving north in large numbers. They followed the north star to freedom.

Slavery's gradual decline in Canada resulted from legislation, the ardent work of black and white abolitionists, a lack of a plantation economy, and long unproductive winters. The relative importance of each of these points is actively debated. What is beyond debate, however, is that blacks played a formative role in building Canada, and directly influenced the abolitionist and desegregation movements in North America.

Black American champions of civil rights, from Frederick Douglass and Sojourner Truth to Martin Luther King, Jr., argued that slavery was in violation of the US Constitution. In this, they echoed the voices of William Wilberforce, John Graves Simcoe, Chief Justice William Osgoode, and other abolitionists. The impact of black contributions, especially during war efforts, was appreciated by liberal reformers north and south. For nearly one hundred years, from the American War of Independence onwards, these contributions helped shape Canada's conflicted relationship with the US.

3

Safe Haven: Myth or Reality?

Canada's reputation as a safe haven for blacks grew during and after the War of 1812. Once again, the promise of freedom, equality, and land brought thousands to Canada. Once again, hopes of renewal were dashed.

The causes of the war, sometimes called "the second American War of Independence," are subject to controversy. Some historians maintain that it broke out over alleged British violations of American shipping rights. Strict control of the seas was essential for imperial Britain, and some American merchant sailors were forced to work on British ships. The US responded by attacking Canada. The ensuing battle was fought both at sea and on land, with Britain claiming many victories in Upper Canada. Other historians argue that "freedom of the sea" issues were really an American excuse to invade and conquer Canada. Since an American conquest of the Canadas raised the spectre of slavery's re-imposition, it is clear why blacks fought against the Americans. In contrast, as British documents attest, much of the newly arrived US white population of Upper Canada was of doubtful loyalty to the Crown.

Thousands of black volunteers fought for Britain, distinguishing themselves in numerous border skirmishes. Most fought in white regiments. However, the first all-black military unit in Canadian history was formed at the outbreak of the war. Captain Runchey's Company of Coloured Men fought in many clashes (Fort George, Niagara Town, Stoney Creek, Lundy's Lane), and played a decisive role in the Battle of Queenston Heights.

The impact of the "Coloured Corps" and other free blacks in the army was not limited to winning battles. News spread of their daring exploits, and of the British promise of freedom and land to escaped slaves. Soon, thousands of black fugitives crossed the border to support the British cause. Though rarely documented as a war to end American slavery, it was perceived as just that by the black community. The burning of the White House by British troops was hailed by blacks as an end to slavery and discrimination. Nearly two thousand "Black Refugees" (so called because most were escaped slaves) came to Halifax in 1813. Valued as manual labourers, they settled largely in segregated districts in Nova Scotia and New Brunswick. Maritime governments were encouraging blacks to immigrate by offering a safer and more profitable existence.

This situation quickly changed as a recession and sudden influx of white immigrants hit Nova Scotia. Expedient politicians argued that there were too many black servants and labourers, and that they were taking jobs away from needy whites. In 1815, the Nova Scotia legislature voted to ban further black immigration. As black unemployment grew, race relations deteriorated. The possibility of meaningful contact between whites and blacks all but ceased, and the emergence of a dependent and impoverished black underclass fuelled the flames of racism. Blacks, fearing racial violence, increasingly took refuge in their own communities.

The War of 1812 also encouraged blacks to flee to Upper and Lower Canada, though in much fewer numbers. Abolitionists like Sir Peregrine Maitland, Lieutenant-Governor of Upper Canada, actively supported black immigration. Angering southern plantation owners, Maitland's government refused to sign an extradition treaty with the US providing for the return of runaway slaves. Job opportunities, especially in land clearance and road construction, benefitted many blacks. However, because they were engaged in mobile employment, active black settlements were difficult to establish. The black community of Upper and Lower Canada had not yet achieved critical mass, a situation that would change dramatically in 1833 when the Emancipation Act abolished slavery in all British territories.

Canada mostly failed in its promises to help the black immigrants re-define themselves north of the border. Segregated, jobless, or given the lowest forms of employment, they were unable to cast off their slave status. Bitterness over this continues to resonate in the Maritimes, where the majority of contemporary blacks are descendants of the War of 1812 refugees. The situation was marginally better for blacks in Upper Canada. Land grants were awarded to black and white war veterans settling in the township of Oro in today's Simcoe County, Ontario, and on a smaller scale in other jurisdictions.

The Underground Railroad

Late in the 1700s New England Quakers began sheltering fugitive slaves, some of whom escaped into Canada. Others, both free blacks and fugitive slaves, moved into the Northwest Territory which, through Congress's passage of the Northwest Ordinance (1787), had been made free. In 1793, the same year that Simcoe's Act was passed in Upper Canada, the US federal government enacted the first Fugitive Slave Law. This law placated agitated southern plantation owners who had witnessed the death of slavery in the North. In essence, it allowed owners and slave-takers to hunt down fugitive slaves and return them to the plantations. Many free blacks, with little recourse before the law, were sold back into slavery by unsympathetic northerners.

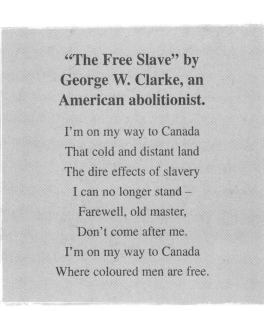

"The Free Slave" by George W. Clarke, an American abolitionist.

I'm on my way to Canada
That cold and distant land
The dire effects of slavery
I can no longer stand –
Farewell, old master,
Don't come after me.
I'm on my way to Canada
Where coloured men are free.

In 1803, the US bought the vast Louisiana Territory, an area which, unlike the Northwest Territory, was suitable for plantation-style agriculture. France, under Napoleon, was involved in costly wars with Britain and Britain's allies. To support her war efforts, Napoleon sold the Louisiana Territory to President Thomas Jefferson for the bargain basement price of $15 million, or four cents an acre. Slavery and the cotton kingdom, which had increasingly become southern institutions, quickly expanded into this new territory, as plantation owners moved north and west.

Both territories bordered Canada, whose own expansion drive west in the early 1800s provided employment opportuni-

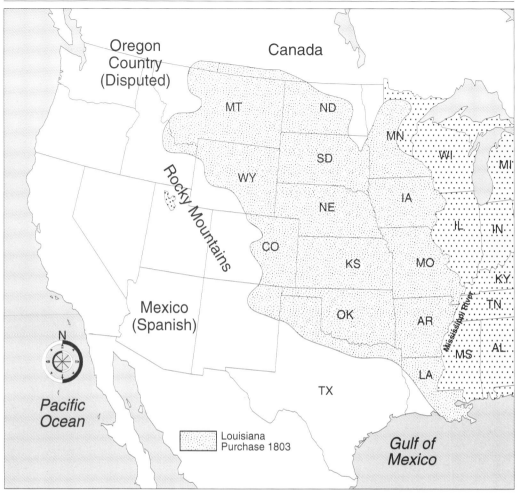

Political boundaries after the Louisiana Purchase of 1803.

ties for blacks. By the time of the Emancipation Act of 1833, which abolished slavery throughout the British empire, the practice of slavery had all but disappeared in Canada. Sympathy for blacks fleeing US slave-holding territories was growing in British North America. Canada, free of fugitive slave laws and refusing to repatriate runaways, seemed an oasis of tolerance.

Black and white abolitionists on both sides of the border had already established an informal network of "safe houses" and secret routes north to protect fugitive slaves. By 1830, this network developed into an organized system called the Underground Railroad (UGR). Though estimates vary, between 1815 and 1860 approximately 80,000 slaves escaped via the UGR, roughly 50,000 of whom came to Canada. In Canada a

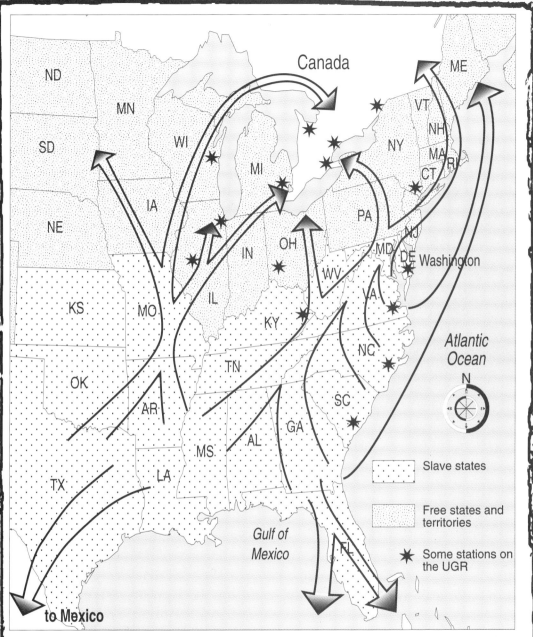

Underground Railroad stations, routes to freedom, and a final termini. *The Niagara Black History Association gives tours through Niagara's "Freedom Trail." The sites include the British Methodist Episcopal (BME) Church in St. Catharines which was the place of worship for Harriet Tubman and the Canadian headquarters of the UGR; the Nathaniel Dett Memorial Chapel (named in honour of a man born in Chatham who became an internationally renowned musician and composer); a safe house in Fort Erie; and the Norval Johnson Heritage Library in Niagara Falls, home to a growing collection of Canadian black history books.*

major centre was St. Catharines, Ontario, the home of Harriet Tubman for some years during the 1850s.

America's second Fugitive Slave Law (1850) heightened the danger of escape and made conditions on the plantations even more restrictive. Nonetheless, it caused a dramatic increase in the number of fugitives seeking salvation in Canada. In Upper Canada alone the total black population ballooned to nearly forty thousand. Three thousand came in the first month after the law's passage.

*From her base in St. Catharines, **Harriet Tubman**, a fugitive slave herself, made 19 journeys south freeing some 300 blacks via the UGR. Believing that slavery was "the next thing to hell," through one perilous journey after another she eluded bounty hunters by travelling at night. Slaves, reluctant to risk death by escaping, were no match for Tubman. She compelled them, sometimes by force, to seek freedom in Canada. During the Civil War, as a nurse, guide, and spy for the Union army, her daring and steely determination was just as evident. Frederick Douglass said of her: "The midnight sky and silent stars have been the witness of your devotion to freedom and your heroism...I know of no one who has willingly encountered more perils and hardships to serve our enslaved people than you have." Harriet Tubman became known as "the Moses of her people."*

Having found freedom, the black community now faced the obstacles of settlement. Hopes ran high, as so many of the new blacks had distinguished themselves by outwitting plantation owners and bounty hunters. The slaves and free blacks who escaped via the Underground Railroad believed that which did not kill them made them stronger. The heroes and heroines of the UGR were the black and white "conductors," who risked federal and state prosecution, and the slaves themselves, who risked death or severe reprisal. Their stories, filled with daring missions, disguise, sacrifice, determination, volunteerism, and ingenious escapes, are epitomized by Alexander Ross and Harriet Tubman.

Ross was a white doctor from Belleville, Ontario. Throughout the 1850s he travelled often to southern plantations, ostensibly to study birds. Ornithology was his disguise, for his real purpose was to help slaves plan their escape. Most often, he provided slaves with provisions and information on secret routes and UGR safe houses, but he also led many to safety in Canada. Ross, like Harriet Tubman, aided the Union cause during the Civil War.

The stories of Ross, Tubman, and other conductors (Calvin Fairbanks, a white abolitionist who spent 17 years in prison for his participation in the UGR; John Mason, responsible for freeing 1,300 slaves; Frederick Douglass, perhaps black America's most influential abolitionist; Levi Coffin and William Still, "presidents" of the UGR) are well documented. What is under-appreciated is that the activity surrounding the UGR years forever changed Canada's relationship with the US. The notion of "Canada the good" and "America the evil" began to take root during these years. Could Canada live up to its self-proclaimed position on the moral high ground?

Early Black Settlements in British Columbia

Governor Douglas travelled widely in the US, and knew of many skilled, educated, and hard-working black communities. San Francisco possessed such a community and, because of severe civil rights restrictions, blacks there were looking for new opportunities. Douglas, of mixed Scottish and Creole parentage, seized the moment and urged them to come north. He felt that in their hands the colony would prosper and remain British.

On April 26, 1858, the first ship carrying black Californians arrived in Victoria. Before that summer ended, 800 black settlers had come north. On

Alexander Ross

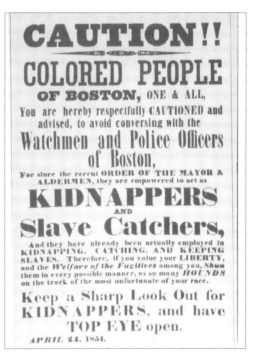

Some unsympathetic and money-driven northerners captured and sold free blacks back into slavery. Such posters alerted blacks and abolitionists to be forever vigilant. Canada, refusing to extradite black fugitives and promising safe haven, came to represent "the promised land."

Douglas' Promise to the Blacks of the Zion Church, San Francisco:

1. Land to be sold at $5.00 per acre;
2. No land taxes would be charged for two years;
3. After nine months of land ownership, they could vote and sit on juries;
4. After seven years they would swear allegiance to the crown and receive full citizenship rights as British subjects.

Mifflin Gibbs was an extraordinary man—some would say, a Renaissance man. As a member of the Victoria municipal government, he was the first black politician in Canada. He was a delegate at the 1868 Yale Convention, a meeting in which it was determined that B. C. would join Confederation. In direct competition with the Hudson's Bay Company, he ran a prosperous hardware store for miners. He built a coal mine in the Queen Charlotte Islands, and the first railway to service a coal mine in Canada. At one point, Gibbs was the acting mayor of Victoria.

Vancouver Island blacks outnumbered whites. Many, having owned businesses or farms in California, had money to invest in the booming B.C. economy. As a group, they were determined to integrate and to succeed as farmers, tradespeople, small businessmen, and gold prospectors. Bahamas-born Henry McDame was as fine a gold prospector as any.

Initially better accepted in B. C. than elsewhere in Canada, the black Californians attended local schools and churches. They settled on Vancouver and Saltspring Islands and on the mainland. The mineral wealth and natural resources of the province also made it appealing to American expansionists. To safeguard against American encroachment and to show loyalty to the British crown, the black community, in 1860, formed the Victoria Pioneer Rifle Company. The "African Rifles," as they were popularly known, was an all-black regiment organized to defend Victoria.

Acceptance soon gave way to segregation. Government legislation suggested that equality prevailed for all people. In truth, convention and the lack of enforcement allowed restaurants and taverns to bar blacks or to establish segregated seating areas, and churches to relegate them to balconies or back pews. Some white church-goers argued that "it is a sin not to recognize the distinction between the races that the creator made" (*Hymn To Freedom,* video), the same basic rationalization for slavery. Businessmen argued that whites would not frequent establishments where blacks were treated equally and with respect. These sentiments were followed by increased restrictions, especially after Governor Douglas was replaced.

British Columbia followed an established pattern. Time and again, blacks were encouraged to emigrate to protect British interests in Canada. Once the threat was over, they were forced to live restricted segregated lives. The case of the Victoria Pioneer Rifle Company is illustrative. (The Company required approval from London to become an established regiment in the the British Order of Battle. No such approval was forthcoming, and no reason was given.) After it became clear that Americans were more interested in gold than storming Fort Victoria, the "African Rifles" faded into distant memory.

Victoria Pioneer Rifle Company
Even though some members served as police officers and others ran successful businesses, the regiment was barred from public ceremonies.

Self-Segregation: the Only Choice?

Even though blacks were one of the largest groups to enter Canada during the nineteenth century, they have received only minimal recognition. Canada was not yet a united country. Its disparate, and often divided, regions were being settled mostly by white Europeans and Americans. As provincial histories show, these regions progressed economically, socially, and politically in their own unique fashions. However, the marginalization of black communities from coast to coast represents one of the few examples of consistency in early Canada.

Many factors contributed to this marginalization, black segregation in distinct settlements being perhaps the most important. As early as 1798 there were 40 black settlements in Upper Canada. Many grew into active communities, proving that black people could accept the responsibilities of freedom and carve out lives for themselves. But, life was hard and insecure in these settlements. As time wore on, Upper Canadian blacks faced the critical question of accepting segregation or pushing for integration.

Wilberforce, established by blacks from Cincinnati in 1829-1830 and named after the British abolitionist, was the first sizable all-black settlement in Upper Canada. Beset by ineffective management, it lasted only six years. Its failure sent a chill through the black community and solidified the white belief that black attempts at community living were doomed. Also, many blacks came to view segregated settlements as exacerbating prejudice. They believed that only through integration would blacks achieve equality.

Reformers like Josiah Henson and white abolitionist Hiram Wilson were unwilling to accept that one failed experiment represented historical truth. In 1842, Henson and Wilson set up The Dawn Settlement, an all-black colony.

Josiah Henson and his Wife
The remarkable story of Josiah Henson, from battered slave to leader of his people, stands as one of great hallmarks of black achievement in Canada.

Henry Bibb and Mary Ann Shadd
Henry Bibb was a highly respected lecturer and anti-slavery advocate. Mary Ann Shadd was the first woman newspaper editor in North America.

Unlike Wilberforce, at Dawn training, education, and community planning were firmly entrenched. It became a diverse settlement, complete with a school, sawmill and brickyard, and considerable farmland. Black integrationists disputed the apparent successes of Dawn. They argued that, because it received donations from white charities to purchase land and erect the school and sawmill, it could not accurately be described as a black initiative.

Two influential black newspapers contended for the minds and souls of black people. *The Voice of the Fugitive,* established in 1851 by former slave Henry Bibb, argued strenuously against white charity and for segregated land settlements supported only by the black community. *The Provincial Freeman,* founded in 1853 by another former slave, Samuel

With his parents, **Samuel Ringgold Ward** *escaped slavery in 1820 at the tender age of three. After being educated in New York, he became a minister and, years later, founder of the* Provincial Freeman.

Ringgold Ward and editor Mary Ann Shadd, stressed with equal resolve that black people must integrate. Former slaves were improving their lot by working in masonry, carpentry, and in other small businesses in Toronto, Hamilton, Niagara Falls, and St. Catharines. Integrationists like Shadd maintained that these positive advances proved that successful intermingling was possible.

The Elgin Settlement and Buxton Mission

Fuelling this debate was the extraordinary work of the Rev. William King, white abolitionist and Presbyterian Church minister. In November, 1849, King and fifteen former slaves began building the Elgin Settlement and Buxton Mission. The slaves, in an ironic twist of fate, had been left to King as part of a property inherited from his father-in-law, a rich southern plantation owner. Working with fugitive slaves in Upper Canada since 1846, and witnessing the initial success of the Dawn Settlement, prompted King to offer refuge in Canada to the fifteen men and women left in his charge. They all accepted his offer, a testimony to the belief that blacks could realize their dreams north of the border.

In 1849, the legislative member and school commissioner for the Chatham district was Edwin Larwill, a powerful politician and ardent segregationist. In a classic *not in my backyard* campaign, Larwill rallied whites in opposition to King's attempt to locate Elgin on a 3,600-hectare plot of land near Chatham. The campaign was overtly racist. By arguing that blacks were inferior, that their presence would drive down property values and drive away white settlers, and that whites, especially white children, would be endangered by having free blacks roam the streets of Chatham, Larwill appealed to the most base characteristics of the human soul.

At a public meeting on August 18, 1849, King debated Larwill about the

Rev. William King

settlement. As described by Daniel Hill in *The Freedom Seekers* (1981), this event, and Larwill's misreading of his supporters' reaction to his zealous pursuit, represent a turning point in Canadian history:

> Over 300 people gathered, including a group of Blacks whose presence assured King's support and safety…The threatened violence did not break out, but only a few of his audience supported King's defence of his proposed settlement…In October Larwill and his supporters persuaded the Western District Council to send another protest to Parliament. Without the Council's knowledge Larwill added several recommendations of his own: that Blacks should be barred from public schools and public office; that they should pay a poll tax; that the whole question of allowing them to vote should be examined; that they should be required to post bonds if they wished to stay in Canada. Taking this independent action hurt Larwill, for many of his supporters concluded that he was an extremist and gradually withdrew from his campaign…William King moved into the Elgin Settlement with the first settlers, his 15 former slaves, on November 28, 1849.

Isaac Riley

The Elgin Association, headed by King and twenty-four distinguished directors, was incorporated on June 8, 1850. It handled all matters pertaining to the secular life of the Settlement. The Mission, with Presbyterian Church assistance, oversaw the community's chapel and schools.

The enterprising original fifteen settlers started by building homes and roads, clearing trees, farming, and encouraging others to join them. Many did, following the example of Isaac Riley and his family. Riley had walked 500 kilometres from St. Catharines to

The Elgin Settlement.

join the settlers. He and his family are believed to have been Elgin's first inhabitants.

By 1854, the Settlement featured 480 hectares of cultivated land, large livestock herds, grain and tobacco farms, two sawmills, a brick-making company, a pearlash factory, a grist-mill, and a profitable farm-supplies store. Elgin blacksmiths, carpenters, cobblers, and coopers made products for the Settlement and for sale in American markets. Trade in raw materials, farm products, and manufactured goods gave Elgin the economic self-sufficiency necessary to grow and prosper.

Most precious to blacks in the Canadas was, as property-owning settlers, the right to vote. This, along with the rights to testify and take legal action in courts of law, distinguished Canadian blacks from their American counterparts. They had gained these rights through persistent struggle and, even though court challenges against anti-black discrimination were rare, the "paper fact" of legal protection offered hope to early settlers.

Leading a coalition of black groups from all over Kent County, the settlers forced Larwill out of office in 1856. Elected to the Legislature in his place was a known abolitionist, Archibald McKellar. McKellar's support by many Chatham whites suggested a more promising future for race relations in the region. From any quarter, it was hard to reject the accomplishments of Elgin. Engaging in political campaigns proved that the Elgin settlers were not content to remain secluded in their utopian community. They wanted a stake in Canada. Soon, other black communities began using the ballot box to push for reform.

Education and the Buxton Mission

> Got one mind for the boss to see,
> Got another mind for what I know is me.

> *– Mississippi Delta blues spiritual.*

Most fugitive slaves came to Canada without any formal education. Slave traders and buyers kept captured blacks "ignorant" by separating them from people who spoke the same language. On the plantations slaves were denied education. Laws prevented "benevolent" slave owners from educating their chattel. The conventional belief was that educating slaves, or allowing slaves to educate themselves, would break down the master/slave relationship and induce rebellion. The twin pillars of American society, "Christianity" and "the rule of law," served as dependable instruments in promoting and maintaining white hegemony.

Slaves, however, found many avenues around these restrictions. Most plantation owners allowed their slaves to attend white church services where the gospel was used to justify slavery and to subdue black discontent. Blacks used these services as education meetings, and put their own spin on the sermons delivered. Also, slaves met during secret late-night vigils to spread community news, educate, and practice their brand of Christianity. A profound oral tradition and a wealth of great black writing have their roots in resistance to the dicta of slavery.

Black students, most of them sons and daughters of slaves, were often barred from the common schools of Canada West. As a result, in church basements and people's homes, Christian abolitionist groups created separate educational facilities for young blacks. Private teachers were hired, stretching the groups' financial resources. Segregated education of this kind was a hit-and-miss proposition, and many black students fell through the cracks.

It soon became obvious to most black parents, desperate to see their children educated, that something substantial had to be done. They lobbied the government and, in 1850, the Common Schools Act provided for the establishment of separate schools for blacks. The first of these schools appeared in 1851 at Amhertsburg. Though worded to calm black parent protest, the Act was more assuredly passed to placate the bigoted white community. It legalized segregation in education. While some black schools were successful, almost all were beset by financial difficulties. Government funding was insufficient, teachers were underpaid, black educators hard to find or employed in trades, and curriculum resources scarce. The schools were forced to rely heavily on volunteers and outside charity, and many folded shortly after opening their doors.

Teacher and students of school section #13, North Buxton, Ontario, about 1910.

Into this fragile mix came the Buxton Mission School. Funded by the Presbyterian church, with trained teachers from Knox Presbyterian College in Toronto, the school opened in April, 1850. Its curriculum included reading, writing, mathematics, religion, rote learning, Greek, Latin, and professional training. Elgin-style self-discipline was demanded of students and teachers alike. From the beginning the Buxton school was integrated, accepting students of different religious faiths and skin colours. Some white students attended, their parents believing that Buxton offered the best education available. By 1857, 250 students had attended, and the Mission School had a growing international reputation.

The Buxton Mission School's mandate was to train students for lives in the professions and trades, ignoring the prevailing belief that blacks were only capable of service and manual labour. The school also trained teachers, many of whom took jobs in other black communities, and some of whom taught overseas. Though the Elgin Settlement was disbanded in 1873, the integrated school continued operating successfully well into the 1900s. It stood as a benchmark for what blacks in Canada could achieve.

Dred Scott, John Brown, and Canadian Reactions to American Prejudice

We tend to associate the struggle for civil rights through courts of law with the black American experience. Landmark US Supreme Court decisions played a critical role, both negatively and positively, in the centuries-old black struggle for freedom. Before Confederation, important legal challenges were also waged by black Canadians, who tended to receive greater support in the courts. The promise of legal protection was a major factor in black emigration to Canada.

In 1857, the US Supreme Court ruled against Dred Scott. Scott, a slave from Missouri, was moved to the free state of Illinois, and then to the Wisconsin Territory which, under the Missouri Compromise, had banned slavery. When Scott's owner moved him back to Missouri, he sued for his freedom. The case raised three critical issues. One, was Scott a citizen? The justices ruled that he was not a citizen because, they argued, the US Constitution did not apply to blacks. Two, did the fact of his residence in a free state entitle him to freedom in Missouri? Here the laws of commerce superseded those of civil rights. Scott was deemed a non-person, a piece of property, and the Court maintained that a person could not be deprived of transporting his or her property. Finally, was the Missouri Compromise constitutional? The Court ruled that it was not.

This case began in 1846 and divided Americans for eleven years. The black community and northern abolitionists were enraged by the Court's judgement. Whatever gains made to defeat slavery were now placed in jeopardy. Southern plantation owners celebrated the ruling as both victory and vindication. Some influential blacks, like Frederick Douglass, believed that the ruling was so outrageous it would actually help the abolitionist cause. Most black Americans were unconvinced. For them, the facts were plain: the combined forces of the Supreme Court ruling and the Fugitive Slave Act provided little hope. They became more receptive to calls for direct action against slavery and discrimination, or for refuge in Canada.

On May 8, 1858, white abolitionist John Brown met with a group of former slaves in Chatham, Ontario. He, and 13 "friends from America," had been in Chatham for ten days: meeting, marching, and performing military drills in Chatham's

Tecumseh Park. Brown knew of the successes of Canadian black communities, particularly Elgin, from newspapers and word of mouth. To him, these communities represented a model of what free American blacks could achieve. The fact that blacks in Canada had the right to organize and associate, made John Brown's mission possible. He came north to launch a revolution for black people.

Brown's ultimate goal was to destroy slavery. Having no faith in American justice or government, he believed it necessary to establish a provisional government for US blacks. The central piece of his program was an attack on the federal arsenal at Harpers Ferry, Virginia. Though some Chatham blacks branded him a dangerous lunatic who would imperil blacks on both sides of the border, many in the free black communities of Canada West were sympathetic.

With the support of the Shadd family, Isaac Holden, Osborne Anderson, Alfred Whipper, J. M. Bell, and others, Brown tabled The Provisional Constitution and Ordinances for the People of the US. It was a Constitution for a new black nation to be established in the Virginia mountains. On May 10, 1858, his 34 supporters officially adopted this Constitution and elected officers for the provisional government.

John Brown believed that only through direct violent action would slavery be defeated.

On October 16, 1859, Brown led a group of 18 white and black men on a dramatic raid of the federal arsenal at Harpers Ferry. Osborne Anderson, a black and a congressman in Brown's government, and Stewart Taylor were the only Canadians to take part in the raid. After the capture of the arsenal, and guns and army supplies worth millions of dollars, emissaries were sent out to lead a mass slave uprising in Virginia and Maryland. Brown and his militia stayed at Harpers Ferry. Led by Robert E. Lee, later the commander of the

Freedom-fighter, adventurer, and writer, **Osborne Anderson.**

Confederate troops during the Civil War, federal marines stormed the arsenal the next morning. They killed or captured all who were trapped inside.

The hoped-for slave uprising never occurred. Found guilty of conspiracy, treason, and murder, Brown was hanged on December 2, 1859. Northern abolitionists turned Brown into a martyr. No longer perceived as a "madman," in Canadian and American newspapers he was described as a hero and true Christian in the cause of justice. Osborne Anderson escaped back to Canada and wrote, with Mary Ann Shadd, a memorable booklet entitled *A Voice From Harpers Ferry.*

Canadian sympathies for Brown and the anti-slavery movement grew after his execution. Far from putting the final nail in the coffins of anti-slavery societies, the daring adventure of John Brown and his men provoked abolitionists on both sides of the border to step up their activities. Most believed that an armed conflict over American slavery was inevitable, and there was little doubt that black and many white Canadians would line up on the side of freedom.

4

The Struggle for Education

Local trustees would cut their children's heads off and throw them across the roadside ditch before they would let them go to school with niggers.
— *D. G. Simpson.*

In 1995, forty black students in two Toronto high schools were asked to identify the above quotation as "American" or "Canadian." Thirty-eight guessed American; the other two were lucky! When informed that this statement was "made-in-Canada," all forty were surprised. The history of black education in Canada contains many surprises.

Race relations in the territories of Canada-to-be began with slavery. Opposition to slavery resulted in legislative and judicial action. After the Emancipation Act of 1833, the key battle-ground for blacks in Canada became education. Canadian legislatures did not enact discriminatory anti-black laws, with the sole exception of legislation legalizing segregated schools. Outright exclusion and/or segregating blacks in back rows of classrooms was the norm in school districts from coast to coast. In Upper Canada black students were barred from attending most public schools. Upper Canada's Common Schools Act of 1850 had its practical parallel in Halifax in the 1870s when the City Council passed a by-law excluding blacks from common schools. Facing racist legislation reflective of American-style slave codes and legalized segregation, black parents responded by taking schooling into their own hands. They had no other choice.

With a few notable exceptions, all-black schools suffered from a lack of money, staff, facilities, curriculum resources, and decent accommodations. They were separate and unequal. As a result, the black community's resolve for integration in education grew. Local school boards operated as relatively autonomous bodies and had legal jurisdiction over their schools. Most petitions, therefore, were heard by boards of education.

During legal challenges by black parent groups the Common Schools Act was generally interpreted as giving school boards the right to enforce segregation. In other words, boards could create segregated schools and compel black students to attend them. After the passage of the Act black attendance in common schools declined dramatically. The courts even sanctioned segregation in schools established prior to the Act.

School segregation in both Upper Canada and the Maritimes followed the establishment of black settlements. A rapid influx of blacks into these two regions led to fears of unhealthy intermingling between the races. These fears were most pronounced when white children were involved. Blacks were thought to be uneducable, half-human, dirty, and overly sexual. How could family-respecting white parents be expected to expose their children to such "mysterious savages?"

The black settlements were a double-edged sword. On the upside they provided a safe haven for blacks; on the downside they made integration, especially school integration, difficult. Public schools cater to local populations, and few were located near black settlements. Transporting their children to far-away white schools was beyond the means of most black parents. Nor could black parents be expected to expose their children to open, and often hostile, bigotry. The lack of meaningful contact between blacks and whites reinforced prejudice and fear.

The black mission schools were both an attempt to provide education for a disenfranchised population, and a determined effort to overcome racism. While educational reformers such as Mary Ann Shadd or William King who ran successful schools were true heroes, the fact remained that across early Canada roughly half of all black children received little or no education. Clearly, mission schools could not do the job that needed to be done.

While blacks were winning victories against discrimination in other walks of life, all legal challenges to educational segregation failed. Again, white Canadian society seemed willing to give blacks "a place in the sun" in venues except those their children daily frequented. For decades, black parents were frustrated in their attempts to bring about educational integration.

Having come up from slavery, where many had been stripped even of their names, they knew too well that without education there would be no freedom. To blacks, education once gained was the one thing that could never be taken away.

The example of Toronto provided a ray of hope. There, schools were integrated from the beginning. Anti-slavery sentiments ran high in the city. White progressives like George Brown of the *Globe* newspaper, and the masters of Knox Presbyterian College, wielded influence in support of black causes. Toronto did not experience a sudden influx of black immigrants. Rather, its black population grew slowly and integrated into a more diverse city life. It seemed out of context, therefore, to impose segregation in schooling when integration existed elsewhere.

Many of the black graduates of integrated Toronto schools committed themselves to serving their community by pushing for integrated schools outside Toronto. This work paralleled that of prominent Buxton Mission graduates, some of whom were successfully transplanting the Buxton model in other jurisdictions. By 1861, there was some reason to be optimistic about the cause of black education in the provinces.

Unfortunately, broad-based educational reform did not occur. Toronto and Buxton remained islands of hope in a sea of discrimination and segregation. Discriminatory education legislation remained on the statute books in Ontario until 1964. Nova Scotia had segregated schools until the 1960s. In America, the famous *Brown vs. Board of Education* decision made racial segregation in public schools unconstitutional in 1954! Many factors contributed to this embarrassing legacy. Most important among them was the US Civil War (1861–1865), an event which forever changed black Canada. Greater issues overtook the black drive for educational reform.

Exemplary black achievers from Toronto integrated schools:

1. Emaline Shadd, in 1855 first-prize winner at the Toronto Normal School.

2. Anderson Ruffin Abbott, in 1857 first black graduate from the Toronto Medical College.

3. W. P. Hubbard, 1860s honoured student of the Toronto Model School.

4. A. T. Augusta, 1860 graduate of the Toronto Medical College.

5. Peter Gallego, student at Upper Canada College, and 1860s graduate of the University of Toronto.

Dr. Anderson Ruffin Abbott was born in Toronto in 1817, and graduated with a medical degree in 1861. In 1863, he became a surgeon for the Union army during the Civil War. (For his distinguished service, the scarf which Abraham Lincoln wore at his Presidential Inauguration was donated to a museum in Abbott's honour.)

The Civil War was fought between the industrial northern or Union states and the agricultural southern or Confederate states. Following the 1860 election of Abraham Lincoln as president, some southern states seceded from the Union. The Confederacy, founded in early 1861, sought to establish itself as a separate and independent country. It had the backing of wealthy plantation owners and others who wanted to preserve the slaved-based southern economy and social structure. Fighting began in April, 1861 with the Confederate attack on Fort Sumter. It ended, four years later, with the 1865 surrender of Confederate General Robert E. Lee. Roughly 40,000 blacks died in the war.

The US Civil War and its Impact on Black Canada

There is an active debate among historians about when the Canadian black community reached its zenith. A good case can be made that the high point of hope and opportunity occurred during the 1850s. In that decade, black communities across the land were putting their stamp on Canada-to-be. In contrast, the US was on a collision course over slavery and the preservation of the Union. The crash came with the Civil War, one of the bloodiest conflicts in history.

At first, blacks were prevented from participating in the war. Many tried to enlist, but were turned down. Fears over arming "inferior and potentially dangerous Negroes" and the ironic belief that this was "a white man's war" kept blacks on the sidelines. Also, critical to the Union's success was the support of slave-owning border states who opposed black enlistment.

Frederick Douglass and other abolitionists demanded that blacks be allowed to serve. In 1861 and 1862, the Union militias suffered many defeats and were in desperate need of additional support. Finally, the government changed its policy with an Act of Congress that permitted recruitment of black soldiers. At the same time, Lincoln suggested to his cabinet that passing a law freeing all slaves would severely undermine the Confederacy as blacks would desert the plantations.

Although the Emancipation Proclamation came into effect on January 1, 1863, for slavery to be abolished the war still had to be won. The call to free their American brethren so moved black Canadians that some 30,000 took the Underground Railroad in reverse to join the Union army. Josiah Henson and Osborne Anderson recruited men from Canada West to serve in black Union regiments. The Elgin Settlement alone provided seventy men. The cause of charting a new course for black people in Canada took a back seat to this new urgency.

Some 186,000–fugitive slaves and free blacks–from all over North America enlisted. These blacks turned the tide for the Union, a fact which history, long maintaining that this conflict was a white man's war, ignored until recent times. There were perhaps an equal number of blacks who were compelled to assist the Confederacy, though not generally as soldiers. Holding their families hostage, southern militias forced black men into service, sometimes using them for fatally

Frederick Douglass represented the moral conscience of nineteenth century America. Freed from slavery by virtue of his gift with language, he was the first black to be nominated as a vice-presidential candidate (1872) and presidential candidate (Republican convention, 1888). In 1889, Douglass served as the US minister to Haiti. His classic autobiography, The Life and Times of Frederick Douglass, *remains essential reading for all those interested in black history.*

dangerous missions to free white southern prisoners. The war also presented the horrifying irony of free blacks having to kill enslaved blacks. It was as much a black war as it was white.

The war and the promises of Reconstruction (1865–1877) led to a massive depopulation of Canada's black community. "Had not William King himself concluded that 'there will be one great black streak reaching from Elgin to the uttermost parts of the South' once the slaves were freed?" (Robin Winks, *The Blacks In Canada,* 1971). The drama of the Civil War left blacks in Canada a largely forgotten community. In the 35-year period after the war, sixty to seventy percent of them left. Canadian authorities did nothing to stem the tide.

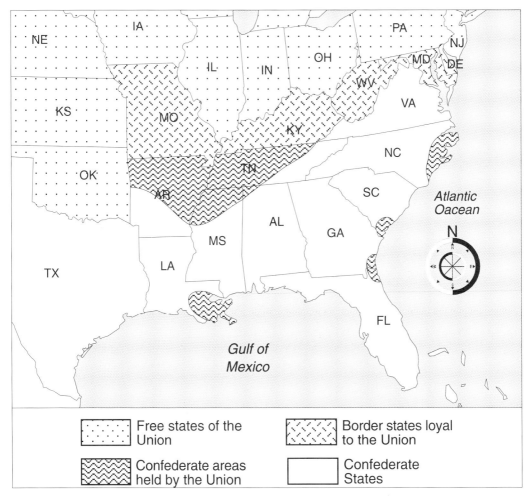

The free states of the Union, slave-owning border states loyal to the Union, and the Confederate states.

This mass exodus cannot alone be explained by the perception of an improved situation for black people in the US. White Canadians, fearing a great migration north, lobbied the government to close the border to all black war refugees and/or former slaves. Campaigns were launched to repatriate blacks to the US. Public school access was further restricted.

Hope surrounding Reconstruction, reunification with family and friends, and return to homeland, are the generally accepted reasons for the black migration south. As previously noted, to these pull factors must be added the equally significant push factors. In 1901, there were fewer than 18,000 blacks in Canada, roughly three-quarters of whom were under twenty-one years old. For forty years only a handful of blacks emigrated to Canada. The history of relatively open immigration to blacks ended with the Civil War, as did Canada's policy of providing a safe haven for blacks.

The Schooling of Black America After the Civil War

In the seventeenth century Africans were initially brought to America as indentured servants and, generally, were released once their period of servitude was over. The idea of slavery as a permanent condition arose years after twenty black captives were first landed at Jamestown, Virginia on August 20, 1619. Whatever their official status, blacks–from the very beginning–were denied education.

> ### The US Reconstruction Amendments:
>
> 1. 13th Amendment (1865): Forbids slavery in any state of the Union.
>
> 2. 14th Amendment (1868): States that all persons born in the United States are US citizens and cannot be deprived of "life, liberty, (or) property, without due process of law" nor be denied "equal protection of the laws."
>
> 3. 15th Amendment (1870): Forbids states to deny the right to vote to male citizens "on account of race, color, or previous condition of servitude."

Those who learned to read and write on their own were the exception, not the rule. Free blacks in the North, and some in the South, took advantage of scarce educational opportunities, and many rose to prominence. However, before the Civil War the total number of educated black Americans was alarmingly small. Education for Canadian blacks before Confederation was limited, but, in general, they fared better than their American counterparts. In Toronto's integrated schools, at Buxton, and elsewhere, blacks excelled academically. This tangible evidence of black academic success might have served as a building block had the Civil War not driven Canada's black community into obscurity.

In the initial years of the Reconstruction period southern blacks, despite white backlash and a campaign of terror, were filled with hope. Denied education for centuries, they knew that no greater task faced America after the war than that of educating its black citizens. Former slaves sought salvation through education and America was compelled to respond. (In this context it is important to note, as Neil Postman observes in *The Disappearance of Childhood* (1994), that–following the emergence of childhood as a distinct entity–the drive to educate children was one of national proportions. He writes, "The period between 1850 and 1950 represents the high-watermark of childhood. In America…successful attempts were made to get all children into school and out of factories.")

Before the war ended the US Congress established the Freedmen's Bureau. Its main purpose was to provide food and clothing to former slaves, and to help them locate jobs and accommodation. By 1867, the Bureau had set up nearly 4,500 schools across the southern states. To help finance the building and operation of Bureau schools parents had to pay tuition. Thousands of impoverished blacks sacrificed whatever they had to enrol their children. In the 1870s Bureau schools came under the jurisdiction of the public systems, and both black and white students enrolled.

The impact of the Freedmen's Bureau schools and, after 1870, integrated southern schools, left its mark on black Canadians. Many black parents, frustrated by their failure to gain access to public education, now wondered if their children wouldn't be better off in schools "back home." The exodus from Canada that began with the Civil War continued throughout Reconstruction, and the perception that educational opportunities were now available in a reformed America was one chief reason for it.

In 1865, America restored its Union. In 1867, Canada became a new country. This new country, unlike the US, reserved no significant role for black people. Blacks in Canada found themselves "sliding down an inclined plane from mere neglect to active dislike" (Winks, 1971). Those who remained in Canada engaged in private pursuits, drawing as little attention to themselves as possible. Lobbying for educational reform, legal justice, and the like, all but ceased. Such active lobbying required a stable and significant population.

After Confederation Canada's national obsession became settlement of the West, to secure it from expansionist America. Western settlement was achieved by aggressively recruiting Anglo-Saxon immigrants. The fact that blacks were leaving in large numbers fed the national belief that they were ill-suited to Canada's harsh climate, that their stay here was only temporary, and that it was only natural that they return home.

After basic survival, the central issue for the remaining black Canadians became immigration. Without a critical mass of people blacks would have little hope. The fact that the majority of those who stayed were young and unestablished made their situation even more desperate. Compounding the problem was a new and potentially devastating theory, the science of race.

The "Science" of Race and its Impact

After the Civil War American blacks were granted citizenship rights. Nonetheless, America's first immigration law, which limited citizenship to "aliens being free white persons," remained on the statute books until 1952. As a result, generations of immigrants from around the world attempted to prove, in order to gain entry into the US, that they were white. (Large numbers were successful in this enterprise, and today, across North America, more and more "white" people are rediscovering their black or coloured ancestry.)

In alarmingly similar ways the politics of colour left its mark on immigration and education policies in all former British colonies. In Canada, the West Indies, and the US, the national priority vis-à-vis immigration was for white settlement; for education it was segregation. As Canada was moving towards Confederation this prejudice was justified on scientific grounds. Negative missionary accounts from Africa, a growing thirst for rational explanations, studies linking cranial capacity to intelligence, Charles Darwin's comparisons between savages and apes, all conspired to produce a scale with white northern Europeans at the top and blacks at the bottom. In Canada and elsewhere, the same basic questions were being asked: "Why admit an inferior race into our country?" "Why teach the unteachable?"

Racism–a scientific theory which holds that all races are part of the slow process of evolution and can be categorized in terms of intelligence, behaviour, or physical type–belongs to the nineteenth century. It came to replace religion, in a more secular age, as the main justification for slavery. Science provided a rational explanation for slavery and imperialism by demonstrating that hierarchical relationships (i.e. master/slave) were a fundamental law of nature. Though Charles Darwin opposed

"'The Orang-Outang carrying off a Negro Girl.' *The eighteenth-century fable of intercourse between apes and African women represented as fact. Beings between apes and humans appear in the background as the offspring of such relations and suggest the missing link in the scale of creatures. Britain, 1795" (Pieterse, 1992). During the nineteenth and early twentieth century racist myths were often presented as fact. Images linking black people to apes were part of the stock and trade of a virulent brand of racism which spanned the continents. Such images were used to bolster claims of a race hierarchy with blacks firmly entrenched at the bottom. Clearly, the intent of such a sustained bombardment of negative images was to squash black advancement, especially after slavery's decline.*

slavery, his theory of evolution was seized by many as the perfect explanation for the sorry state of blacks the world over.

In Canada, three other factors combined to produce restrictive anti-black immigration policies: the abolition of slavery, concerns over assimilation, and fears about race mixing. "Science" had shown that blacks only responded to authority, and thus were natural slaves. The responsibilities of freedom were simply too much for genetically inferior black people. So, the reasoning went, if it was against the law to enslave blacks, there was no reason to allow them in. Again, the pull to the US was augmented by the push from Canada.

After Confederation, Canada, given its need for western settlement, was compelled to address the immigration question. At the time most blacks lived in segregated communities, suggesting that they did not easily assimilate. Government officials ignored the history of imposed segregation and the successes of integration in Toronto, Buxton, and British Columbia. Taking a purposefully selective view of things, they argued that blacks were unassimilable. This view, combined with the desire to populate the west with northern Europeans, led to new restrictions on black people and a virtually closed door to future black immigration.

A Single Drop of Negro Blood and Canada's Missed Opportunity

Many European countries had formally recognized race hierarchy scales. Spain, for instance, the dominant imperial power in the sixteenth century, had 16 official categories. Though customs broke down and there was much intermingling between racial groupings, this delineation or ranking of races was essentially transplanted to the New World.

Intermingling between whites and blacks on plantations led to a small but significant mulatto population in the southern US. Before the Civil War, some states allowed these people to define themselves as white or half-white. Guilt over the rape and abuse of many house-slave women on the plantations no doubt played a role in this leniency. (Certain personal histories maintain that a mixed-race child would have a greater chance at upward mobility, for in both the North and South light-skinned blacks were accorded more privileges and respect than people of a darker

hue. A similar phenomenon occurred in the West Indies.) After
the Civil War, however, tolerance for mixed-race people dissi-
pated. In time, a "single drop of Negro blood" was enough to
forever mark a person as black. (In this, the West Indies differed
from America.) It was a view consistent with the race science of
the day.

Most states followed this restrictive view and, after
Reconstruction, many passed laws prohibiting inter-racial marriages and stipulating how much "Negro blood" a person could
have (in Virginia, less than one-sixteenth) to be classified as
white. Though Canada passed no such laws, it was clear from
1867 onwards that racial mixing would not be tolerated.
Politicians accepted the white supremacist argument that such
mixing would dilute the Anglo-Saxon stock. White children,
especially, had to be protected and the colour line was strictly
enforced. The surest method of dealing with the "black menace"
was to keep it out.

In early Canada, the only form of segregation recognized in
law was in schools. By not listening to the sincere black and
white voices of school integrationists, Canada made an egregious error of omission. By listening to the racist fear-monger-
ing of school segregationists and the pseudo-theories of race
science, Canada made an equally egregious error of commission.

By dismantling school segregation Canada could have honoured the promises made to scores of black refugees. It could
not have misunderstood the importance of education to black
people. Ignoring the consistent voices for integration and reform
proved costly. The imposition of segregation in education and,
increasingly, in other walks of life, caused Canada to miss a glo-
rious opportunity. In short, Canada could have kept its vital
black communities. For one hundred years, it paid the price for
not doing so.

Black Educational Reform in the US

American white supremacists clearly understood the potential
impact of education for blacks. The burning of black schools
was a major plank in the Ku Klux Klan campaign of terror. In
the face of threats, intimidation, and actual burnings, the black
community's resolve remained strong. America experienced a

dual history of terror and destruction on the one hand, and faith and construction on the other.

Black churches were instrumental in keeping the faith alive. Through fundraising, community development, and "teaching on the side," they rallied the community. Schools and churches were burned to the ground, but doggedly rebuilt. Religious belief and education were two things that could never be taken away. A solid grounding in both became the black community's ethos.

Housed in segregated, underfunded, and poorly equipped schools, black students took up the challenge. Literacy and numeracy rates soared. By the turn of the twentieth century a full 70% of American blacks could read and write, twice as many as before the Civil War. Blacks were overcoming the limitations resulting from centuries of slavery and servitude and were succeeding in spite of segregation.

Perhaps the greatest educational achievement was the founding of black colleges and universities. Prior to 1865 only five black colleges and universities existed in America, all of them in the North. Between 1865 and 1915, seventy-four black colleges or universities were founded, most of them in the South. Many were supported by federal government grants and the Freedmen's Bureau, but they all relied on financial support from the black community.

The Hampton Institute, Tuskegee, Howard University, Spellman College, Wilberforce University, Shaw University, and others provided quality higher learning for thousands of black students. Hampton, in Virginia, continues to attract many of the finest black students in America. Gaining acceptance there is as difficult as at any Ivy League school, including Harvard and Yale. Howard, in Washington, D. C., has trained many of the nation's top

Booker T. Washington
Born into slavery, Booker T. Washington graduated from The Hampton Institute. He became director of the Tuskegee Institute, built, from the ground up, by Washington and his staff.

black politicians, lawyers, doctors, dentists, scientists, and engineers. Spellman, the first college for black women, has a one-hundred-year tradition of academic excellence. Other universities, like Wilberforce, trained its students in religion, reflecting the close link between religion and education in black America.

Across America the building of each black university or college was cause for celebration. By 1915, every state south of the Mason-Dixon line, except Kentucky and West Virginia, had at least four black colleges or universities. Mississippi, arguably the most regressive state of the old Confederacy and the site of much anti-black violence, had nine. During an era when race science was at its height, US black colleges and universities were producing graduates of great academic distinction. These graduates, up from slavery, would deliver black people from a history of oppression and bring them to the promised land of freedom and prosperity. They signalled a different tomorrow.

Great Post-Civil War Black Achievers

Daniel Hale Williams: In 1893, he performed the first successful heart transplant in history; Edmonia Lewis: One of the few recognized black women sculptors of her time; George Washington Carver: An agricultural scientist and inventor, he is credited with bringing crop diversification to the South; William Christopher Handy: Brought blues music to general public attention.

Having defeated slavery, black America would not be defeated by segregation. The success of black colleges and universities was paralleled in other walks of life. Many black inventors, poets, novelists, artists, agriculturists, entrepreneurs, athletes, classical, jazz, and blues musicians, and the Negro Baseball Leagues, rose out of the Reconstruction period. Enjoying the fruits of increased liberty, blacks were making their mark in mainstream society. No longer hidden on plantations, they were finally being noticed and their contributions appreciated. W.E.B. Du Bois' notion of the "talented tenth" leading black people to the promised land of wealth, prosperity, and, most importantly, freedom, was bearing fruit.

Ironically, the harsh segregation laws of the late nineteenth and early twentieth century were not the result of black inferiority; rather they were passed because blacks were succeeding. When the laws failed to "keep blacks in their place," violent white supremacists were to take justice into their own hands.

In Canada, black issues were relegated to the back burner, forgotten in concerns over western settlement and the division of powers between the provinces and the federal government. It would take decades before the black community began, once again, to assert itself north of the border.

Elijah McCoy
Between 1873 and 1894, seventeen blacks were admitted to the Mississippi law bar. Three of those admitted were from Canada: Garrison Shadd's son, W. A Shadd; Charles V. Roman (who helped establish the National Medical Association); and the great black inventor, Elijah McCoy. McCoy was the son of slaves who escaped to Canada. He invented the lubricating cup, a device which allowed machines to be oiled while still running. This time-saving advance was so important that many manufacturers demanded that purchased machinery be equipped with "the real McCoy."

5

Black Canada: the Dormant Years

Separation and division are recurring themes in New World black history. First, African slaves were separated from their homelands. Then, on the plantations of America and the West Indies, they were divided into field and house slaves. (Malcolm X summarized this division, in terms of living in different physical and psychological worlds, with his famous reference to the "field nigger" and the "house nigger.") Some black men of "sturdy build and quiet constitution" were removed from the flock and used as breeders. Some desirable black women were used, in order to maintain a consistent slave population and to decrease the costs of importation, as birthing chambers. Black escapees (fugitive slaves, economic refugees, immigrants) carried the hurt of separation in their souls.

Stripped of nationhood, next of kin, identity, culture, religion, language, and name, blacks under slavery were animate things: bought, sold, manipulated, and killed in the manner of domesticated animals. Like a cow or pig, slaughtered and hung for bleeding, many blacks were destined for the kind of brutal treatment only poets can describe:

> Southern trees bear strange fruit
> Black bodies hanging in the Southern breeze
> Blood on the leaves
> And blood at the root.
> —Lewis Allen (lyrics), sung by Billie Holiday,
> *Strange Fruit.*

During Reconstruction, southern blacks, having been granted voting rights, became politically active. Supported by the presence of the US army, black men went to the polls in unprecedented numbers. In the South they represented the vast majority of Republican voters. Between 1865 and 1877, 600 blacks were elected to southern state legislatures; 20 served in the US House of Representatives, and there were two black Senators. Such widespread political representation gave blacks hope that Reconstruction promises would materialize. The federal government assurance of "40 acres and a mule" offered a real possibility that impoverished former slaves could become independent farmers and help re-build a devastated southern economy. Blacks were encouraged to stay in the South with the understanding that, for the first time in history, their labour would be rewarded financially and through personal fulfilment.

To Canadian and other blacks, the South looked like a land of opportunity. Reconstruction governments built public schools and hospitals in poor black and white communities. Many state legislatures outlawed the Black Codes and extended services to former slaves. Black churches sprang up across the land, as congregations saved money to buy property and build places of worship. The role of black ministers, "men of words," took on a new importance. These men were expected to lead their communities, and many of them moved from the pulpit to government office.

Jim Crow and the Reign of Terror

The emergence of well-organized inter-state societies like the Ku Klux Klan and local anti-black vigilante groups grew out of the Union victory and black political progress during Reconstruction. As schools and churches for blacks were built, these groups burned them down. Black activists and white sympathizers were terrorized in their homes. Across the South, kidnapping, cross-burning, and/or the lynching of innocent blacks became an almost daily occurrence. It was a reign of terror that federal officials did little to stop, and that many southern state representatives openly supported.

There were early signs that all was not right in the South. Many bitter whites believed that they must take justice into their own hands. Secret societies like the KKK and the Knights of the White Camellia spread throughout the region. Their aim was to "win back the South" through a campaign of terror. In the two years after the Civil War nearly 5,000 blacks were murdered, many of them lynched.

Jim Crow Laws:

1) Georgia passes segregated schools legislation (1870), separate seating areas on trains (1891), separate parks (1905), and separate baseball fields (1932).

2) South Carolina has separate railroad cars for blacks (1900), segregated work areas in factories, and a law justifying unequal education spending (1915).

3) City of Baltimore establishes separate living districts for blacks (1910).

4) Louisiana segregates seating at public performances (1914), and provides no state money for integrated schools (1965).

5) Oklahoma passes separate phone booths legislation (1915), and outlaws certain mixed race recreational activities (1935).

6) Mississippi enacts separate public transportation legislation (1922).

Dozens of other laws were passed, all with the intent of establishing a strict separation between blacks and whites.

The subsequent withdrawal of federal army forces turned the South into a racial battleground. The 1875 Civil Rights Act, which outlawed racial discrimination in public places, was ignored in many jurisdictions. Blacks who dared to vote were particularly targeted, and most stayed away from the polls. One southern Republican after another lost his seat to a white Democrat, and the balance of power shifted dramatically. By 1877, white southerners were in a position to win back the cherished goals of the Confederacy.

Citizenship rights gained during Reconstruction were lost as southern states freely passed laws disenfranchising blacks. Thirst for rapid national economic expansion overshadowed concerns regarding civil liberties. The promises of Reconstruction gave way to *Jim Crow,* the term used to describe a system of segregation laws establishing strict separation between blacks and whites. Barriers to voting included a property test, which stipulated that every voter had to own property; a poll tax or voter's fee; a literacy test, requiring that all voters know how to read; and a grandfather clause which waived certain other requirements if the voter's grandfather was eligible to vote before the Civil War. These laws were passed specifically to block black involvement in politics. Few could fulfill their stringent requirements. In 1898 in Louisiana, only 5,000 blacks voted, a 95% drop from the previous state election. By the turn of the twentieth century the black cause ceased being addressed in southern legislatures.

With whites firmly in control of state legislatures, Jim Crow and vicious intimidation campaigns, where thousands of blacks were jailed and/or lynched, made many wonder if life for blacks wasn't better, or at least more secure, under slavery. Moreover, the federal government promise of 40 acres and a mule proved empty as most blacks received no financial support from Washington, itself a largely segregated city. Forty acres, a mule, and independence gave way to sharecropping, a system which further impoverished blacks.

Sharecroppers farmed small plots of other people's land. They received a share of the crop and lived on credit until harvest time. White landowners and storekeepers (often one and the same) acted as creditors, keeping sharecropping families fed and clothed. Debts accrued over the year were paid back through a percentage, large or small depending on the total amount borrowed, of the harvested crop. Prices on staple products were fixed and blacks were prohibited from selling their crop margins to the highest bidder. A cycle of dependency developed wherein blacks found themselves permanently indebted. Sharecropping became another form of slavery, another form of economic exploitation. The master/slave relationship was replaced by a landowner/debtor relationship.

Black Canada: Towards the Twentieth Century

In 1901 there were fewer than 18,000 blacks left in Canada. The census of that year showed that nearly three-quarters of these were under the age of twenty-one. The post-Civil War push and pull factors had reduced Canada's black population to an insignificant phantom, a distant memory.

Their contributions to nation-building and protecting Canada from American encroachment all but forgotten, black Canadians were regarded as minstrel-type caricatures from romantic comedy. Blacks who didn't buy into the happy Negro stereotype, singing and dancing on minstrel stages, were persecuted. The choice was plain: understand your role as a subject for white amusement, or leave. The undercurrents of bigotry, reinforced by race science and stereotypical depictions of blacks, moved from the shadows.

In the press and in professional journals blacks were consistently portrayed as pleasure-seeking sexual beasts, indolent,

US black iron workers in cast house of Dominion Iron and Steel Company blast furnace, Sydney, Nova Scotia, (circa 1902).
Between 1901 and 1904, several hundred skilled black steel and iron workers from the southern and western US came with their families to Cape Breton. During the same period other American black labourers, business people, and single women emigrated to Cape Breton. These blacks established a vibrant community complete with a church, school, and recreational facilities. By 1905, however, housing difficulties and a lack of employment drove all but a few off the island.

smelly, unreliable, incapable of assimilation, and dependent. Though much depleted, the black population, young, marginalized, segregated in "peculiar kinship settlements," and cast in the light of gross inferiority, was considered a threat. Described as "niggers," "sooties," "dinges," and "jigaboos," blacks retreated into the shadows.

Late nineteenth and early twentieth-century Canadian historians either denied the existence of slavery in Canada or blamed it on the Americans. Canada assumed a position of innocence, denying its legacy of black mistreatment. Positive black achievements (the humanitarian work of abolitionists, the critical role of blacks in the military, Buxton and the Elgin Settlement, Victoria's black community, John Ware's rodeo, and so forth) became mere footnotes to Canadian history.

Increasingly blacks left their small settlements for the cities. Though slave auctions had been held in York (now Toronto), the city also served as a hide-out for black refugees escaping slave chasers who entered the settlements. The city grew into an abolitionist centre and meeting place for black organizations. The municipal government's St. Lawrence Hall provided space for black community agencies.

In contrast to recent times (i.e. the police killings of Anthony Griffin on November 11, 1987 and Marcellus François on July 3, 1991; and the demonization of peoples of colour by then Parti Québécois leader Jacques Parizeau following the narrow "No" victory in the 1995 referendum on sovereignty), Montreal seemed better able to integrate black people. Although in Montreal, as in Toronto, blacks tended to settle in their own communities. The Union United Church on Atwater Street in Montreal's St. Henri district became a critical unifying institution. Successive

Turn-of-the-Century Press Descriptions:

1) …Negro "peculiarities…so abnormal that…he sinks to the level of the animal," being fond of gin and fried liver, of outlandish religion, witchcraft, sex, and song. (The *Windsor Mail,* Nova Scotia, 1876.)

2) Canadians wished to see the Negro "work out his own intellectual, moral, and economic salvation if he is to be saved." (*The Week,* Toronto, 1887.)

3) …there were said to be one hundred and thirty-eight "dusky houchie kouchie girls" from the "jungles of Africa" who did "business by the gleams of a red torch" upon black skin. (Vancouver, 1903.)

4) …the "dangers within, not without" already posed by too many Jappy-Chappies, Chinks, and Little Brown Brothers who could not be assimilated. There were "dangers of dilution and contamination of national blood, national grit, national government, national ideas,"…for self-seeking "Jews and Pollacks and Galicians" would corrupt Canada. "Theoretically…the coloured man should be as clean and upright and free-and-equal and dependable as the white man; but…practically he isn't." As for inter-marriage, "we do not propose poisoning the new young life of Canada." (Agnes C. Laut, "respected popularizer of Canadian history," *The Canadian Commonwealth,* 1915.)

Robin Winks, *The Blacks In Canada.*

Clearly, other immigrant groups "of colour" suffered under the lash of race science and its colour scale theories. This "science" made its way from academe to all sectors of society.

church ministers acted as counsellors, immigration consultants, and black community advocates. Eaton's Department Store agreed to hire its first black worker as a direct result of pleas from the Union United Church and the Coloured Women's Club of Montreal. The Church was an instrument of education. It, along with the Negro Community Centre, were focal points for blacks in Little Burgundy.

These institutions had their parallels across Canada, especially in the Maritimes. In 1900, James Robinson Johnston

James Robinson Johnston
Urban black communities were held together by stalwart leaders like William P. Hubbard, Toronto alderman and acting mayor; Anne Packwood of Montreal's Coloured Women's Club; and James R. Johnston, Halifax lawyer and civil rights activist.

opened his law office in Halifax. A superb criminal lawyer, Johnston has been referred to as the "Martin Luther King of Nova Scotia." Halifax had many active black churches and associations. In 1903, the influential black journal *Neith* was founded in Saint John by Abraham B. Walker, another lawyer of considerable distinction. Johnston, Walker, and others provided a ray of hope to the disenfranchised.

The title of Peggy Bristow's book *"We're Rooted Here and They Can't Pull Us Up": Essays in African Canadian Women's History* (1994) neatly captures the essential role of black women in Canadian history. Their struggle to overcome the double discrimination of systemic sexism and racism is marked by incredible determination. Without the dedicated work of black women, in churches, community and advocacy groups, schools, and in the home, it is unlikely that Canadian blacks would have survived the racist hurt of turn-of-the-century Canada.

Immigration: "Exodusters" and "Sodbusters"

While education became the central issue for America's black community, for Canada's dispirited blacks immigration was the primary concern. Not having a substantial number of individuals united under a common cause meant certain destruction of the community.

As, under Jim Crow and the dismantling of Reconstruction reforms blacks were being lynched by the thousands in the South, white Canada began to fear a "return exodus" of blacks north of the border. Conventional wisdom held that the surest way of avoiding a "black problem" was to restrict entry. Politicians across the country were petitioned by their constituents to "keep the Negroes out." Statements advocating a whites-only immigration policy ensured electoral success. A misunderstanding of sharecropping's economic exploitation led white Canadians to believe that blacks were predestined to be a dependent underclass. Canadian newspapers occupied themselves with negative stories, leaving black American successes unreported.

When climate was added to the growing list of rationalizations for barring black immigration, white Canadians could smugly maintain their innocence, ignore Canada's history of black mistreatment, and do an about-face on the positive legacy of encouraging blacks to seek refuge within their borders. Blacks, it was felt, should be kept out for their own good. In this context, there was no need for discriminatory laws to keep blacks in their place: their place was determined by the racist theories and conventions of the time. Increasingly, whites fell prey to a *not in my backyard* syndrome, believing that the best place for blacks was outside Canada's borders.

Between 1879 and 1881, 50,000 blacks, most of them sharecroppers escaping indebtedness and KKK terror, fled the South. Two former slaves, Henry Adams and Benjamin "Pap" Singleton, organized the initial groups of escapees. They named themselves "Exodusters" after the Biblical story of the Israelites' fleeing Egypt for the Promised Land. The promised land in this case was the Midwest where blacks believed they could settle, prosper, and govern themselves.

*Born into slavery, **John Ware** moved from Texas to Alberta in 1882. A superb cowboy, he has been credited with introducing longhorn cattle to Canada and pioneering the development of the rodeo.*

Several thousands opted to live in all-black communities in Kansas and Oklahoma, choosing self-segregation due to a total distrust of the white man. They established towns not unlike the black settlements of Canada West in the 1850s. Most, however, integrated with the white population whose greatest concern was environmental disaster, not racial bigotry. Flooding, livestock disease, and frequent droughts were commonplace. Trees

Benjamin "Pap" Singleton was a black slave from Tennessee. Like many blacks, he was migratory. He lived, among other places, in Windsor, Ontario. There is a strong possibility that Singleton was influenced by the success of black settlements in southwestern Ontario, and he strongly advocated all-black settlements in Kansas. When the US Congressional Committee held its meeting to investigate the causes of the 1879 exodus, Singleton boasted, "I started it all; I was the cause of it all."

were so scarce that migrants, black and white, built houses out of prairie sod, hence the name "Sodbusters."

Within a few years the promise of land in the American Midwest was bearing fruit. Land prices were within reach and black farmers, determined to achieve economic independence, successfully cleared and cultivated their acreage. Black farms dotted the landscape. The community, experiencing the heartache and joy of all pioneering settlers, swelled with pride. Some pooled their savings, formed companies, and bought huge ranches, home to thousands of cattle. Most blacks settlers on the Great Plains were self-supporting within one year, a dramatic turn of events given their community's history.

How did Canada Respond?

Black Americans were proving their ability to settle agricultural territory. Land ownership was the key. So too was the opportunity to have their children attend integrated schools, which existed throughout the rural Midwest. Whites in Kansas recognized the need for settlement, industry, and increased population, and many supported the blacks. These stories of peaceful coexistence and positive race relations did not make their way into Canada.

At the time of the Great Plains settlement, large numbers of blacks were migrating into northern US cities. While this migration did not reach its height until the 1910s, by the 1890s negative accounts of blacks in cities near the border appeared in Canadian newspapers. That Canada chose to focus on this aspect of black American migration, rather than the achievements of the pioneering Exodusters, speaks volumes about ingrained fears and prejudices. After all, a primary goal in Canada was western settlement, and blacks were successfully settling prairie-type land just to the south.

Canadian immigration authorities were having difficulty attracting settlers to the Prairies. They feared losing these virgin lands and their vast economic potential to the Americans. Previously, Canadian governments had brought blacks north to protect Canada from American encroachment and the "Manifest Destiny" designs of US federal politicians. How would they respond this time?

Thousands of black Americans had participated in the California Gold Rush (1849) and the Colorado Gold Rush (1857). They continued their trek west throughout the 1870s and 1880s, settling farm land in Nebraska, the Dakotas, Montana, and other states. Life was difficult, but many prospered. The US government knew that such westward expansion was critical to the economic health and security of the Union, and it encouraged adventure-seeking Americans to populate the west.

The expansion was so rapid, however, that land soon became scarce. Land prices in the states bordering Canada skyrocketed. Increased mechanization left many labourers unemployed. An opportunity to attract American farmers to Prairie Canada opened up, and Canadian authorities seized it. Beginning in 1897, Canada set up immigration offices in over twenty American cities.

*Freed from slavery after the Civil War, **Nat Love** headed for Kansas. He became one of the most famous cowboys in American history. For 20 years he drove cattle from Texas to Kansas. After winning the roping and shooting contests at the Deadwood Rodeo, he became known throughout the Midwest as "Deadwood Dick."*

By 1900, land prices in Dakota were twenty-five times higher than in neighbouring Saskatchewan. Unemployment was running high. As part of an all-out campaign to attract farmers, advertisements offering great opportunities and cheap land were placed in American newspapers. "Six hundred thousand Americans responded. Since Sifton [Sir Clifford Sifton, federal minister responsible for immigration in Laurier's government] mentioned no restrictions, and since the *Saint Paul Broadax,* a Negro newspaper, in 1901 ran articles in which the premier of Manitoba extended cordial invitations to all readers…the Negro

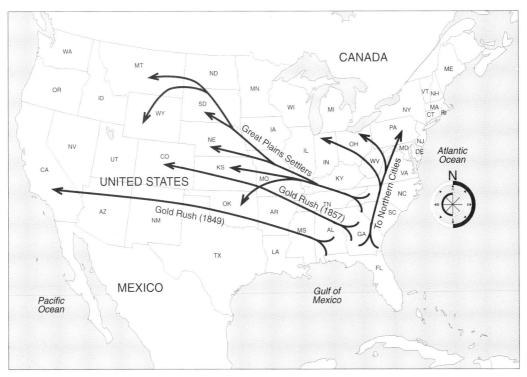

Movement patterns of southern blacks (1850–1900).

American assumed that he was welcomed. He was not" (Winks, 1971). White American settlers were welcomed, blacks were not. Many were turned away. Only a trickle penetrated Canada's border. It would be ten years before they arrived on the Prairies in any significant numbers.

During the fifty-year period from the Civil War to 1910, Canada only welcomed blacks in cases of emergency. Yet, looking back, contemporary black Canadians can take heart in some delicious ironies. On April 4, 1909, as Canadian authorities were contemplating strict legislation to bar black entry into the Dominion, the North Pole was discovered. The first person to reach the top of the world was Matthew A. Henson, a black American from Maryland, and a member of Admiral Robert E. Peary's expedition force. Canada's restrictive immigration policies of the early twentieth century were based primarily on the notion that blacks could not tolerate the cold. Climate did not seem to worry Matthew Henson!

In 1905, black intellectual and civil rights leader W. E. B. Du Bois met with delegates from thirteen states and the District of Columbia in Fort Erie, Ontario. At this meeting the Niagara Movement, precursor to the National Association for the Advancement of Colored People (NAACP), was founded. The delegates were barred entry to hotels in Buffalo, New York and chose to meet near Niagara Falls, Ontario partly because of the area's history as an important terminus on the Underground Railroad.

The meeting itself, not attended by any Canadian blacks but with the local black community's support, produced a radical agenda for change in America. An immediate end to all forms of racial discrimination, equality before the law, fair accommodation practices, and full voting rights for black men, were the cornerstones of the Niagara Movement's platform. A photograph of Niagara Falls in the background and the delegates in the foreground symbolized the Movement's agenda for change.

In Canada, a growing number of stalwart blacks adopted the notion that nothing was gained by taking flight.

Matthew Henson
The glory for discovering the North Pole has gone to Admiral Peary, not Matthew Henson or the Canadian aboriginals who were part of the expedition. In like fashion, though the praise has gone to Sir Edmund Hillary, Sherpa guide Tenzing Norkay was actually the first person to reach the summit of Mount Everest on May 29, 1953. Often, Eurocentric media create world-wide images favourable to its culture and, in these two examples and many others, diminish the roles of achievers from non-European cultures.

They had been down that road before. With firm resolve, they decided to stay and fight for what was rightfully theirs.

6

Racism on the Plain

Different governmental systems, geography, social safety nets, contrasting judiciaries, Canada's constitutionally recognized bi-culturalism (English and French), and notions of a multicultural mosaic, versus America's mono-cultural society and melting-pot, are often cited as differences between Canada and the US. Canadian nationals cherish these differences. They make "us" different and, subtextually, better than "them." But the steamroller of American culture in politics, television, and other walks of life has penetrated Canada's borders, has raised fears that our differences are shallow and vulnerable, our similarities deep and ingrained. Perhaps we let the steamroller in because it is "us."

More than a common border links Canada to the US. Historically, the most important shared attribute is our British heritage. Protecting this heritage from outsiders was considered equally necessary in both countries. Those "deemed unsuitable" were enslaved, segregated, discriminated against, or pushed out. Blacks suffered most from American and Canadian policies of exclusion, policies tied to the expansionist white ethos of empire-building Britain.

Westward expansion also inextricably linked Canada to the US. In both countries, settling the west ensured our survival as nation states. While acknowledging these and other similarities, Canadians maintain that in terms of race relations our countries have historically charted different courses, and are

For a period of one year from and after the date hereof the landing in Canada shall be and the same is prohibited of any immigrants belonging to the Negro race, which race is deemed unsuitable to the climate and requirements of Canada.

Government of Canada:
Order-in-Council no. 1324,
12 August, 1911.

presently radically different. Indeed, the differences are stark. Canada was free of white supremacist-inspired lynching campaigns. However, there are parallels to be drawn.

Indian and Black Oklahomans

The history of America's involvement with its Native Indian populations is one of wars, attempts at cultural genocide, and domination. As in Canada, however, these populations were often necessary for nation-building, and reciprocal agreements were struck. In both countries Indians enslaved blacks. Some American Indian bands adopted harsh slave codes, inherited from white slavery; others practised a far more lenient form of subjugation and control. The two communities have survived this history and, especially in the US, often work in common purpose.

Long before Canada returned vast tracts of land to its Native Indian populations, the Americans created the Indian Territory, now Oklahoma. Black slaves first appeared in the Indian Territory in the 1830s. They remained there until their slave holders freed them after the Civil War. A bond between the groups developed, based primarily on anti-white feelings, and mixed Indian-black marriages were common. As William Loren Katz explains in *Black Indians: A Hidden Heritage* (1986):

> Among Creeks, Seminoles, and Cherokees, black people made economic strides they could rarely duplicate in US society. African-Cherokees owned barbershops, blacksmith shops, general stores, and restaurants. Some had become printers, ferry-boat operators, cotton gin managers, teachers, and postmasters.

In both Canada and the US, the politics of skin colour superseded the legacy of Indian enslavement of blacks and brought the two communities together.

Free blacks of the Indian Territory were joined by Exodusters when the Territory opened up for settlement in 1889. Growth in black land ownership, farming, trade, and commerce continued apace. But when in 1907 the Territory, against the wishes of its coloured populations, became the State of Oklahoma, state sanctioned segregation took place almost

The peaceful co-existence between blacks and various Indian bands was threatened when, in 1907, the Indian Territory became Oklahoma. Jim Crow laws immediately proceeded the achievement of statehood.

immediately and Jim Crow laws were passed. Before long Oklahoma fell under the influence of the Ku Klux Klan. Racial violence erupted across the state, and in 1910 black Oklahomans were disenfranchised. Powerless and increasingly vulnerable, "move north or be lynched" became a common sentiment among black settlers.

The Old South had moved into Oklahoma and, once again, Canada was perceived as a safe haven. This perception was based largely on newspaper articles and advertisements encouraging American farmers to settle in Canada. These articles were supported by the Liberal government of Sir Wilfrid Laurier, and the initial pleas made no colour distinctions. A trickle of blacks joined thousands of white farmers settling the Canadian Prairies.

In 1905, Oklahoma City newspapers ran advertisements offering 160 acres of Canadian Prairie land for ten dollars. The

Proctors, a large black family, picked 250 pounds of cotton a day to finance their trip north. In 1906, they landed in Winnipeg, moving on to Edmonton by train. From there, the family trekked behind their loaded wagons for 106 miles to Junkins, Alberta. They received title of their Junkins homestead only after clearing the woods laboriously by hand. Their struggle was emblematic of black determination in Prairie Canada.

A few other black families journeyed north and settled near Maidstone, Saskatchewan in 1905 and 1906. At first, they were barely noticed amongst the hundreds of thousands of new white immigrants. This would soon change, for after Oklahoma achieved statehood, more black families moved to the Prairies, settling in Maidstone, Wilkie, Athabasca, Junkins, Breton, Clyde, and Amber Valley. Some of these homesteading trailblazers, like Henry Sneed, returned to Oklahoma and various other districts to organize larger parties of potential black emigrants. Benjamin "Pap" Singleton thought it possible that blacks could colonize the Canadian Prairies. By 1909, hundreds of blacks had settled in small isolated communities from Alberta to Thunder Bay, Ontario. The Prairie black community was achieving visible status.

Sneed successfully encouraged blacks from Oklahoma and southern districts to move north. He gathered two groups of two hundred men, women, and children in Weleetka, Oklahoma. The group leaders had determined, through appeals to Washington and Ottawa, that nothing in Canadian law could be used to bar their entry.

Sneed's first group arrived at the Canadian border in 1911. News of the group's intentions had filtered into Canada, and immigration officers were prepared. The black refugees were subjected to a battery of medical, literacy, character, and financial examinations not applied to other incoming groups. The blacks were equally prepared, having heard of these new restrictions

At the time of the black migration north, Canada and the United States were attempting to hammer out a Reciprocity Treaty allowing for freer trade and open markets. Prairie farmers would gain greater access to American markets through this agreement, and Prime Minister Laurier needed their electoral support. In 1911, the deal was signed, and Laurier called an election.

through the underground black press. As they were healthy Americans with sufficient money and property, existing regulations could not keep them out. Also, immigration officials feared that barring their entry would damage relations with the US and put in jeopardy the imminent free trade agreement. When Sneed's groups arrived, via the Great Northern train, at Emerson, Manitoba, both were admitted into Canada.

"Plain Racism"

Much Canadian history suggests that northern Europeans settled the Prairies. In fact, the largest group were white farmers from south of the 49th parallel. Though cheap farm land was the main reason for emigrating, many chose Canada because it did not have a "black problem." They came to Canada to escape contact with blacks. This, combined with the entrenched Victorian-era racism of northern Europeans, made for an explosive mix of hostility towards blacks in Prairie Canada.

Prairie whites' reaction to the 1910–1911 influx of black immigrants was chilling. The hostility shown towards free blacks was unparalleled. It was "plain racism," a virulent strain of bigotry which combined southern white values and the deep colour prejudice of Victorian Britain, overlaid with profound sexual and religious connotations. With a few notable exceptions, the press joined white groups, associations, and chambers of commerce in sending one single unified message to Ottawa: "Keep our Land White."

Anti-black racism spread like a Prairie fire across Canada. It reached its height in April, 1911. On April 4, Hazel Huff, a fifteen-year-old girl from Edmonton, accused a black man of assaulting her in the family home and stealing her ring and some money. Two days later J. F. Witsue was arrested.

The news snowballed across the country. Typical of the coverage was the *Lethbridge Daily News'* article entitled "The Black Peril." Most reports traded on the age-old fear of the promiscuous and sexually aggressive black man. White parents of daughters were warned to beware of the "Negro menace" within Canada's borders. Women's groups and others linked the attack directly to black immigration. "*The Saskatoon Daily Phoenix* announced the incident… in a front-page item with a large headline: 'A Negro Atrocity–White Girl

1911 Press Clippings and Other Statements:

1) "Whether well-founded or not, we have to face the fact that a great deal of prejudice exists against the coloured man and that his presence in large numbers creates problems from which we naturally shrink" (*Edmonton Journal*, March 27).

2) J. H. Woods, editor and managing director of the *Calgary Herald*, concluded that the black immigration was the first fruits of reciprocity with the United States. Teddy Roosevelt's question of what to do with the blacks was being answered...by sending them to Alberta. "Reciprocity...means that Canada is anxious to take all that America does not want." (March 25.)

3) "...we would like to add that the numerous instances of the lynch law in the southern states, about which we read almost daily and which deal almost exclusively with crimes likely each committed by Negroes, these instances should convince us, apart from other reasons, how undesirable such an increase is to our population" (Winnipeg, *Der Nordwesten*, German language newspaper, April 26).

4) Describing blacks as "...that special element, the worst of all," Arthur Fortin..of Quebec, contacted Frank Oliver to assure him that any government action to stop the influx would meet with the approval of that part of French Canada..."to prevent or at least control the immigration of Darkies into the Dominion. Just as it does for the Chinies–the Hindoes–and the Japs."(April 5).

5) William Thoburn, the Conservative member for the Ontario riding of Lanark North, asked Oliver whether...it would not be preferable "...to preserve for the sons of Canada the lands they propose to give to niggers?" (April 3).

6) "The assault made by a colored man upon a little girl in Edmonton should open the eyes of the authorities in Ottawa as to what may be expected regularly if Canada is to open the door to all the colored people of the republic and not bar their way from open entry here"(*Calgary Albertan*, April 5).

R. Bruce Shepard,
*Plain Racism: The Reaction Against Oklahoma Black
Immigration To The Canadian Plains* (1985).

Flogged and Assaulted by Late Arrivals at Edmonton'" (Shepard, 1985).

Nine days after the alleged assault and robbery, Hazel Huff admitted to fabricating the entire story. She had been afraid of being punished for losing her ring! A mythological black assailant became her escape. Witsue was freed, but the damage was done.

In microcosm this story represents white attitudes towards blacks in the Prairie provinces. Against incredible odds 1,500 blacks emigrated to Canada between 1909 and 1911. This relatively minor black population growth was enough to set off a chain of events that exposed Canadian racism in bold face. Racism, as a political strategy, was used to curtail black immigration. As R. Bruce Shepard states, in *Deemed Unsuitable* (1996), "The racist response to the African-American migrants insured that there would be only a few dark complexions in the region during the settlement era on the Canadian Plains. There should have been many more of them."

The Hazel Huff fabrication bears a striking resemblance with that of Susan Smith from Union, South Carolina. In 1995 Smith, having rolled her car into a river with her two young sons in it, claimed that they had been abducted at gun-point by a black man. After several suspects had been picked up, she recanted her testimony.

The Political Bind

Federal Cabinet ministers like Frank Oliver, Minister of the Interior, maintained an icy, almost eerie silence. The black Oklahomans were experienced farmers, many had money to invest, their stay in the American Midwest had proven their capacity to contribute economically free of government support, and they were sure to be loyal Canadians. In short, they would strike any objective observer as ideal settlers. None of this seemed to matter. To whites, they were nothing but a menace.

Fear that the Sneed groups represented a thin edge of the wedge, a mass black exodus north, became a Prairie obsession. The federal government, many of whose members supported the Prairie white community, did nothing to denounce this "un-Canadian" bigotry.

Laurier, having lost out to the Americans in a long-standing dispute over the Canada-Alaska border and, in the process, incurring the wrath of Canadians from coast to coast, desperately needed to push through a free trade agreement with the US (or so he believed at the time). The deal would be backed by Prairie farmers in all three provinces. Also Laurier, facing a revived Conservative Party and bedeviled by the old French-English split over imperial issues–which this time took the form of a fractious dispute on how to respond to Britain's request for naval assistance against the rising German threat–decided to seek a limited free trade deal with the US.

Laurier felt that he could not alienate the Americans by openly restricting black access to Canada. And yet, something had to be done to quell the rising tide of made-in-Canada anti-black hatred. If free trade was an election winner, not stemming the influx of black immigrants was clearly a loser.

Fear of alienating voting blacks in Ontario and the Maritimes necessitated a subtle campaign. Immigration officials, one of whom was a black doctor from Chicago, were sent to the South to discourage black migrants; higher immigration standards for blacks were invoked; US railways were petitioned to deny blacks access to Canada; and border officials were rewarded for disqualifying blacks. This campaign was sealed by the Liberal government's August 12, 1911, Order-In-Council prohibiting black immigration for one year. It was an all-out campaign designed to win the trust of Prairie whites, without blatantly offending black voters elsewhere. Nevertheless Laurier, thought to be disloyal to the British empire on the naval issue, and seemingly threatening the tariff-protected business establishment of central Canada with his reciprocity proposal, lost the ensuing election.

Immigration and the Law

Prior to these attempts to keep the Prairies white, British Columbians had launched a successful campaign to rid the province of its "yellow scourge." In 1876, the B. C. government responded to numerous petitions by passing a resolution stating "it is expedient for the Government to take some steps (at as early a date as possible) to prevent this Province being overrun with a Chinese population to the injury of the settled population of the country" (B. C. Legislature, *Journals, 1876*).

Chinese Americans entered British Columbia in the 1850s during the time of the Fraser River gold rush. Their numbers were small and, given that they worked mostly in abandoned or back-country mines, hardly warranted a backlash. Nonetheless, provincial restrictions were placed on employment and settlement opportunities. In 1884 and 1885 the B. C. legislature passed statutes prohibiting future Chinese immigration, and placed a $50 head tax on the few allowed to enter. These restrictions were struck down by the federal government who had final jurisdiction over immigration.

B.C.'s response to Confederation was often hostile and the federal government was forced to listen to western protest. In 1885, Ottawa passed an Act To Restrict And Regulate Chinese Immigration Into Canada, adding a blatantly racist restriction to Canada's first (1869) immigration legislation. It also exposed an unsettling parallel between Canada's treatment of Chinese and black immigrants.

Between 1869 and 1885, "approximately 15,000 Chinese immigrants were admitted specifically as a source of inexpensive labour for the construction of the western portion of the transcontinental railway" (*The Advocates Manual,* Law Union of Ontario, 1987). The promise of a rail-link to eastern Canada was instrumental in bringing B. C. into Confederation. Without such a link, the reasoning went, the new territory would inevitably fall to the Americans. As blacks were brought to Canada to fight wars, to protect the British empire, and build the nation, so too were the Chinese. In both cases, after the job was done, once their specific contribution had been made, Canada went to great lengths to push them out.

Chinese immigration to B. C. fell off sharply after the passage of the Act. In 1903, the head tax, first $50 then $100, was raised to $500, a huge sum at the time. Clearly, Canada did not want "yellow folk" within its borders. The drive to keep the Dominion white stretched from coast to coast.

Prairie whites used this precedent-setting legislation to bolster arguments favouring similar restrictions on blacks. The federal government had supported B. C.'s campaign, how could it not support the Prairie's? After all, as many Prairie whites believed, they were trying to exclude a group even lower on the colour scale!

Perhaps the chief defect of the 1867 Constitution Act, Canada's defining document, was its silence on equality rights. The Act gave primacy to trade and commerce, and gave courts of law little opportunity to defend human rights. Even if political will and the cultural climate had been on the side of equality, Canadian progressives were hamstrung by Canadian legislation.

Chinese Railroad Labourers
"Canada is a big country. How we got that much of the earth's surface, put it together politically, continue to hold it (more or less), is in itself, without our quite realizing it, a major achievement" (The Illustrated History of Canada, 1986). *This statement is certainly true, but what isn't often acknowledged is the means by which we created this "major achievement."*

By 1912, restrictions on would-be black immigrants ended the flow north. The campaign of exclusion worked its magic, and Laurier's Order-in-Council was never proclaimed. That Canada was able to stop black migrants from entering the country without enacting specific racist policies fed, and continues to feed, the notion of white Canadian innocence. True enough, except in the area of education, Jim Crow laws are not part of our historical record. But are we any more innocent? Or simply more subtle?

Stories of the many remarkable black achievers who helped settle the Canadian Prairies are documented in R. Bruce Shepard's *Deemed Unsuitable* (1996), a study of the black Oklahomans in Canada. This book is an important record of black achievement. Without it, Canadians would remain ignorant of a formative episode in Canada's development.

Often lost under the great sweep of continental events is the history of individual people and their families. Appreciating this

social history, or history in microcosm, is essential for understanding macroscopic change. If greater tolerance and acceptance did eventually come to the Prairie provinces of Canada, it
did so because of the determination of the Mayes family and
other black settlers. Their ability to overcome incredible obstacles stands as a monument to black potential.

It takes people to build a nation, people like the Mayes' and
their descendants. The Proctors, Robinsons, and Browers, to
name just a few, contributed mightily to Canada's growth and
prosperity. Prairie blacks were determined settlers who wanted
nothing more than an even chance to succeed. Racism and a
selective view of history prevented Canada from having more of
them.

Viewing History Selectively

Comparing and contrasting ourselves with Americans is a
staple of Canadian discourse. It has always been so. The
Edmonton Board of Trade, perhaps the single most influential
group involved in closing the door to black migrants, in its 1911
petition to Ottawa, stated:

> We cannot admit as any factor the argument that these peo-
> ple may be good farmers or good citizens. It is a matter of
> common knowledge that negroes and whites cannot live in
> proximity without the occurrence of revolting law-lessness,
> and the development of bitter race hatred. We are anxious
> that such a problem should not be introduced into this fair
> land at present enjoying a reputation for freedom from
> such lawlessness as has developed in all sections of the
> United States where there is any considerable negro ele-
> ment. There is no reason to believe that we have here a
> higher order of civilization, or that the introduction of a
> negro problem here would have different results.

Canada accepted as absolute truths international stereotypes
about blacks, particularly black men. The Canadian Imperial
Order of the Daughters of the Empire reflected these prejudices
by stating, in numerous petitions to Ottawa, that white women
must be protected from the sexual aggressiveness of black men.
Pre-occupied with racist myths, supposed black inferiority, and

After the upheaval of the American Civil War a Georgia-born woman named Mattie moved with her family to Tennessee. There she met and married Joe Mayes, a Baptist preacher. Within a decade Mattie and Joe headed west to the area then known as the Indian Territory, in what would later become the state of Oklahoma.

There Joe became the head of a small Baptist congregation and farmed to support their growing family. By 1909 Mattie and Joe had heard of good land available north of the international border on the Canadian Plains. For a ten-dollar fee you could homestead a quarter section and, providing you lived on it for three years and made improvements, the land would become yours. The Mayes family and some of Joe's congregation decided to trek north.

The Indomitable Mattie Mayes

The migrants took wagons to Tulsa, Oklahoma, and then caught the train north: St Paul, Minnesota; Winnipeg, Manitoba; and (by March, 1910) North Battleford, Saskatchewan. After studying maps and discussing possible homestead sites, they chose the Eldon district, fifty miles north-west of North Battleford, and eighteen miles north of Maidstone, along the North Saskatchewan River.

The land they chose was not easy to farm. Some had to be cleared of bush, and the tough plains sod had to be broken for crops. But hard work paid dividends. By the 1920s their farms were well established.

A church, constructed in 1912, became a focal point for the community, and Joe Mayes became the first preacher of the new congregation. In 1913 the first baptism was held at a nearby lake, and the first funeral was held in the little cemetery next to the church. The growing number of children pressed the Oklahomans to look into developing a school district. In 1915 the Eldon School was built and served the area until 1951, when it was consolidated along with other small schools in the area into a larger unit.

In 1950 Mattie left the Eldon district to live with one of her sons in Edmonton. Her son George stayed in Saskatchewan. His son, Murray, opened an automobile body shop in North Battleford. Murray's family grew, and are now found across Canada and the United States.

Murray's son Reuben became an outstanding football player, a Rookie of the Year in the National Football League. He played with the New Orleans Saints, and later with the Seattle Seahawks. He also obtained a degree in administration, and currently operates a job placement service in the Seattle area. Reuben's brother Christopher also obtained a degree in administration and works with his father in the family business. Their sister, Lucille, manages a restaurant in North Battleford.

Other members of the family have taken on a variety of challenges. Lisa is a high school teacher in Vancouver. Mary Ann is in Toronto studying to be a nurse. Chrystal is a candidate for the Royal Canadian Mounted Police. Charlotte completed her doctorate in veterinary medicine at the University of Saskatchewan, and recently gave birth to her first child.

R. Bruce Shepard,
Deemed Unsuitable (1996).

a rapid influx of southern blacks into US cities close to the border, Canada conveniently ignored post-Civil War black progress in America. So much so that, in 1929, a "senior government official could write totally inaccurately, that the settlers had all failed and left Canada" (Walker, 1985). In fact, many stayed. Their legacy lives on.

For a country to be distinct, it must define itself on its own terms. The Constitution Act of 1867 reflects the received wisdom of England, a country which also failed to recognize how important immigration would become to its lifeblood. After the American Civil War, the Fathers of Confederation were determined to chart a course different from the "dis-United States." They failed to take heed of the positive changes resulting from the war. They failed to notice that America was, at least on paper, attempting to mend the errors of its ways in regards to race relations.

In terms of race relations, America laid down foundation stones of change which directed black protest for one hundred years. Paper documents produced an agenda for US black activism. The targets of racial injustice (segregation, denial of

Teacher, Mabel Lockhart Hemmings, and students at Silver Fox School, Amber Valley, Alberta, 1921.

voting rights, discrimination in employment) stood out and could be directly challenged because they violated America's own laws and Constitution. By the turn of the twentieth century, with blacks uniting behind their leaders, the civil rights struggle was on.

Canada, having excluded blacks from its birth as a nation until, arguably, the 1950s, saw no need for either protective or (apart from immigration and education) discriminatory legislation. Racial discrimination was evident in all walks of life, but the targets were "moving" (Winks, 1971). Some schools, restaurants, and workplaces integrated, but others did not. With no legislation around which to base a movement and little recourse before the law, the cause of black Canada went into remission. After WW I (1914–1918) over 2,000 blacks, many of them talented and influential members of their community, left Canada for the US. This final exodus left black Canada at its lowest ebb.

> Perhaps more effectively than anyone else, Martin Luther King, Jr. would remind America of its "paper promises:"
>
> *Fivescore years ago, a great American, in whose symbolic shadow we stand today, signed the Emancipation Proclamation. ... But one hundred years later, the Negro is still not free;... So we've come here today to dramatize a shameful condition. In a sense we've come to our nation's capital to cash a check.*
>
> - Martin Luther King, Jr.,
> *I Have A Dream speech,*
> Washington, D. C., August 28, 1963.

Presently, our country is facing new and pressing race-relations challenges. The real question is, "Are we now ready for positive, constructive change?" Are we ready to define and re-define ourselves as circumstances dictate? As Stephen Lewis articulates in his *1992 Report On Race Relations In Ontario,* the challenges before us are great:

First, what we are dealing with, at root, and fundamentally, is anti-Black racism. While it is obviously true that every visible minority community experiences the indignities and wounds of systemic discrimination throughout Southern Ontario, it is the Black community which is the focus. It is Blacks who are being shot, it is Black youth that is unemployed in excessive numbers, it is Black students who are being inappropriately streamed in schools, it is Black kids who are disproportionately dropping-out, it is housing

communities with large concentrations of Black residents
where the sense of vulnerability and disadvantage is most
acute, it is Black employees, professional and non-profes-
sional, on whom the doors of upward equity slam shut. Just
as the soothing balm of "multiculturalism" cannot mask
racism, so racism cannot mask its primary target...As one
member of the Urban Alliance on Race Relations said:
"The Blacks are out front, and we're all lined up behind."

Canadian Innovations and the Challenge Ahead

The Lewis Report, and other reports since, suggest alarming
parallels between Canada and the US in terms of race relations,
discrimination in the administration of justice (e.g. the over-
policing of black communities), black student "underachievement" and drop-out rates, and so forth. While it is true that, in
the 1990s, nearly one out of every four black males in America
between the ages of 20 and 30 has spent some time in jail; it is
also true that the per capita spending on education for black
youth is between 20 and 25 percent less than it is for white children and teenagers. The reasons for this inequity may be mani-
fold and complex; but the result, in terms of a cause-and-effect
relationship, should be obvious.

Canada justifiably prides itself on more equal publicly
funded education systems; but, as statistics clearly indicate, it
has not escaped problems associated with black students
"disidentifying" (Claude Steele) with school, not achieving to
their potential, and/or dropping out. The wisdom of the Lewis
Report is that–echoing the voices of people like Dr. Sheldon
Taylor and Metro Toronto Councillor Bev Salmon of the Black
Educators Working Group–it asks for an examination of the
causes, as opposed to a pre-occupation with the symptoms, of
black disengagement with the learning process. It points to a
positive course of action, and has helped spur the development
of specific anti-racist initiatives, English programs which
include black authors, and black history courses in Ontario
schools.

Indeed, across Canada black community groups are taking
up the challenge. In Nova Scotia, the dedicated work of the
Black Learners Advisory Committee has led to far-reaching
constructive reforms. In Quebec, the Quebec Board of Black

Educators, the Black Studies Centre, the Black Community Council of Quebec, the Black Theatre Workshop, and other organizations all provide essential educational services for black students. Similarly, the Afro-Caribbean Association of Saskatchewan, the Alberta Black Heritage Studies Association, British Columbia's Junior Black Achievement Awards, and many other associations all play critical roles in recognizing black achievement, providing positive role models, and ensuring the community's longevity.

At the time of the Lewis Report release, a multi-racial grade nine class from St. John's High School in Winnipeg was midway through conducting interviews and writing biographies on 44 distinguished blacks from Manitoba. With financial support from the province, the federal government, and black community groups; through the inspired organization of Linda McDowell (Social Studies Consultant, Winnipeg School Division No. 1), Zeeba Loxley (IDEA Centre), and the Afro-Caribbean Association of Manitoba; and, the thoughtful editing of Pat Graham and Darryl Stevenson, the 21 students completed their task. In 1993, *The Black Experience in Manitoba: A Collection of Memories* was published. As per its mission, the project has fostered a "general understanding of the historical and contemporary black experience in Manitoba," created a "cohesive identity for black students," and helped recognize the contributions of a group largely ignored in Canadian history books.

Any comprehensive study on black Manitoban history must now include this important book. As the students discovered, one finds in the 44 interviewees a vast reserve of determination and talent. *The Black Experience in Manitoba* stands as a model of educational excellence–a model which in the ensuing years will no doubt be replicated elsewhere. For many it has opened a new chapter on African-Canadian contributions to Canada's evolving democracy. For all this project demonstrates the value of cultural pluralism in education.

The achievements of these groups, and others like them, speak to the spirit of cooperation between associations and governments which Canadians of all ethnic backgrounds hold dear. Shrinking budgets may be used to justify re-configuring this relationship, but not to dismantle it. To do so would be to do

Frances Atwell
Gerry Atwell
Tony Ayre
Edward and Helen Bailey
Edward Bent
Ed Blackman
Duane Brothers
Wayne Cadogan
Carmen Cameron
Herb Carvery
Toby Chase
Patricia Ann Clements
Heather Daley
Cherrlyn Duhard
Dave Duncan
Gordon Earle
Mike Gaston
Pauline Grant

The

BLACK

EXPERIENCE

Louis Ifill
Dr. June James
Dr. Ralph James
Angelina Olivier Job
Stella Zola LeJohn
Harold Marshall
Charlotte Martin
Norm McCurdy
Mr. and Mrs. Mekonnen
Yvette Milner
Monica Naherny
Titilola Olude
Darryl Patterson
Willard Reaves
Hugh Rowe
Keith Sandiford
Janet Scott
Tony Scott
Del Simon
Inez Stevenson
J.R. Stevenson
Esme Stewart
Carl and Anna Tynes
Lee Williams

in Manitoba:

A Collection of Memories

Those remembered in The Black Experience in Manitoba *are listed on the book's cover.*

irreparable damage to the pursuit of equality. On this issue the challenge facing Canada is articulated by Madame Justice Abella:

> Equality and its handmaiden human rights are about fairness, an ethereal objective. But it is a realistic vision. To have the benefit of diversity is to have the benefit of heterogeneous input–human, intellectual, economic, cultural and political. It is to appreciate that the social orchestra, conducted by a democracy, sounds best when it is harmonious. The sounds blend, they do not merge. It is a symphony, not a concerto. All the players expect to contribute to the melodious whole, and are interdependent on one another for support. It is a solidarity based on understanding the unique value each different instrument brings to the whole orchestra. It is a solidarity we must never strop trying to achieve.

> – R. S. Abella,
> *"Human Rights in the Twenty-First*
> *Century: A Global Challenge."*

7
The Black Community's Quest for Self-Definition

Before WW I fewer than 20,000 blacks lived in Canada. Much of the community had been born in Canada. The black Oklahomans were the only significant group of recent immigrants, and for thousands of them the entire North American continent seemed hostile to their needs and wishes. The failed promise of the Canadian Prairies spurred a back-to-Africa movement in Oklahoma, not unlike the one based in Nova Scotia over one hundred years earlier. Alfred Sam, a native African, encouraged blacks, some of whom returned from Canada, to set sail for Africa. Sam's mission (not unlike the one later proposed by Marcus Garvey) of repatriating blacks to their true homeland had many followers. His enterprise, however, interrupted by the outbreak of WW I, never materialized.

The war united Canadians around a common cause. Intense feelings of nationalism and patriotism filled the air. The issues and concerns of black Canadians were pushed to the margins.

The Story of Africville

For decades, Africville, a small black community in Halifax, had been quietly working on its own quest for self-definition. Many of its successes paralleled those of other black settlements; many were unique to itself. In the 60 years between 1850 and WW I Halifax doubled in size. Thousands of white immigrants poured into the city and it became a vital trading port for Canada. Residents of Africville, created as a separate black community through a land purchase in 1848 and located in the north end of the city, contributed directly to the 19th-century growth of Halifax.

After establishing eleven Baptist churches throughout Nova Scotia, in 1854 Richard Preston founded the African United Baptist Association at Granville Mountain. Serving as a parent organization for twelve Baptist congregations, the AUBA became one of the most vital black associations in Maritime history. Importantly, these churches acted as a "Christian link" to the white community. They were also instrumental in furthering black education, many of them doubling as schools. To this day, the AUBA represents the needs and interests of black Nova Scotians.

From the beginning Africville was a church-based community. Regular attendance at church was taken for granted, as it was in most black communities up from slavery. While church served as a linch-pin for the soul, the men and women of Africville were also industrious. They worked as labourers and in service jobs in Halifax. Black stonemasons helped construct many of the city's public buildings.

Halifax's industrial growth was largely based on trade. Here too, Africville residents played an impor-

Richard Preston *escaped slavery in Virginia and arrived in Nova Scotia in 1816. He became a Baptist minister and helped found the Cornwallis Street African Baptist Church in Halifax, later establishing 11 Baptist churches.*

tant role. "Most of the people who reported themselves as seamen had worked the ships travelling between Halifax and the West Indies, and they had subsequently settled down in Africville" (Clairmont, *The Spirit of Africville*, 1992). Pride in community led to the creation of Africville businesses and organizations. For years, Africville was a vibrant community representative of the Maritime black struggle.

Industrial growth proved a mixed blessing for Africville residents. In the 1850s, land was expropriated from the community for railroad tracks and sewage disposal pits were relocated there. A pattern developed wherein the city placed institutions not wanted elsewhere in or around Africville. Against the community's protests, this pattern continued into the twentieth century. "They said the people in Africville encroached on the

Africville, Nova Scotia
For many, Africville came to represent the black quest for self-definition. Its history is one of ardent community involvement and, sadly, a battle to overcome white hegemony: a battle which was ultimately lost.

government but I say the government encroached on the people" (Africville resident). In the mid-1950s the City Council moved a large open dump to within a stone's throw of the community. Soon after, Africville's residents were relocated and the community destroyed.

The Rallying Spirit of Nationalism

As preparations for WW I intensified the "black problem" disappeared from Canada's national consciousness. The struggle of blacks, fewer than 20,000 and strung out in isolated communities, became immaterial. Canada was in the process of defining itself as a nation by suiting up for war. It was a quest for self-definition; for defining itself from within, not without. As Robin Winks (1971) explains:

The nadir for the Negro in Canada came at the moment when the nation as a whole at last felt itself to be emerging as an identifiable culture on the world scene. Having rebuffed the United States by rejecting a reciprocity treaty that Canadians had been seeking for fifty-five years, having made abundantly clear that Indian, Negro, and Oriental immigrants were not wanted, and having rallied to the defense of God, Country, and Empire, Canada now stood at Armageddon. The moment was an emotional one–and a magnificent one. For the greatest efforts of patriotism, of commitment to long-voiced if not oft-defended ideals, and of physical sacrifice were drawn from the Canadian people, at Vimy Ridge, at Passchendaele, and at home…The Negro stood outside this new drama.

Essentially, Africville was a community with an exceptional sense of historical continuity, but its residents lacked political power and influence with city officials…outsiders, black and white alike, could not see Africville as viable and its existence as desirable.

Donald Clairmont,
The Spirit of Africville.

And yet, blacks clearly wanted to be part of "this new drama," clearly wanted to break through the hegemony of exclusion. Across Canada scattered black communities were not to be denied. Would their dedicated service in the war effort alter perceptions at home and abroad?

The Struggle to Enlist

Recruiting volunteers was the job of local commanding officers and, by 1915, a few blacks were allowed to enlist in white regiments. Black leaders like Arthur Alexander from Buxton, J. R. Whitney (reporter with the *Toronto Canadian Observer,* a major black newspaper), and William A. White (the only black chaplain in the British army during the war), continued to press for greater black involvement. These and other blacks realized what was at stake. Not participating in battle would reinforce anti-black prejudice, and young black men made determined efforts to enlist.

In 1916, Canada set an ambitious target of one-half million recruits and the number of available white volunteers was drop-

Collection of statements made by white military officers:

1) I have been fortunate to have secured a very fine class of recruits, and I did not think it fair to these men that they should have to mingle with negroes. (Commander, 104th Overseas Battalion at Saint John.)
2) Neither my men nor myself, would care to sleep alongside [Negroes], or to eat with them, especially in the warm weather. (Commander, 106th Overseas Battalion at Halifax.)
3) Nothing is gained by blinking at the facts. The civilized negro is vain and imitative; in Canada he is not impelled to enlist by a high sense of duty; in the trenches he is not likely to make a good fighter; and the average white man will not associate with him on terms of equality. In France, in the firing line, there is no place for a black battalion, C.E.F. It would be eyed askance; it would crowd out a white battalion... (Major-General W. G. (Gwatkin, Chief of the General Staff at Ottawa.)

Robin Winks, *The Blacks In Canada.*

ping. Thousands of blacks had volunteered but been rejected. Official government policy stated that "There is no colour line; coloured battalions are not to be raised; coloured men are to be allowed to enlist in any battalion of the Canadian Expeditionary Force." Nonetheless, most recruitment officers used the old arguments regarding black-white intermingling: enlisting blacks would drive potential white volunteers away, whites could not be expected to fight alongside blacks, and so forth. Shut out at recruitment offices, blacks renewed their attempts to form all-black regiments.

Black Canadian leaders persisted and, in what was viewed as a human-rights victory, forced the issue to be debated in the House of Commons. Finally, authorization was given for the creation of an all-black unit. In 1916 the Nova Scotia No. 2 Construction Battalion was formed, its black soldiers recruited from across Canada. Clearly, this was a compromise move by Ottawa, but an important first step for blacks.

The Nova Scotia No. 2 Construction Battalion was indeed a concession. Barring blacks from enlisting was deemed anti-democratic. The only solution was to give them a regiment of their own, albeit one ruled by white officers. It was a temporary measure which allowed the Canadian military to circumvent more difficult issues of inclusion and integration. Once again, it appeared that exceptions would be made during war-time, but after the conflict ended the status quo returned.

Even though several blacks served with distinction in white regiments, there was never any intention of allowing the "No.

With the publication of Canada's Black Battalion No. 2 Construction 1916–1920 (1987), *Nova Scotian historian **Calvin Ruck** set the record straight on black Canadian contributions to the war effort. Blacks were determined to participate, never accepting the notion that WW I was a "white man's war." Roughly 300 of the 600 soldiers in the No. 2 Construction Battalion came from Nova Scotia. Ruck's research also details the phenomenal exploits of black "fighting men" like Jeremiah Jones of the 106th Battalion. Jones single-handedly captured a German machine gun post, killing a number of German soldiers and capturing others in the process. Perhaps this, and other dramatic acts of bravery, failed to be included in Canadian history books because black men like Jones never received distinguished conduct medals.*

2s" into battle. From their base at Truro, Nova Scotia they were sent to Liverpool, England, where they joined another group of volunteer blacks, the South African Labour Corps. After a brief period in England they were dispatched, as part of the Canadian Forestry Corps, to France. During war-time, and the demobilization period which followed, these black recruits were subjected to numerous physical attacks by white soldiers and civilians. There was little indication that their loyal service brought about greater acceptance.

Between 1914 and 1918, black Canadians at home were actively involved in the war effort. Black associations, on their own and in cooperation with white groups, launched fundraising campaigns and distributed propaganda leaflets. Some black

agencies were founded specifically to help Canada during these
years of crisis. Blacks worked in war factories, or volunteered
as free manual labourers and in hospitals as nurses. "Ironically,
Canada's white soldiers marched into battle in uniforms, the
buttons for which were manufactured by the only Montreal
company that extensively employed West Indian labour after
1911" (Winks, 1971).

The War Years in Black America

The US entered WW I in 1917 and more than four million white
workers were conscripted into the army. Desperate for labourers,
American company officials combed the South luring blacks
north with promises of jobs paying five times what they could
possibly earn at home. Without a new labour force the US war
economy (steel mills, railroads, meat-packing, textiles, brick-
yards, loading docks, army tanks, battleships, trucks, and uniforms) would grind to a halt. Southern blacks, restricted in their
movement by curfews, living under prejudice and the threat of
Jim Crow laws, and fearing lynching, were a receptive audience.

This was especially true for dispirited sharecroppers. The
market for southern cotton was in steady decline, and few of
them could support their families. Never before had they been
presented with so a promising offer. Also, the north retained its
reputation for greater tolerance and acceptance. The black rural
existence in America had been one of constant disappointment.
So, when the cities beckoned, their promise was irresistible.

W.E.B. Du Bois rallied black support for the war. "If this is
our country, then this is our war," he stated. As in Canada, most
American blacks drafted served in segregated labour battalions.
They were put through their paces in segregated southern
camps.

The Navy and Marine Corps refused to train blacks for battle, using them only in war service industries. American army
generals questioned the fighting ability of blacks and believed
that whites would not fight alongside them. Jim Crow infected
the American military from the top down.

In August, 1917, a street fight erupted between black army
recruits and a gang of white civilians in Houston, Texas. The
blacks were responding to taunting and racist insults. Twelve
whites were killed. In a celebrated military trial thirteen blacks

were found guilty of murder and ordered hanged, fourteen others were sentenced to life in prison. No whites were charged. News of this trial spread quickly through black America. Black leaders demanded an end to the brutal treatment of blacks in military camps. They doggedly championed the cause of real black involvement in the armed forces. Eventually the army agreed to let blacks serve in a fighting capacity.

Over 100,000 men served in mostly all-black regiments. (The officers were white, as blacks were not trusted with commissioned rank.) In France, they gained widespread respect for participating with distinction in one bloody battle after another. Trench warfare was not for the weak of heart. Black women served in army medical corps both at home and abroad.

By helping to protect world democracy, Du Bois and the NAACP believed that blacks would become valued citizens of America. But the respect gained overseas was not being translated into good relations at home. In 1917, race riots broke out in 26 cities across America. In St. Louis, Illinois, 39 blacks were killed. The rapid influx of blacks into northern cities was a test of American democracy. While winning the battle for rights and freedoms in Europe, they were losing it at home.

Black military heroes became civil rights heroes. After the war, thousands returned and were celebrated in huge parades. The most significant of these was held in New York City where one million people lined Fifth Avenue. Harlem's all-black 369th Infantry Regiment, cited eleven times for bravery and awarded top military honours, marched with pride to cheering white and black spectators. Was it the dawning of a new era?

1920s: the Harlem Renaissance

Over two thousand blacks migrated from Canada to the US in the years directly following WW I. Following an established pattern, Canada's loss was America's gain, as many who left were talented and educated. Most went to northern US cities, where opportunities for blacks seemed brighter than ever before. Black pride was sweeping America. Nowhere was this more evident than in Harlem, New York. Black writers, thinkers, artists, musicians, athletes, and entrepreneurs, from all over the US and, to a lesser extent, Canada and the West Indies, moved to Harlem to be part of the scene.

In August, 1920, over 50,000 blacks gathered in Harlem, marching in solidarity to mark the opening of the International Convention of Negro Peoples of the World. White America stood by as blacks triumphantly raised their tri-coloured black, red, and green international flag: black standing for their race, red for their blood, and green for their hopes. This march signaled a renaissance, a re-birth of black America.

Marcus Garvey
With his famous slogan "One God! One Aim! One Destiny!" Marcus Garvey led the first mass black movement, the UNIA, in North America. To this day, many black activists wear the label "Garveyite" with pride.

Leading the march was Marcus Mosiah Garvey, a Jamaican who promised to "organize the 400 million Negroes of the world into a vast organization to plant the banner of freedom on the great continent of Africa." Garvey's ideas amounted to a black nationalist platform and were perceived by many whites as directly challenging integration. Blacks, according to Garvey, had to take care of their own affairs, had to become independent. If this independence meant creating black homelands, either in North America or in Africa, then so be it! In time, Garvey's call for "pride in blackness" would have a dramatic impact on Canadian blacks.

Not all blacks shared Garvey's vision. Though discrimination continued to be a fact of life, and thousands of blacks lost their war-time jobs to returning white veterans, many others were making their mark in mainstream society, or on their own. The success of the Negro Baseball Leagues, for instance, before, during, and after the war, suggested that black enterprises could survive in a white world. The teams, with black owners and managers, not only beat the best white teams on the playing field, they often out-drew them at the ticket window!

Emboldened by their war-time contributions and with the protection and support of large urban populations, black artists came out from the shadows. In night clubs, art galleries, literary gatherings, theatres, and sporting venues, black culture asserted itself. The racist conventions discouraging black-white intermingling broke down as whites flocked to Harlem, South Chicago, and other black communities across America, to hear first-hand the blues and hot jazz of black musicians. Cities, as the enigmatic king of delta blues, Robert Johnson, rhapsodized in "Sweet Home Chicago," encapsulated the hopes and aspirations of millions of black Americans.

The era of black minstreling was over. No suggestion of buffoonery or "gettin' down on bended knee for Massa" was evident. The talent of black musicians, singers, writers, artists, actors, and actresses was being widely recognized as art of the highest order. The hip white crowd was buying black and were proud of it. Louis "Satchmo" Armstrong ushered in the Jazz Age, bringing his band from New Orleans to Chicago in 1922. By the 1930s, Armstrong was, arguably, the most popular American musician in the world. Over two million copies of Bessie Smith's 1923 recording *Down Hearted Blues* were bought by black and white Americans. Paul Robeson's career as spirtual singer, scholar, actor, athlete, and civil rights activist, was launched in the 1920s. Duke Ellington, Ethel Waters, and other talented black musicians and actors packed Harlem night clubs and Broadway stages.

> ### Harlem Renaissance Writers
>
> Much has been said about the oral tradition sustaining black people and black history. While this view has merit and a degree of historical accuracy, it sometimes obscures the glorious tradition of black writing. During the Harlem Renaissance, blacks such as Langston Hughes, "the poet of black America;" Zora Neale Hurston, novelist and cultural anthropologist; Claude McKay, Jamaican poet, short story writer, and novelist; and, Jessie R. Fauset, critic, essayist, novelist, and literary editor of the NAACP's *Crisis* magazine, carried on this tradition.

Self-Definition and the Leadership Issue

Strung out across the country and facing the more subtle aspects of Canadian racism, blacks had difficulty uniting behind a common cause and a common leader. The lack of recognized black spokespeople with a national focus threatened to keep the community in its restricted place. Canadian blacks, if they were to survive a hostile environment, needed to organize. City life came to represent their only hope.

By the 1920s most Canadian blacks lived in cities. Job opportunities, the emergence of the KKK in small towns, city excitement, and the growth of black pride movements brought blacks from rural areas to Halifax, Montreal, Toronto, and Vancouver. Also, in the heady days of the 1920s the loosening of immigration restrictions resulted in small groups of American and West Indian blacks entering Canadian cities.

Marcus Garvey's "pride in blackness" served to encourage hope of independence. In 1914, Garvey had founded the Universal Negro Improvement Association (UNIA) in Jamaica. His belief was that blacks could gain equality only through economic, political, and cultural independence. Between 1916 and 1920 chapters of the UNIA were established in numerous American cities. They were linked by the Association's newspaper, *Negro World,* and Garvey used their resources to start black-run businesses.

The UNIA fell on hard times, and Garvey was found guilty of mail fraud. He spent two years in prison and, after his release, was deported. (Some maintain that Garvey was sent to jail on trumped-up charges by those fearful of black economic power.) Between 1919 and 1923, however, chapters of the UNIA were established in all Canadian cities with sizable black populations. Garvey gave rousing speeches in an attempt to unify black Canadians behind the cause of economic self-sufficiency and pride in their African heritage. The Montreal, Halifax, and Toronto chapters were especially active. In these cities the Association became the voice of protest for thousands of blacks.

Strains on Black Urban Culture

Canadian whites, witnessing the influx of blacks into northern US city ghettoes, were fearful of similar developments occurring in Canada. Montreal was Canada's dominant city, and some developments there struck the conservative white establishment as "too American."

During the 1920s the train from Montreal to New York was usually packed. By the same token, Montreal's reputation as the Paris of North America brought equal numbers of New Yorkers north of the border. They came to sample fine French cuisine, theatre, black cabaret, and the hot jazz at Rockhead's Paradise.

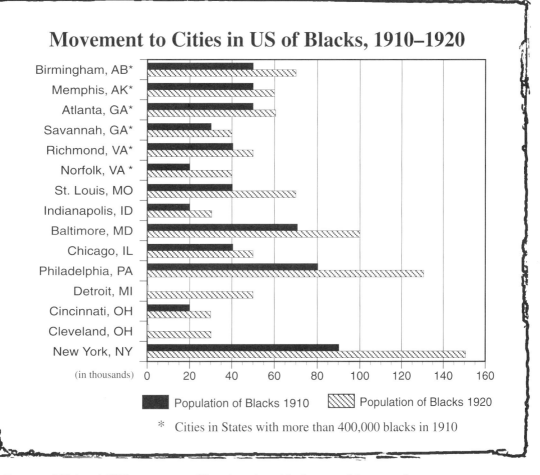

Movement to Cities in US of Blacks, 1910–1920

(in thousands)

Population of Blacks 1910   Population of Blacks 1920

* Cities in States with more than 400,000 blacks in 1910

Between 1914 and 1929, over one million American blacks moved from rural settings to cities. On a much smaller scale, a similar migration occurred in Canada. The Depression dampened the spirit of most, and made the dream of economic self-sufficiency impossible for all but a few.

Montreal was a culture capital and black families, many of whose households centred around a piano, played no small part in its development. In 1925, Oscar Peterson, considered by many the greatest jazz pianist in the world, was born in Montreal. He is a product of his milieu.

Montreal in the 1920s was special in other ways. A large percentage of black men (forty percent by some estimates) were married to, or cohabiting with, white women, a phenomenon which was also occurring in France. The national average for this form of mixed-race union was roughly seven percent. What did this high rate of miscegenation represent? Did it have more to do with class than colour? What factors unite all people suffering from economic impoverishment? What factors separate them? How was it viewed by the black community and white community? Is inter-racial marriage or cohabitation the ultimate breaking of the colour line?

City administrations became concerned about blacks escaping US prohibition by moving into Canadian cities. In 1922 in Montreal, the Nemderoloc Club ("coloredmen" spelled backwards) gained a reputation as a black den of iniquity. Negative stories about the club's activities caused a rift among blacks. As in other Canadian cities, the presence of new blacks with different ideas and cultural frames of reference placed a strain on indigenous black communities. These communities, struggling to survive and make inroads into mainstream society, did not want any disapproving attention. Many whites, who wrongly believed that "all blacks must be the same," were somewhat bewildered by these new black voices.

The Coloured Women's Club of Montreal, founded in 1902 by the wives of black railroad workers was, and still is, representative of stability. So too was the Union United Church. These institutions served as essential filters for the black community. Over the years they have helped thousands of blacks adjust to their new lives in Canada. Their memberships, conservative, dedicated, and hard-working, stood in sharp contrast to the black thrill-seekers entering the city in the 1920s.

Following a pattern established in America, Montreal blacks found themselves increasingly living in run-down apartment buildings. In the States, whether it be Harlem, Chicago's South Side, or the black community of Boston, rents were so high that several black families shared single apartments. Unscrupulous "slumlords" gouged their tenants, threatened eviction, and allowed their buildings to deteriorate. The strategy was simple: charge high rents, pack as many blacks into a building as possible, allow it to deteriorate and then sell the complex to industrial interests. In Montreal a similar strategy led to similar results.

Small groups of West Indian immigrants began arriving during and after WW I. Many settled in the Maritimes where they worked as industrial labourers. Those who moved to the cities tended to support Marcus Garvey's platform, which many blacks and whites increasingly viewed as a threatening segregationist agenda.

As the decade wore on, UNIA supporters and conservative blacks grew further apart. Garvey's statements about racial purity and attacks on light-skinned blacks alienated many, for inter-racial marriages between blacks and whites, and blacks and Indians were quite common at the time. Also, his back-to-Africa appeals and sponsorship of the African Orthodox Church failed to resonate with those who now considered Canada home. How would such divisions benefit the Canadian state? In diversity there can be strength. There existed, however, two related problems: a leadership vacuum in the Canadian black community; and the white establishment's inability or unwillingness to accept a plurality of black voices.

List of UNIA Achievements in America:

1. Harlem chapter founded in 1916. Chapters soon follow in other cities.
2. The Negro World newspaper develops a wide readership. It appeals to black pride by relating stories about black American heroes.
3. The Black Star Line and the Negro Factories Corporation founded in 1919. Both appeal to black nationalist sentiments by starting black businesses.
4. The UNIA raises an estimated $10 million to support its initiatives.
5. By 1920, Garvey claims to have four million black American supporters.

Garveyism was not providing a unifying message. When he returned to Toronto in 1936, Garvey "alienated yet more Canadian followers by indiscriminate attacks on ex-Prime Minister R. B. Bennett, W. E. B. Du Bois, Richard B. Harrison, and parliamentary government" (Winks, 1971). Nonetheless, Garveyism remained a potent force in Toronto, the Maritimes, and elsewhere, and has done much to further the goal of self-definition for Canadian blacks. Stalwart Garveyites are still among us, and doing much for black pride.

Over the following decades various organizations attempted to fill the leadership vacuum. Stepping into the breach and assuming a national focus was especially complex in Canada because regional histories and patterns of discrimination differed significantly. Breaking down barriers in one province did not necessarily lead to advances in others. In the east, for instance, where discrimination was the most overt and persistent, black frustration was reaching the boiling point. Racism and discrimination appeared as "moving targets" in

Canadian history, making coalescence around a common cause difficult. Keeping black Canadians uncertain of both their place and their rights proved a fruitful strategy in diffusing activism.

The Brotherhood of Sleeping Car Porters

As Nelson George describes in *The Death of Rhythm & Blues*, (1988) rail porters in the US were instrumental in spreading black news and culture throughout the land. Early tapes of Mississippi Delta blues, black newspapers, and other cultural products, were brought by these porters to black five & dime stores across America. In this manner, news spread fast and disparate black communities were connected.

Though such trade in products was minimal in Canada, black Canadian porters did provide an essential communications link from coast to coast. Canadian railways joined Canada east to west and made Confederation possible. Black porters on their long trans-continental trips helped unify disparate groups of black Canadians. Winnipeg, with its central location, became an important meeting and resting place for black porters.

Canadian railway companies began hiring black porters in large numbers early in the 1900s. When the Canadian Pacific Railroad established its headquarters in Montreal, and the Canadian National created a hiring office there, the city became a magnet for most would-be porters from America, the West Indies, and Nova Scotia. A railway porters' community developed around the St. Antoine Street district in Montreal, with parallel, if smaller, communities in Toronto, Windsor, Winnipeg, Calgary, and Vancouver.

These communities were held together by extraordinary individuals. In Winnipeg, for instance, the late Piercy Haynes (railway worker, boxer, jazz pianist) and his wife, the late Zena Hayes (jazz singer), owned and ran the great Haynes Chicken Shack, where Prime Ministers Diefenbaker and Manley (of Jamaica) dined. The restaurant was a vital cultural institution and meeting place. Along with parallel "institutions" in cities across Canada, Haynes Chicken Shack represented "putting down roots" and was a source of pride for the community. So too was the Bailey family, also railway workers, who diversified to red-cap service at the Winnipeg airport gaining, over time and through dedicated work, a virtual monopoly on this business.

While establishing businesses was critical to the black community's growth and status in Winnipeg, it was religion which served as the essential unifying force. As Professor Donald K. Gordon (University of Manitoba) argues, "The role of the quintessential black church, Pilgrim Baptist Church (41 Maple Street) cannot be over-stated. It has been a unifying fulcrum for blacks–American, Canadian, Caribbean–especially during the long tenure of the Reverend A. R. McCarver." For black people, like the porters and their families, church services provided respite from a life on the run. They also provided the opportunity for the sharing of information necessary to tackle the challenges ahead.

Though portering was a widely respected occupation in the black community, it was, on balance, a demeaning job. Porters made considerably more money than other black working groups, but often the price paid in emotional terms was high. Separated from their families for weeks and sometimes months at a time, the porters were viewed as a mobile and expendable class. They carried luggage, made beds, and shined shoes for whites, not all of whom were appreciative. A customer's complaint could result in immediate dismissal. Knowing this, some whites tested the porters by launching racial slurs and insults at them. The humiliation was too much for some; a few committed suicide, others resigned. Some were charged with "Uncle Tomism" by more strident blacks. But with their families' support the porters displayed grit, determination, and a firm resolve to act as ambassadors for the black community. If they got a job they tried to keep it, both for themselves and their people.

The black porters' struggle for unionization and equality is one of the great achievements of Canadian black history. By and large, blacks had been shut out of labour unions both in the US and Canada. After a bitter struggle, A. Philip Randolph founded and became president of the Brotherhood of Sleeping Car Porters in America. Shortly thereafter, Canadian porters, an overwhelmingly black group, were given union status by the Canadian Brotherhood of Railway Workers. Years later, the union's struggle for equality would win them access to more lucrative jobs such as rail-diner waiter (previously an all-white preserve) and, in 1954, the right to become conductors.

Randolph's experiences organizing black American porters made him an important labour leader in America. In 1941, he used his leverage by threatening President Roosevelt with a mass demonstration on Washington unless the President passed legislation giving blacks access to defence industry jobs. Worried about the political fall-out of such a demonstration, Roosevelt capitulated. That year a law was passed which made discrimination in US defence industries, job training programs, and government agencies, illegal. Enforcement mechanisms were also established, giving teeth to the legislation.

In Canada portering represented one of the few areas where meaningful contact between blacks and whites was possible.

Black porters were on the vanguard of civil rights reform in Canada.

Such contact is one of the surest ways of breaking down prejudicial stereotypes. The black men of the Canadian Brotherhood of Sleeping Car Porters, through persistent lobbying both within their employment area and as citizens outside of it, were instrumental in causing positive change for blacks in Canada. Their story, as workers, proud Canadians, and civil rights advocates, is described in *A Black Man's Toronto 1914–1980: The Reminiscences of Harry Gairey* (1981).

The KKK in Canada

The post-World War I black quest for self-definition and post-war optimism soon gave way to grim realities. Employment for blacks became increasingly restricted. Men worked as general labourers, janitors, waiters, barbers, and porters. Even jobs as security guards, today an opportunity accepted by many, were closed to blacks. Women found themselves trapped in job ghettoes with even less chance of upward mobility. As domestic servants, chambermaids, or waitresses, most worked a double shift, eight hours on the job followed by at least eight hours at home.

Worse still, a virulent strain of racism from south of the border was gaining a foothold in Canada. In the States a revived Ku Klux Klan expanded its attack. The targets now included any group not of Anglo-Saxon stock. Jews, Catholics, Asians, Indians, blacks, and even socialists, were all labelled "corrupt" and a direct threat to Protestant racial purity. In their propaganda papers the KKK described cities as places of loose morals and unhealthy racial mixing, a view widely accepted in rural and small town settings. By 1928, Klan Klaverns were established in most Canadian provinces.

The KKK in Canada operated on two fronts: first, spreading racism through direct action and Klan newspapers: second, by supporting the campaigns of white supremacist politicians. Some Roman Catholic churches in Quebec and Ontario were burned or bombed by members of "the invisible empire." High-ranking politicians in Saskatchewan were linked to the Klan.

On February 28, 1930, the Klan marched openly through the streets of Oakville, Ontario, and burned a cross to protest the anticipated marriage of a local white woman to a black man. The normally secretive Klan, who relied on night-time fear and intimidation tactics, would only have come out from the shadows if assured of broad-based support.

As in the past, these activities were a response to perceived immigrant success. The Klan in Canada appealed to "Canadianism" and the values of rural settlement. Cosmopolitan cities, which attracted an increasing number of immigrants throughout the 1920s, were viewed as places of vice. The Klan's association with segregationist American Klan organizations forced many immigrants to give up on notions of integration and seek refuge in small, but protective, enclaves. The government's inability or unwillingness to prevent Klan activities was a clear signal to blacks and other immigrant groups that they must seek their own protection.

Black Women and the Church

Through the "dormant years" blacks survived on faith and determination. Peggy Bristow in *Black Women in Buxton and Chatham, 1850–65* (1994) states that "white promoters of the

Elgin Settlement saw their experiment as part of a larger mission to Christianize Black people." This was undoubtedly true, and consistent with aims of the Buxton church and school into the 1900s. The role of black churches in Canada, however, always encompassed more than merely keeping the faith alive. Christian social reform has long been a hallmark of black churches, and black women have been behind the struggle from the beginning.

Though the ministers were men, the black churches and their affiliated social services were generally sustained by women. Inspired by religion, belief in ultimate deliverance through prayer, and (because the men often had to work away from home) greater immediate contact with children, black women were the guardians of their communities. Strong, determined, and often uncompromising, many worked a triple shift: at home, at work, and at church.

Certainly one reason for the strength of the black baptist tradition is that ministers were elected by parishioners. The church gave blacks the opportunity to actively participate in a democratic institution, an experience (especially for black women) they were otherwise denied. The fact that church leaders often doubled as community spokesmen made such participatory democracy vitally important, a civic duty seldom ignored.

While the increasing industrialization of Canadian society from 1900–1929 clearly benefited white women, black women remained in the employment ghetto of domestic service. At the outbreak of WW II, at least 80 percent of black women in Canadian cities worked as domestics. The increased unionization of the Canadian work force during the 1930s and beyond did not help these women. As isolated employees, their wages remained stagnant. Most began domestic work as teenagers, earning one dollar a day or less. They had no bargaining power, and were often subjected to the arbitrary demands of their employers. Lack of extended formal education restricted many to a lifetime of domestic service. The church, where they could connect with others suffering a life of degradation, became an essential meeting place. It offered one of the few means of participating in their community's life.

Labour shortages during WW II finally opened new employment doors for black women. Thousands leapt at the opportunity. The recruitment of white men into the armed services also created openings in teaching, some of which were filled by experienced black women.

Black churches took part in the social Christianity movements. As primary social agencies, they were active in the cause of reform. Gains made during WW II did not simply occur because of economic necessity. Nonetheless, the post-war treatment of blacks, many of whom lost their war-time jobs to returning veterans, did suggest that the black place in Canadian society was inextricably linked to economic demands.

For a disproportionately high number of black women the only available work after the war was back in domestic service. One step forward was followed by two steps back. However, the

The Executive Committee, African United Baptist Association of Nova Scotia, 1919-1920.

experience of war-time employment in factories and offices would have a lasting impact. Blacks, having contributed directly to the war effort, would not willingly return to their marginalized position. Black women, often working behind the scenes, were instrumental in bringing about post-war reforms. This involvement paralleled their counterparts' role in the US.

A Lost Opportunity

Problems of Confederation dogged Canada from its inception. At the end of WW I Newfoundland was independent. Whether it would remain so, fall to the US, or join Confederation, became a consuming question for Canadian parliamentarians. Before the war, there had been plans to forge a union with the British West Indies. Many believed that such a union would bring Newfoundland, and possibly some Caribbean islands, into Canada. On January 1, 1919, Prime Minister Borden announced that a union would benefit Canada by providing its civil service with administrative opportunities. Nevertheless, he rejected the plan out of concern that black West Indians would demand representation in parliament. This, he maintained, would be unacceptable to white Canadians.

Borden and others bolstered their position with statements about the "backward" nature of mixed-race West Indian societies. Such heterogeneity was presented as a threat to Canadian values and democracy. An opportunity to expand the Canadian nation-state died on the shoals of racism. Newfoundland would not join Confederation until 1949.

The turn-of-the-century Jubilee Singers and Orchestra brought negro spirituals to the Canadian stage and overseas.

8

Blacks, Human Rights and Legislation

In the territories of Canada-to-be, race relations between blacks and whites were determined by slavery. In courts of law slaves who had committed criminal acts were given stern sentences. Robbery often resulted in hanging. Legal proceedings, however, also provided slaves with the opportunity to describe the sorry social and economic conditions of their lives. Such public airings resulted in some positive developments.

The celebrated case of Marie-Joseph Angélique resulted in a ban on torture. After the abolition of slavery in Upper Canada, courts upheld the principle "that every person is free who reaches British ground" and consistently refused to extradite fugitive slaves to the US. These, and numerous other examples, gave Canadian blacks the impression that they would be protected in courts of law.

The February 16, 1861 overturning of an extradition order against John Anderson, a black man found guilty of murder in Missouri, proved the point. In the initial judgement, the fact that Anderson had committed murder in his attempt to flee slavery mattered little to the court. Though Canadian precedent for denying US extradition orders was well established, the court argued that it must draw the line if a criminal act like murder had been committed.

For the black community, and especially the Toronto Anti-Slavery Society, Canada's reputation as a safe haven would be judged on this

As one confused youth observed, in Canada he was "half free and half slave," having British justice and no job. In the United States the Negro was somewhat more sure–sure of where he could go and could not go, of when to be meek and when to be strong. In Canada he was uncertain. Robin Winks, *The Blacks In Canada*.

case. Outraged by the verdict, the Society fought for an appeal. The case was re-opened and the Appeals Court ruled that Anderson "should have been charged with manslaughter since, under British law, a slave could not be accused of a crime if the act was a necessary part of escape. This judgement set Anderson free" (Hill, 1981). Supporting the Toronto Anti-Slavery Society was Thomas D'Arcy McGee, one of the Fathers of Confederation.

Increasingly, blacks viewed courts as places where their civil liberties might be recognized. The community regularly protested decisions it deemed harmful to the cause of freedom and equality. As persons, blacks had legal rights and they were determined to exercise them. Had historical circumstances been different, this trend may have resulted in the ending of segregationist educational legislation, arguably the largest stumbling block to black advancement in early Canada.

Racial Discrimination and Canada's Constitution

Prior to Confederation and the signing of the British North America Act (BNA Act–until 1982 Canada's Constitution), blacks were gaining some measure of equality in courts of law. The BNA Act dealt, primarily, with the division of powers between the federal and provincial governments. It established, among other divisions of power, federal jurisdiction over immigration, and provincial jurisdiction over the franchise, employment and business opportunities, education, and land ownership–areas of vital importance to all immigrant groups trying to gain a foothold in a new land. However, apart from protecting the rights to form and attend certain religious schools, the Act made no reference to equality rights. This omission, and the fact that the Judicial Committee of the Privy Council considered racial discrimination not a basis for invalidating provincial legislation, left all ethnic minorities in a precarious position, especially since British common law did not generally serve their interests.

In terms of legal restrictions on governments, courts had a role only in cases where the federal government or the provinces overstepped their jurisdictions. So, for instance, when a complaint was made about a section of British Columbia's Election Act which prohibited "Chinamen, Japanese, and

Indians" from voting, the court ruled that this was not an issue which it could consider. The British Columbia government, though acting in a clearly racist manner, had not overstepped its jurisdiction and could not, therefore, be challenged on constitutional grounds.

Restrictive federal immigration policies, segregation in schools and land ownership, and refusing to hire people on racial grounds, were deemed beyond the court's jurisdiction. These were matters to be decided by federal and provincial legislatures and the voting public, not courts of law. In 1919, a black man from Montreal sued Loew's Theatre for refusing to allow him to sit in an orchestra seat. At Loew's and most other theatres (and, interestingly, in most churches) blacks were restricted to sitting in the balcony. Balcony seating came to be called "Nigger Heaven." On appeal, the theatre was found not guilty because its actions were considered both moral and in the public good.

Many restaurants and bars either refused to serve blacks, or served them only in segregated seating areas. Complaints were made, but in 1924 an Ontario court established the right of restaurant proprietors to restrict access in this manner. This case proved that racial discrimination was not contrary to Canadian law. Just the opposite was true; agents of racial discrimination would, in fact, be protected by Canadian law.

Canadian provinces did not have Jim Crow laws as such, but given the fact that "the general principle of the law of Quebec is that of complete freedom of commerce, and any merchant is free to deal as he may choose with an individual member of the public" (Judge J. Rinfret), the effect was often the same. In all commercial transactions the laws of commerce superseded concern over human rights. This distinction was part of the ruling in *Christie vs. York Corporation,* the first case of racial discrimination to reach the Supreme Court of Canada. In 1940, Christie, a black man, sued the Montreal Forum tavern for refusing to serve him a beer. When he complained to the police, the tavern's manager supported his waiter and explained that the bar did not serve black people.

Christie lost his claim on two grounds: one, the freedom-of-commerce rationale, consistent with the BNA Act; two, because the tavern's actions were not deemed contrary to good morals and public order. In the same year the British Columbia Court of Appeal held that anyone "may conduct a business in the manner best suited to advance his own interests," even if that meant discrimination solely because of race or colour.

By the time of the Great Depression it had become apparent to black leaders that discrimination would only be defeated at the ballot box and through organized political lobbying. The courts, stuck in the mire of determining government jurisdiction rather than creating change, were of little use to the black community.

The Great Depression and Self-Help

The New York stock market crash of 1929 sent shock waves around the world. In southern states, where most black Americans still lived, cotton prices fell by two-thirds. Again, blacks flocked to the cities, but this time there were no jobs and less tolerance. Throughout the 1930s whites took "black jobs." Blacks, shut out of labour unions and without recourse before the law, lost jobs by the millions. By 1932, the black unemployment rate in most cities hovered around fifty percent.

"The Depression had brought everyone down a peg or two. And the Negroes had but a few pegs to fall."

Langston Hughes, black American writer.

Canadian blacks suffered the same degree of misfortune. Losing jobs, lining up at food banks and soup kitchens, and pawning material possessions at rock-bottom prices, became a daily reality for blacks north and south. Neither government believed that it could afford to finance relief. Black communities were on their own. In both countries black churches responded by moving away from saving souls and empowering through education, to feeding the desperately hungry and clothing the needy.

Church-based emergency relief centres also became arenas for political activism. In 1931 and 1932, US President Herbert Hoover exacerbated the situation with grants to big business, arguing that the prosperity of increased employment would trickle down to the most dispossessed in society. Resistance to this policy was intense among newly unemployed blacks, and they launched "Don't Buy Where You Can't Work" campaigns in cities across America.

Given the large numbers of black people in cities like Chicago, New York, and Philadelphia, these campaigns resulted in increased job opportunities for some. The Depression, however, was a sturdy weed, money was not trickling down, and increasing numbers fell into poverty.

Depression-era poverty knew no colour. Most people felt the quiet pangs of hunger and the increased sting of discrimination brought about in times of scarcity. A growing number of leaders argued that blacks must develop a national focus and forge alliances with other groups, particularly with certain elements in the labour movement who had previously rejected black inclusion.

Abandoning quasi-segregationist mandates proved difficult for some black associations. This was especially true in the geographically isolated Maritimes where a strong sense of regionalism prevailed in both black and white communities. Whereas blacks in Toronto and Montreal were gaining considerable support from white liberals–some blacks were moving into white neighbourhoods and black children were attending integrated schools–the Maritime situation was moving from bad to worse. There, blacks were the chief target for persecution and segregation. As Winks (1971) explains:

> When a Negro purchased a house in Trenton, Nova Scotia, in October 1937, a mob of a hundred whites stoned the owner and broke into his home. After being dispersed by Royal Canadian Mounted Police, the mob returned the following night–now four hundred strong–and destroyed the house and its contents. The RCMP would not act unless requested to do so by the mayor, who refused, and the mob moved on to attack two other Negro homes. The only arrest was of a New Glasgow black, who was convicted of assault on a woman during the riot; and the original Negro purchaser abandoned efforts to occupy his property.

Supporting the black cause from the beginning was Roosevelt's wife, Eleanor. Some historians speculate that she was the real impetus behind positive change. By writing newspaper articles in support of total equality for blacks, inviting black leaders to the White House, personally defying Jim Crow laws, and pushing the President to appoint blacks to senior government positions, she became the "darling" of the community.

With events like this occurring in their backyards it is understandable that Maritime blacks had difficulty joining a united national cause. Nova Scotia, especially, came to resemble the Old South; segregation in schooling, housing, and employment being the order of the day. Given this level of hostility, is it any wonder that Garveyism remained strong in the east?

President Roosevelt and the New Deal

The 1932 US election presented black Americans with a difficult choice. The Republicans, led by Herbert Hoover, were the party of black America, the party of Abraham Lincoln, the party that freed blacks from slavery and ushered in Reconstruction reforms. The Democrats, led by Franklin D. Roosevelt, were making the right noises, but they were white America's party, the party of the deep South.

Roosevelt defeated Hoover by a large margin. Black Americans, distrustful and incapable of turning their backs on history, voted *en masse* for Hoover. White America supported Roosevelt's "new deal for the American people." In an ironic twist of electoral fate Roosevelt's New Deal would, ultimately, greatly help the cause of black America. By the 1936 election a near complete reversal of political allegiance had occurred and black Republicans were difficult to find.

The primary objective of New Deal programs was to get people back to work

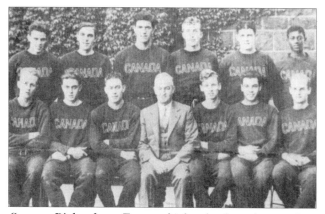

Sammy Richardson, *Toronto high school track sensation, seen here as the lone black representing Canada in international competitions.*

*During the medal ceremony, second place finisher **Lutz Long** gives a Nazi salute as **Jesse Owens** awaits his gold in the broad jump. A crucial moment in the history of black sport occurred at the 1936 Berlin Olympics. With Adolf Hitler, the leader of Nazi Germany and father of the "Master Race" theory in attendance, Jesse Owens, a black American sprinter, dramatically upset the doctrine of white supremacy by winning four gold medals, including the one-hundred-metre dash.*

through government-funded employment initiatives. At first, many of the programs were discriminatory and benefited whites only. Roosevelt needed the votes of southern Democrats to get bills through Congress. This prompted charges of the New Deal being a "raw deal" for blacks. Others criticized it for being too expensive and/or for legislating too much government control over the economy. Roosevelt pushed forward, believing that he must respond to desperate conditions.

In time, blacks began directly benefiting from New Deal programs. Roosevelt established the "Black Cabinet" to advise him. Mary McLeod Bethune, the Cabinet's leader, became director of the National Youth Administration which gave financial support to over 300,000 blacks attending schools. Other Cabinet members were promoted to key government jobs in future administrations.

Under Roosevelt, Congress approved a series of policies and programs prohibiting discrimination based on "race, creed, or color:" Works Progress Administration, Farm Security Administration, and Public Works Administration. Perhaps most importantly, the National Labor Relations Act was used to unionize workers in industries employing large numbers of blacks. In the 1930s, with unemployment growing across the land, unions desperately needed to increase their memberships and, after years of resistance, they opened their doors to blacks. Being a part of politically powerful labour unions gave black workers new status in America. Black Canadians, witnessing these positive changes, began pushing government authorities to take a more activist role.

The Second World War

People come together in hard times. Race relations were definitely improving in Canada. When overtly racist incidents occurred, the Canadian press increasingly rose to the defence of the victims. The Depression was having a sobering emotional effect and whites, blacks, and other ethnic minorities were forging alliances.

The Second World War sped up the process. Like the Depression, it was a national emergency. Though some instances of discrimination certainly occurred, blacks were now accepted into integrated army regiments after training at mostly integrated bases. Many served with distinction on and off the battlefield, and the re-education of whites was underway. As in the US, black contributions to the war effort led to a new resolve within the community. "If we're willing to die for our country, then our country should treat us with equality and respect," became a rallying call north and south of the 49th parallel.

At home, blacks served in numerous capacities during the war. A protest in Toronto resulted in blacks being included in the ranks of National Selective Service (NSS), the main labour pool for war industries. In 1942, the NSS began to recruit women. As Dionne Brand points out in *'We weren't allowed to go into factory work until Hitler started the war:' The 1920s to the 1940s*, (1994) black women, though rejected at first, fought hard to be included. Eventually they won the battle, and job opportunities other than domestic service opened up to them. Through dedicated work, these women broke new ground in race relations and women's rights.

The war effort brought blacks to all four corners of Canada. In less than eight months, beginning in 1942, the US army built a road from Dawson Creek, B. C. to Big Delta, Alaska. It was one of the largest engineering projects in North American history. Nearly a third of the labourers were black, including the 93rd, 95th, and 97th all-black army construction regiments. The road was built to open up supply routes to the northwest and to protect Canadian and American interests against a possible Japanese invasion.

In 1945, the Nova Scotia Association for the Advancement of Coloured People was founded. Blacks were gaining national profile, and by the war's end all regions of the country were playing active roles in a national black organization. Canadian blacks had found a collective voice.

The Birth of Human Rights Legislation in Canada

As previously noted, perhaps the chief defect of the BNA Act was its silence on equality and human rights. When courts of law or the state did not pro-

Harry Gairey (left), with federal court judge Pamela Appelt and Don Moore, was a mentor to many, including historian Dr. Sheldon Taylor.

I said, "Now it would be all right if the powers that be refused my son admission to the Icelandia, I would accept it, if when the next war comes, you're going to say, "Harry Gairey, you're Black, you stay here, don't go to war." But, your Worship and Gentlemen of the Council, it's not going to be that way, you're going to say he's a Canadian and you'll conscript him. And if so, I would like my son to have everything that a Canadian citizen is entitled to providing he's worthy of it. Thank you, Gentlemen of the Council." I think it was in the paper the following day; students from the University of Toronto picketed the place. And it was the first time that the City Council made an ordinance that they must not discriminate because of race, creed, colour or religion. I was the man that caused that ordinance to be passed, with the help of the good white people of Toronto.

Harry Gairey, *A Black Man's Toronto 1914-1980.*

tect people of colour, anxieties were raised concerning British justice. WW II was a race war. The atrocities of that war, most notably the killing of six million Jews in Nazi death camps, could not be ignored. Canadians began to feel ashamed about denying entry to displaced European Jews during the 1930s, about the increased degradation of Native Indians' status, and about the historic mistreatment of blacks. Change was in the air.

Uncertainty prevailed, however. Segregated schools still existed. Blacks continued to be welcomed in one restaurant, but not another. Black women feared that their wartime work in factories and hospitals would not lead to new employment opportunities. Many blacks moved to the US where they seemed more certain of "where they could and could not go," more certain of "when to be meek and when to be strong." Those that remained pressed on. The civil rights movement in America had its parallel in Canada.

Change came in the form of human rights legislation. In 1944, Ontario passed the Racial Discrimination Act, prohibiting the publication or broadcast of anything which discriminated on the basis of race or creed. For the first time a Canadian legislature ruled that racial and/or religious discrimination was contrary to public policy. Commerce and trade no longer protected racists. At least, that was the hope.

Blacks, especially through the Brotherhood of Sleeping Car Porters, had long fought for this type of legislation. The impact of the Act was immediate. In 1945, an Ontario court used the Act to strike down a covenant prohibiting the sale of land to "Jews or persons of objectionable nationality." For Jews, blacks, and other peoples of colour this court enforcement represented a dramatic change in Canadian history. Feelings of victory, however, were short lived as the ruling was reversed in the Ontario Court of Appeal. So, as W. S. Tarnopolsky states in *The Practice of Freedom: Canadian Essays on Human Rights and Fundamental Freedoms* (1979):

> It is no wonder, then, that the provincial legislatures, with no aid from the judiciary, had to move into the field and start to enact antidiscriminatory legislation, the administration and application of which has largely been taken out of the courts.

In 1947, Saskatchewan passed the first Bill of Rights in Canada. It was a wide-ranging Act, protecting everything from free speech to the right of assembly and association. Unfortunately, it lacked strong enforcement mechanisms. Offenders were levied a maximum fine of only $50. Nonetheless, court challenges were launched and, in time, stronger enforcement procedures were adopted.

Bringing in wholesale legislative change, affecting all regions of Canada, was beyond the power of the federal government. Most areas of concern to blacks fell under provincial jurisdiction. In 1950, a coalition of black and other groups presented their grievances directly to Ontario's premier. Ontario responded by passing the Fair Employment Practices Act in 1951. Three years later the Fair Accommodation Practices Act was passed. These two Acts served as prototypes for provincial human rights codes.

While black Canadians fought hard for these changes, they were not enough to eradicate discrimination. Human rights legislation provided a good indication of governments' intentions and public will. However, although "the machinery of the state was placed at the disposal of the victims of antidiscrimination, the whole problem was approached as if it were solely their problem and responsibility" (Tarnopolsky, 1979).

In other words, if a black family was barred from a certain apartment complex because of their race, it was their responsibility to launch legal proceedings. This meant hiring a lawyer and pursuing the matter through an already bogged-down system. For most blacks, this process was simply too expensive and time-consuming. Though the black press regularly reported on examples of discrimination, few legal complaints were made.

Frustration set in, especially in urban black communities, when the police, supposedly the first line of protection, often failed

Anti-discrimination Legislation in Canada:

1. Racial Discrimination Act (Ontario, 1944).
2. Social Assistance Act (British Columbia, 1945).
3. Bill of Rights (Saskatchewan, 1947; Nova Scotia, 1963; Alberta, 1965).
4. Fair Employment Practices Act (Ontario, 1951; Manitoba, 1953; Nova Scotia, 1955; New Brunswick, Saskatchewan, and British Columbia, 1956; Quebec, 1964).
5. Fair Accommodation Practices Act (Ontario, 1954; Saskatchewan, 1956; New Brunswick, 1959; British Columbia, 1963).

to take discrimination complaints seriously. In fact, blacks encountered discriminatory treatment at the hands of an often all-white police force. Property and commerce laws continued to dominate judicial thinking, and judges were disinclined to grant orders which directly impinged on these rights. Simply put, taking to court a racist landlord for preventing certain ethno-racial groups from renting apartments, a department store for exclusionary hiring practices, or a diner for refusing to serve a coloured customer, was beyond the reach of those so victimized.

*"American by birth, Canadian by education and adoption, **Dr. Daniel Hill's** achievements are truly outstanding: Research Director, Social Planning Council of Metropolitan Toronto, 1956-1960; Instructor in Sociology at the University of Toronto; Director and Chairman of the OHRC; Adjunct Professor at the School of Social Work, University of Toronto; President of the Ontario Black History Society; Advisor to universities and governments on multiculturalism and race relations."* (The Freedom Seekers).

The result, in black and other communities, was (and some argue still is) a move towards self-segregation. Certainly, there is always a pull towards settling with your own kind. This is especially true for new immigrants, who move from countries where they are in the majority to countries where they are part of a distinct and highly visible minority. The pull factors, however, are complemented by significant push factors. In Canada, true integration, as opposed to "ethnic box settlements," would require blacks and others to step up the political agenda for total inclusion.

The Ontario Human Rights Code

In 1961, Ontario gave teeth to its human rights legislation by creating the Ontario Human Rights Commission (OHRC). The Commission's main responsibility was enforcing the Ontario Human Rights Code of 1962. Up to that point, most Canadian governmental initiatives in this area followed American models. The OHRC, being able to investigate, adjudicate, and award settlements, broke this trend. Significantly, the

Commission's director was Daniel G. Hill, a black man with a long track record of successful activism.

By 1975, every Canadian province had Human Rights Commissions. In 1977, a federal commission was established to oversee the Canadian Human Rights Act. The definition of racial discrimination used by these agencies followed that provided by the United Nations at the 1965 International Convention on the Elimination of All Forms of Racial Discrimination:

> Any distinction, exclusion, restriction or preference based on race, colour, descent, or national or ethnic origin which has the purpose or effect of nullifying or impairing the recognition, enjoyment or exercise, on an equal footing, of human rights and fundamental freedoms in the political, economic, social, cultural or any other field of public life.

Employing this wide ranging definition the OHRC investigated thousands of cases. Its mandate was to administer existing laws and to promote equality. For people of colour it provided an essential educational resource as to their rights and a "quicker fix" to situations of discrimination. With some variations this mandate was adopted by all provisional Commissions.

In subsequent years, the OHRC (and others) has come under much criticism. The average amount of time for a complaint to be processed is exceedingly long. Also, it has a low budget, and makes relatively small awards. Some argue that the Commissions are a sad excuse for the work courts should be doing. With their development, the courts now have no jurisdiction to hear cases of discrimination, except those raised under the 1982 Charter of Rights and Freedoms. While these criticisms have some validity, there is no dismissing the fact that the creation of human rights commissions was due, in large part, to organized ethnic group protest. Blacks, in concert with other groups, clearly made their mark on Canadian democracy.

9
Revolutionary Times in North America

During the 1940s and 1950s Canada's black community was held together by extraordinary individuals. Two such people, Dr. William Percy Oliver and Pearleen Borden, were married in Nova Scotia in 1936. The Olivers were born in Canada, and they proudly considered it their home. Through years of dedicated service to Maritime Baptist churches, they became committed black civil rights advocates.

Along with their professional and church activities, the Olivers raised a phenomenal family. All of their five sons "obtained at least one university degree, in some cases more, and in one instance a doctoral degree–a remarkable achievement by any standard" (Pachai, 1993). These men obviously benefitted from the early childhood lessons of self-pride, dedication to excellence, and cultural awareness, delivered by their parents.

The founding of the Nova Scotia Association for the Advancement of Coloured People (NSAACP) was a significant event in Nova Scotia and Canada. It signalled a new desire to work in common purpose. The Association began fighting discrimination by launching court challenges. For instance, the NSAACP supported Viola Desmond, a black woman from Halifax, in her 1946 case against a New Glasgow theatre. After purchasing a cheaper balcony ticket, the only kind she was allowed to purchase, Desmond sat in the white section of the theatre. Confronted by the theatre's manager, she offered to pay the more expensive ticket price. Her offer was refused, and she was removed from the premises by the police. Desmond spent the night in jail.

Desmond was found guilty of disorderly conduct. She was fined $20.00 plus court costs, and did not appeal. The significance of the case, however, lay in Desmond's demonstration of non-violent civil disobedience, the exact strategy used effectively during the American civil rights revolution. The NSAACP publicized the

Pearleen Oliver:

1. First black graduate of New Glasgow High School (1936).
2. Distinguished historian of the black experience in Nova Scotia.
3. First woman elected as moderator of the African United Baptist Association of Nova Scotia (1976).
4. First Woman of the Year Award from the YWCA (1981).
5. Honorary Doctor of Letters degree from Saint Mary's University (1990).

Bridglal Pachai, People Of The Maritimes: Blacks.

William Oliver:

1. Holder of two university degrees, and two honorary doctoral degrees.
2. Founder of the Nova Scotia Association for the Advancement of Coloured Peoples (NSAACP, 1945), the Black United Front (BUF), and the Society for the Protection and Preservation of Black Culture in Nova Scotia.
3. President of the United Baptist Convention of the Maritimes.
4. Regional representative with the Adult Education Division of the Nova Scotia Department of Education (1962–1977).
5. Order of Canada recipient (1984), the Human Relations Award from the Canadian Council of Christians and Jews (1985), the Distinguished Service Award of the Alumni of Acadia University (1988).

Bridglal Pachai, People Of The Maritimes: Blacks.

event and court case, and a wide audience, black and white, across Canada took note. Nova Scotia would soon join other provinces in enacting human rights legislation.

In the US, the courts became the main vehicle for advancing civil rights. Ending segregation in public institutions–schools, restaurants, buses, and washrooms–rallied black America behind a common cause. In Canada, political lobbying and union movement advocacy took precedent over other forms of activism. Canada's immigration policies became the target of unified black activism. In both countries, a changing cultural context buttressed the activities of black political reformers.

Black Culture Goes Mainstream

Paul Robeson at Toronto's Canadian National Exhibition
That the US government was not yet willing to accept testimony from independent-minded blacks was proven in the treatment of Paul Robeson. Scholar, linguist, All-American athlete, film, stage, and recording star, and civil rights activist, Robeson's passport was revoked by the US State Department during the McCarthy era. His "crime," visiting the Soviet Union and suggesting–at the height of Cold War paranoia–that blacks there were better treated than in America. New chapters to Robeson's legendary career are still being uncovered. In 1950, at a time when Jewish people were being harassed, tortured, and, in some cases, assassinated, Robeson sang (at the Moscow Concert Hall), first in English and then in fluent Yiddish, the Warsaw Ghetto Rebellion anthem. It was an act of extraordinary defiance, liberation, and solidarity between two persecuted groups. After the Yiddish version, in the words of Robeson's son, "The place erupted; they blew the roof off it" (CBC Radio interview, 1996). *The concert was recorded. But, apparently on the personal orders of Soviet leader Joseph Stalin, the tape was seized and hidden in the deepest of deep vaults, never to resurface. However, as chance and historical circumstance would have it, the tape has been uncovered. It is now part of the historical record. Paul Robeson, the first black to play Shakespeare's* Othello *on an American stage, star of* Porgy And Bess *and the movie* Showboat, *was exiled from his own country.*

During the 1950s two issues came to dominate American political life, the Cold War with the Soviet Bloc, and race relations at home. Continuing a trend from rural to urban existence begun years earlier, two million blacks moved from the south to friendlier environs in the north and west. They migrated for two reasons, jobs and culture. However, while Americans were increasingly supportive of keeping the "Soviet menace" in check, the gnawing issue of black-white relations polarized the nation.

Nevertheless, the colour line was breaking down everywhere. In the 1940s, Richard Wright's novel *Native Son* became the first book by a black writer to achieve bestseller status. It took direct aim at white prejudice. The bebop jazz of Dizzy Gillespie, Charlie "Bird" Parker, and Thelonious Monk revolutionized American popular music. In 1949, Oscar Peterson played to a packed house at New York's famed Carnegie Hall.

Jackie Robinson, after testing the waters in Canada with the Montreal Royals, broke baseball's colour barrier in 1947, the same year that President Truman integrated the American military. Perhaps this momentous civil rights victory would not have occurred had the Brooklyn Dodgers, Robinson's team, not had a minor league franchise in Montreal. Robinson's positive reception by Montreal baseball fans in 1946 convinced Branch Rickey, the Dodgers' owner, that the time was right to desegregate baseball in America. Some argue that this event foreshadowed the end of segregation in all of America's institutions. Baseball, after all, was a more consuming passion than politics.

*Arguably, **Jackie Robinson** and Martin Luther King, Jr. were America's two most influential twentieth century black men.*

In the 1950s, black athletes were being recruited to star on American college sports teams. Quotas restricted the number who could be on the field or court at one time. Some athletic directors purposefully recruited light-skinned blacks in order to beat the quota. It was feared that the lucrative scholarships offered to black athletes attending white universities would threaten the highly successful athletic programs at black colleges. Given the use and abuse of many of these athletes, the jury is still out over whether this form of recruitment has benefitted or damaged black America.

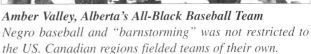

Amber Valley, Alberta's All-Black Baseball Team
Negro baseball and "barnstorming" was not restricted to the US. Canadian regions fielded teams of their own.

Black art continued to make forays into mainstream society. In 1952, a mixed black and white audience of 18,000 from Cleveland, Ohio witnessed the world's first rock 'n' roll concert. All of the performers were black. Ralph Ellison's novel *Invisible Man* and the pain-filled prose of James Baldwin spoke with vision about the black condition in America. Mahalia Jackson brought gospel to the masses and, in so doing, dramatically increased white interest in the "soul" of black churches.

On television Elvis Presley, a white man "singing black," stole the hearts of young white women across the nation and around the world. (The irony of Michael Jackson, perhaps the most "colour-confused" of entertainers, marrying Lisa Marie Presley was not lost on shrewd black culture critics.) Others, more sophisticated and contemptuous of a white appropriator of black music, were checking out jazz and blues musicians in clubs that were previously all-black preserves. Though there was considerable upset over whites making a financial killing off black music–while the artists themselves often went hungry–black aesthetics, in sport, entertainment, and writing, was attracting a mass audience.

The new crossing-over of black culture cannot be separated from the civil rights movements in America and Canada. As jazz great Oscar Peterson said in a CBC radio interview aired in 1995, "It wouldn't have mattered if I bleached my skin. I could play and that is all that counted." The mainstream appeal of black style brought into sharp focus the hypocrisy and injustice of segregation.

History was being made on the streets and it would soon filter into the board rooms of power. Canada was watching black Americans challenge segregation, knowing full well that the results of this challenge would spill over north of the border. The 49th parallel had never been so porous.

The Desegregation of America's Schools

In the late 1950s, the desegregation of public elementary and high schools became the centrepiece of the American civil rights movement. Ontario and Nova Scotia still had segregationist educational legislation. In the US, as in Canada historically, resistance was strongest over the issue of having white pre-teens and teenagers sharing educational facilities with blacks of the same age.

The National Association for the Advancement of Colored People (NAACP) had won landmark victories forcing colleges and universities to integrate. Its lawyers, especially Thurgood Marshall, successfully argued that the 1896 *Plessy vs. Ferguson* decision, was a sham. The *Plessy* ruling, popularly known as the "separate but equal" decision, legalized segregation as long as the separate educational facilities were equal. Of course, the facilities were separate, but in no way equal, as Thurgood Marshall had already proven in the *Sweatt vs. Painter* case.

In winning the Sweatt decision, Marshall argued that separate educational facilities were "inherently unequal." This proved to be an even more important victory than the ruling for George McLaurin in his 1950 case *McLaurin vs. Oklahoma State Regents*. That Supreme Court decision outlawed segregation only in schools that admitted black students. Jim Crow continued to hold sway in the Deep South as many schools refused to integrate, arguing that "separate but equal" facilities existed, or could be made to exist.

For black Americans, **Thurgood Marshall** was a lawyer "who stood up in white men's courts." Educated in law at Howard University, Marshall became, in 1967, the first black American appointed to the Supreme Court. A distinguished career as a Supreme Court Justice ended with his retirement in 1991.

In 1868, the US government passed the 14th Amendment to its Constitution. This Amendment states: "all persons born in the US are US citizens and cannot be deprived of life, liberty, or property, without due process of law nor be denied equal protection of the laws." In *Brown* vs. *Board of Education of Topeka, Kansas* (1954), a Supreme Court case which applied to all cases of segregation in education, Marshall used the 14th Amendment to argue that barring black students from certain schools or segregating them in back rows deprived them of basic citizenship rights and equal protection before the law. The case turned on the acceptance of compelling testimony by psychologists who maintained that segregating black students led to lack of confi-

dence and an overwhelming sense of inferiority. The Court
ruled unanimously for Brown:

> To separate (those children) from others of similar age and
> qualifications solely because of their race generates a feel-
> ing of inferiority as to their status in the community that
> may affect their hearts and minds in a way unlikely ever to
> be undone...Separate educational facilities are inherently
> unequal...Any language in *Plessy vs. Ferguson* contrary to
> these findings is rejected.

Canadians, black and white, followed these Supreme Court
cases with keen interest. By the 1950s the civil rights movement
had become a television revolution. The horrors of civil rights
abuses (segregation in public washrooms, hotels, restaurants,
and schools) were brought, via television, into people's living
rooms. Graphic reports of lynchings, KKK intimidation and
propaganda campaigns, and violent reactions to peaceful black
protests, shocked Canadians. It also fuelled the white belief that
racism was a made-in-America problem. Black Canadians
thought otherwise. To them there was a north-south continuum
with differences of degree, not substance.

"Buying Power:" the Montgomery Bus Boycott

Black Americans had their "eyes on the prize," and the prize
was freedom. As in Canada, American civil rights organizations
went after local targets with national implications. One such target was the segregated bus system in Montgomery, Alabama.

Throughout the South city and interstate buses were segregated. Blacks had to sit in the back of all buses. If a bus was
crowded they had to relinquish their seats to white passengers.
This was the law.

On Friday, December 1, 1955, Rosa Parks, secretary of the
Montgomery branch of the NAACP, refused to give up her seat to
a white passenger on a city bus. When she and three other blacks
boarded the bus it was not crowded and they took their seats in
the "colored section." The bus soon filled and a white passenger
was left standing. At this point the bus driver approached Rosa
Parks. She recounts the following conversation:

Bus Driver: "Stand up and let me have those seats." [No one moved.] "You all make it light on yourselves and let me have those seats."

Police Officer: "Did the driver ask you to stand?"

Rosa Parks: "Yes."

Police Officer: "So, why don't you stand up?"

Rosa Parks: "I don't think I should have to. Why do you push us around?"

Police Officer: "I don't know, but the law is the law and you're under arrest."

Parks was arrested and jailed. After posting her bail E. D. Nixon, branch president of the NAACP and, with Parks, former activist with the Brotherhood of Sleeping Car Porters, said to Parks, "With your case we can break segregation on Montgomery buses." Parks agreed. Her act of non-violent civil disobedience planted the seed for an idea that would rock the nation.

The NAACP, in conjunction with Dexter Avenue Baptist Church minister and leader of the Montgomery Improvement Association, Dr. Martin Luther King, Jr., decided to launch a one-day black boycott of Montgomery city buses. For the boycott to succeed all of the city's 40,000 blacks had to be alerted. This job was assumed by Jo Ann Robinson, president of the Women's Political Council, and two associates. Through a massive leaflet distribution campaign and word of mouth, the task was completed overnight. Blacks represented at least

KKK recruitment meetings were held across the south. Dr. E.B. Slay of Atlanta, "an apostle of hate," predicted a klan of 18 to 20 million members in 10 years."

two-thirds of Montgomery's bus riders, and the next day, a working Monday, not one of them boarded a bus.

That night blacks met at a packed assembly in the Holt Street Baptist Church. They voted unanimously to continue the boycott. To rousing cheers E. D. Nixon stated, "For all of these years I've been fighting so that my children wouldn't suffer as I've suffered. Well, tonight I've changed my mind. Hell, I want to enjoy some of this stuff myself!" The keynote speech that evening was delivered by Martin Luther King, Jr. He described a political and philosophic platform which would turn into a moral crusade:

> Reaching out for the daybreak of freedom and justice and equality...The only weapon that we have in our hands this evening is the weapon of protest. That's all...And we are not wrong in what we are doing. If we are wrong, the Supreme Court of this nation is wrong. If we are wrong, the Constitution of the United States is wrong. If we are wrong, God Almighty is wrong!

The next day black people walked to work. They would continue walking, while empty buses passed alongside them, for 381 days. The protest nearly bankrupted the city bus company, and it resonated throughout the South. Black buying power had within it the capacity to undo segregation. In 1956, the Supreme Court ruled that bus segregation was unconstitutional. The next day blacks boarded integrated buses.

Little Rock, Arkansas

It seemed that every civil rights advance was followed by a white backlash. In 1957, the same year that Congress passed the first civil rights law since Reconstruction, Arkansas state troopers stopped Elizabeth Eckford's attempt to enter Little Rock Public High School. Claiming state jurisdiction over schools, Governor Orval Faubus chose to ignore the Supreme Court's *Brown vs. Board of Education* desegregation ruling. Using the state's National Guard was necessary, Faubus argued, to ensure the protection of blacks.

With a white mob massed outside the school, some threatening to lynch Eckford, Faubus seemed to have a point. The real

*In 1960, six-year-old **Ruby Bridges** braved the threats of screaming white adults to attend school in her home district of New Orleans. This painting by Norman Rockwell captures the emotion of the times.*

reason for the state militia's presence, however, was to prove Arkansas' resolve in maintaining segregated schools. Eckford was spirited away by a white bystander, and Faubus seemed to have gained the upper hand.

President Eisenhower, fearing a prolonged conflict between the Arkansas and federal governments, assumed control of the state National Guard and sent in the 101st Airborne Division. Little Rock resembled a city under a state of siege. Faubus responded by closing down all of Little Rock's high schools. To Canadians it appeared that little had changed in the South since the Civil War.

The Little Rock situation proved that the courts and the Constitution would not alone protect black Americans. The struggle against discrimination needed other, more far reaching campaigns. The courts became one plank in a movement which made black resistance to segregation the domestic issue of the 1950s and early 1960s.

Sitting, Riding, and Marching for Freedom

Eisenhower's weak Civil Rights Act had little effect in the South. So slow was the integration of schools, many blacks left. Lynching, which Truman had wanted to make a federal crime, was still common in many jurisdictions. Blacks lived under constant threat of KKK violence. The KKK's campaign of terror and intimidation was openly supported by many southern politicians.

Black Civil Rights Organizations:

1. National Association for the Advancement of Colored People (NAACP).

2. Southern Christian Leadership Conference (SCLC).

3. Student Nonviolent Coordinating Committee (SNCC).

4. Congress of Racial Equality (CORE).

Still, black organizations continued to mobilize around the theme of meeting violence with non-violence based on the teachings of India's Mahatma Gandhi. Martin Luther King, Jr. summarized the civil rights movement's strategy: "To resist without bitterness; to be cursed and not reply; to be beaten and not hit back." This frustrated many southern whites who were hoping either for open conflagration, or that the numerous black organizations would break down because of internal disputes.

In 1960, using King's philosophy as inspiration, black students of the SCLC launched sit-ins in segregated restaurants across the South. The strategy was simple. Groups of black students walked into restaurants and peacefully sat down in white sections, usually on bar stools at the counters. They sat in silence and waited to be served. Service was not offered. Invariably white patrons would protest, throw food at them, pour drink over them, and, in many cases, beat them. The students remained silent, and never fought back. When the police arrived they were forcibly removed from the premises.

Close to 70,000 black students and their white supporters took part in such non-violent demonstrations. Many were charged with civil disobedience and/or breaking Jim Crow laws and spent time in jail. Their acts were widely reported in local and national newspapers, and on radio and television. They were gaining widespread sympathy both on the street and in the corridors of power.

"Freedom rides" became another form of non-violent protest. Court orders had ruled that segregated interstate buses were unconstitutional. CORE freedom riders tested the court's authority by boarding interstate buses destined for the deep South. Many such buses were met by angry white protesters, who, in some cases, set buses on fire and beat the freedom riders. In Birmingham, Alabama, Eugene "Bull" Connor, the city's police chief, unleashed his police force on the freedom riders. They were beaten, thrown in jail, and then transported out of state.

Being thrown in jail had become a badge of honour gladly assumed by thousands of civil rights workers. Increasingly, southern politicians blamed the north for inciting radicalism and sending protesters south. America was a nation divided.

On April 12, 1963, Bull Connor threw Martin Luther King, Jr. into his Birmingham jail. King was in Birmingham to organize a march celebrating the 100th anniversary of the signing of the Emancipation Proclamation. While incarcerated he wrote his famous *Letter from a Birmingham Jail,* a pointedly direct answer to the white southern establishment, who viewed him as little more than a trouble-maker.

*Non-violent protests, like this one led by **King** and **Rev. Ralph Abernathy,** spurred violent white attacks.*

Upon release, King and his supporters, in open defiance of the Birmingham police, resumed their marches. They marched every day for nearly two weeks, encountering hostility, jeering crowds, but no violence. Most black school-aged children of Birmingham were bewildered by these marches, but many understood their meaning and wanted to join. On May 2, King decided to include them in a mass demonstration. It was a struggle of titanic wills, and Bull Connor was determined to save face. He confronted the black protesters, including children, with fire hoses and a police force itching to fight. Police rage erupted and unarmed blacks were savagely beaten with billyclubs. Fire hoses battered the protesters. Attack dogs unloaded their venom. Close to one thousand school children were imprisoned. It was a civil war in the streets of Birmingham, television images of which were sent across the continent.

"I Have A Dream"

In a tightly contested election John F. Kennedy became President in 1961, largely because of the overwhelming support he received from black America. For the first time in history, blacks voted in large numbers for a Democratic candidate. Fearful of losing southern democratic support, Kennedy hesitated to bring in civil rights laws. The events in Birmingham, however, compelled him to push through a civil rights agenda. He became an open advocate of the black cause in America.

Martin Luther King, *I Have A Dream* **Speech Conclusion:**

And when we allow freedom to ring, when we let it ring from every village and hamlet, from every state and city, we will be able to speed up that day when all of God's children–black men and white men, Jews and Gentiles, Catholics and Protestants–will be able to join hands and to sing in the words of the old Negro spiritual, "Free at last; thank God almighty, we are free at last."

Perhaps the crowning moment of the civil rights movement occurred in Washington D. C. on August 28, 1963. Blacks from across the continent came to hear Martin Luther King Jr.'s "Dream" and to pressure Congress into passing President Kennedy's civil rights bill. Over 250,000 blacks came to Washington that day to witness a defining moment in US history. Would America follow King's Dream?

On November 22, 1963, Kennedy was assassinated. He did not see his civil rights bill passed through Congress. His death, along with the assassination of Medgar Evers, a leading black civil rights activist from Mississippi, was the beginning of a series of assassinations that would shock America, Canada, and the world.

Building a Collective Consciousness in Black Canada

Black Canadians did not passively observe this American drama. A new militancy took root in Canada as well. On a smaller scale similar kinds of protests, less publicized but no less meaningful, were occurring on a daily basis. Black Canadians did not have the advantage of a flexible Constitution and a judiciary which waded into the troubling seas of human rights. Nonetheless, they marched, organized, sat in white sections, and built a collective consciousness.

Political assassinations rocked America during the 1960s. Medgar Evers and President John F. Kennedy in 1963; Malcolm X in 1965; Robert Kennedy and Martin Luther King, Jr. in 1968, all fell to assassins bullets. These assassinations proved that black leaders, and white leaders sympathetic to the black cause, were involved in a life-threatening campaign. A sickness had taken hold in America.

The 49th parallel was porous, but the disruptions in America did not send Canadian blacks into hiding. Canadian human rights legislation, passed in the 1950s and 1960s, was largely the result of direct black protest and/or the coordinated lobbying of blacks with other ethnic groups.

Typical of the new politicization was the Canadian Negro Women's Association (CANEWA). Founded in 1951, the CANEWA evolved out of a black women's social network in Toronto. No longer content with doing fundraising and charity activities, the women of the CANEWA, spearheaded by leading black Canadian actress Kay Livingstone, involved themselves directly in politics. The experience of work in factories, hospitals, offices, and schools during WW II made a lasting impression on black women across Canada. With truce declared and veter-

*Ground-breakers like **Kay Livingstone** helped re-define the position of black women in Canada.*

Internationally acclaimed contralto, **Portia White**

ans returning home to assume their jobs, domestic service was starring black women in the face. They would not, however, willingly give up gains made during war-time.

This new black consciousness was partly based on a fusion of culture and politics. Nowhere was this more evident than at the United Negro Improvement Association (UNIA) headquarters in Toronto. In the early 1940s, black patrons and musicians were barred from the Palais Royale and other night clubs. They responded by heading to the third floor at 355 College Street (UNIA building) for Tuesday, Saturday, and Sunday evening jam sessions. This location became known as "The land of jive. The home of happy feet!" It provided a venue for local jazz talent and for musicians from other destinations, especially Montreal.

Montreal, thanks in large part to the Jazz Workshop, had become a focal point for jazz musicians, black and white. Though Oscar Peterson was stealing headlines, Canada had a wealth of other great black jazz artists. Nelson Symonds, born 1933 in Hammond's Plains, Nova Scotia; Oliver Jones, born 1934 in Montreal; Wray Downes, born 1931 in Toronto; and, Sonny Greenwich, born 1936 in Hamilton, Ontario–to name just a few.

In 1953, the legendary alto saxophonist Charlie Parker came to Canada to play with the musicians of Montreal's Jazz Workshop. Later that year, he was joined by Toronto musicians and the internationally acclaimed Dizzy Gillespie, Bud Powell, Charles Mingus, and Max Roach at Massey Hall for "the greatest jazz concert ever." As told by Mark Miller in *Cool Blues: Charlie Parker in Canada 1953* (1989), the performances in Montreal and Toronto were "Canadian stories, no matter that many of the principals involved, Charlie Parker first and foremost, are American." Indeed, from coast to coast jazz clubs or associations were showcasing Canadian talent, albeit often in segregated venues.

Toronto's UNIA headquarters was much more than a musical meeting place. It was there, and at similar locations across Canada, that black culture and politics fused. Young and old met to discuss the issues of the day and to celebrate black talent. Strategies for change were hammered out in these meetings. Blacks understood that they had to both protect their community and find ways to make it grow. Importantly, a tremendous amount of transgenerational respect (a hallmark of indigenous West African education and apprenticeship systems) was engendered at these meetings. This relationship, between young and old, would prove essential in the years to come.

Without the numbers to launch effective economic boycotts, and without the identifiable targets of totally segregated regions, black Canadians coalesced around a more subtle form of racism, immigration policy.

Egon Letchner, Archie Alleyne, and Bernie Saunders (l to r) at the House of Hamburg, Toronto, 1953

Walk into Archie Alleyne's living room and you enter a music museum. Through artifacts, traditional instruments, pictures, posters, and, of course, music itself, "cool" jazz merges with "hot" Caribbean rhythms and both with their African heritage. In a space no larger than 10 x 15 feet, one feels the timeless power of black culture and its direct connection, as a sustaining force, to black history.

Toronto drummer Alleyne is one of Canada's Jazz greats. He counts Billie Holiday, Lester Young, Zoot Sims, Chet Baker, and Mel Torme with whom he has worked and performed. Like Wynton Marsalis, he is dedicated to bringing jazz to young people. He is so dedicated because jazz is rooted in the black experience, and because the demands of the music–improvisation, syncopation, call and response, and respect of a knowing audience–are essentially democratic. In 1989, Alleyne and other Canadian jazz artists toured Africa, bringing jazz and its history back to its homeland. In 1992-1993, he and producer Rudy Webb staged The Evolution of Jazz concerts, a series adapted into The Evolution of Jazz School Program, *a first-rate teacher's guide for Toronto-area schools.*

Archie Alleyne's career gives vivid testimony that in music, as in other areas of cultural expression, integration and respect between black and non-black performers is the rule, not the exception. Wynton Marsalis argues, "Now, one day the entire world will be the home of everybody. That's not yet, but it's what people in the arts strive for" (Utne Reader, *April, 1996). Society at large has much to learn from artists who embody history and, in the words of Alleyne, "bridge divides and put their stuff out there."*

Anna Gollinger, Ken Jacobs (piano), Auburn Trottman (sax)
Black Canadian musicians strutted their stuff in places like Toronto's UNIA headquarters, a place where those in the know flocked to swing and "take down" cool jazz.

Though segregation continued to exist, especially in education, it was the need to end discriminatory immigration policies that united the community.

One of the strengths of black people, north, east, south, and west, is their ability to "put a fresh spin on activities elevated and prosaic." As Nelson George, after seeing a "roundball" game at Madison Square Gardens, explains in *Elevating The Game: The History & Aesthetics Of Black Men In Basketball* (1993):

On the subway home we laughed about those two moves, compared them to past moments, and savored these improvisational flights as intensely as any jazz aficionado might listening to a riff by Miles or Bird or Trane. Or any b-boy would be hyped by the rhymes of Rakim or Chuck Dee or L.L. Cool J. Or the righteously born again might shout "Amen" at the rigorous rhetoric of Dr. Martin Luther King or Jesse Jackson. What links these basketball moves with rapping, sermonizing, and soloing is that they all manifest a particular–and shared–African-American aesthetic. My unknown Brownsville dunker, like NBA players Mark Jackson and Otis Thorpe, didn't simply score, he personalized the act of scoring just as African-Americans, in everything from music to jump rope to slang, have put a fresh spin on activities elevated and prosaic.

George is describing what binds black Americans to each other. Those bonds made the civil rights revolution possible. For black Canadians similar ties that bind allowed them to overcome differences and fight the common cause. In many areas, their civil rights victories preceded those of their American counterparts.

There are parallels to be drawn between Sammy Richardson and Jesse Owens. There are equal similarities between the stories of Viola Desmond and Rosa Parks, or Herb Carnegie and Jackie Robinson, or Stanley Grizzle and E. D. Nixon, or Rosemary Brown and Shirley Chisholm, or Austin Clarke and Richard Wright, or between the great black jazz musicians north and south of the border. True, Canada never had a Martin Luther King, Jr. But black Canadians had to fight many of the same battles as those fought in the US, and black culture made inroads in Canada for the same basic reasons: talent, skill, achievement, and pride. The only real difference, following an intriguing national characteristic, is that Canadians, black and white, recognize their heroes in a comparatively muted fashion.

CLUB LINCOLN

Presents a

JAZZ CONCERT
AND

DANCE

FEATURING THE

SKY LINE TRIO
THE KEY NOTES
NORM. *"Mr. Blues"* HARIS
Rubber Leg WILLIAMS
AND OTHERS

175 - 7th. St., New Toronto

Thursday, June 22, 1950

Admission 50c

Produced by Alan McLeod

10

Immigration: the Next Frontier

Feelings of shared experience prompted black Canadians
to identify with their American brethren, the dispossessed in the West Indies, and liberation movements in
Africa. Allied with other groups, black activists petitioned governments to end discrimination in employment, education, housing, and recreational facilities. Because their
protests were mostly verbal or written petitions they went
largely unnoticed, especially compared to the drama south of
the border.

Racism has many different guises. Some are obvious and
apparent to all. Some are not. More subtle forms can be every
bit as humiliating as the blatant ones. Segregated hotels in
Montreal, segregated schools in Nova Scotia, and "nigger heav-
ens" in churches and theatres across the land, were constant
reminders of state-sanctioned notions of racial superiority and
inferiority. They became, in the 1950s, flash-points for black
civil rights activism.

In 1954 Daniel Braithwaite, born in Sydney, Nova Scotia, of
Barbadian parents, launched a campaign to rid Toronto public
schools of *Little Black Sambo*. The book painted black people in
a derogatory manner, and did much to foster racial stereotypes
in young minds. Its existence as part of the Toronto Board of
Education's curriculum gave tacit legitimacy to racist beliefs.
Braithwaite knew of this from personal experience. He wrote:

> I was taunted by this Sambo business when I was small
> and vividly remember when a big white boy grabbed hold
> of my neck and rubbed his hand in my hair, saying, "Hello
> da Sambo."
> As I grew older, I became involved in community work,
> and I also vowed to myself that if I had a son and he was
> bothered with this derogatory story of *Little Black Sambo*,

I would go to any lengths to have this book removed from the school's curriculum. (*The banning of the book "Little Black Sambo" from the Toronto Public Schools 1956,* 1987.)

Braithwaite did have a son who in December, 1955, at age five, was shown the film version of *Little Black Sambo* during a school fundraising event. Braithwaite immediately stepped up his campaign. Here was an identifiable target around which the black community could mobilize, and mobilize it did. A flood of letters, petitions, and speeches by Braithwaite and other prominent blacks led, finally, in February, 1956, to the banning of both the book and film from Toronto schools.

The black community's resolve to topple discrimination in Canada was indeed strong, was indeed a tie that bound. The size of the target matters little, it's the passion that is important. Canadian school boards might consider placing *The Banning of the Book "Little Black Sambo" from the Toronto Public Schools 1956* on school curricula. It stands as an important historical document.

The Critical Issue of Immigration

During WW I over two thousand blacks left Canada for the US. No such migration occurred during WW II. In fact, many black Americans came north and served in black construction regiments. Canadian voices of opposition to discrimination began being heard in the 1940s. In 1953, *The Canadian Negro* was founded in Toronto. This national newspaper reflected a new consciouness among blacks. They were exhibiting a determination to work together to carve out their rightful place in Canadian society.

Political change often depends on having a critical mass of people, a voting bloc that cannot be ignored. Since the 1850s immigration policies had kept the Canadian black population from growing substantially. To attract immigrants host countries must put out the welcome mat: Canada established immigration offices in countries with "desirable" populations. Few of these countries had many black people. Until the 1960s, most blacks had been born in Canada.

Black history cannot be separated from black culture. In 1949, Montreal's **Oscar Peterson** *launched his international reputation as one of the world's great jazz pianists by playing to a packed house at New York's Carnegie Hall. No doubt, his popularity helped spur changes in the political arena. Oscar Peterson–Companion of the order of Canada and Juno and Grammy awards winner–continues to be one of Canada's most respected ambassadors. During roughly the same period, Truro, Nova Scotia's* **Portia White** *(1911–1968) was also breaking down barriers by giving concerts on major stages at home and in the US.*

In the US, "Don't Buy Where You Can't Work" (1930s) and "Buy Black" (1950s) campaigns were successful because urban black Americans, by their sheer numbers, had economic clout. These campaigns led to civil rights advances as, in order to avoid bankruptcy, white store owners opened their doors and hired blacks. Such opportunities were not available to black Canadians. Nonetheless, they pressed on and, through constant petitioning, effected real change. Despite smaller numbers, the human rights advances in Canada preceded those in America.

The flurry of activity around human rights legislation in the 1950s was making immigration restrictions more unacceptable.

Black leaders understood that unless their population grew, advances in human rights legislation would be threatened at the ballot box. Under the Immigration Act, black British subjects from the West Indies were denied the rights which whites had to emigrate. The Act was clearly discriminatory. Immigration thus became the critical issue facing the community. It was an identifiable target with international implications.

A Black United Front

On April 27, 1954, a delegation of 35 black activists from the Negro Citizenship Association (NCA) met in Ottawa with federal cabinet members to discuss Canada's anti-black immigration policies. Led by Don Moore and Stanley Grizzle of Toronto, the delegation presented a brief to Walter E. Harris, Minister of Immigration. The group's presentation, thoroughly researched, articulate, and defiant, changed the course of Canadian history. Many of the delegates had been active for years. By helping thousands of blacks settle, find jobs, unionize workers, meet contacts, and avoid deportation, people like Moore, Grizzle, Harry Gairey, Lenore Richardson, and many others, were building the community from the ground up. Stanley Grizzle summarized Canada's immigration policy vis-à-vis blacks as a "Jim Crow Iron Curtain." Don Moore stated:

> You have kept them out because they are black. If I were a Communist, there is opportunity for me to change and become a decent, respectable Canadian citizen. But I am born black, God has made me that way.

Donald Willard Moore (1891-1994) at age 100

Barbados-born Don Moore migrated to Canada in 1913, and immediately, without bitterness, set out to improve the circumstances of black people. At a meeting he convened in January, 1951, with pioneers Harry Gairey, Dr. Norman Grizzle, and George King, the Negro Citizenship Committee (later the NCA) was established. This group would ultimately succeed in persuading the Canadian government to open its doors to black people from the West Indies. Don Moore, like Harry Gairey, is an Order of Canada recipient. He richly deserves a place in the civil rights pantheon of heroes.

You are asking me to undo what God has done. (*Donald Moore: An Autobiography,* 1985.)

Recommendations of the Negro Citizenship Association's (NCA) Brief to the Minster of Immigration. The Negro Citizenship Association respectfully requests that the Government of Canada:

1. Amend the definition of "British subject" so as to include all those who are, for all other purposes, regarded as "British subjects and citizens of the United Kingdom and Commonwealth."
2. Make provision in the Act for the entry of a British West Indian–without regard to racial origin–who has sufficient means to maintain himself until he has secured employment.
3. Delete the word "orphan" from the regulation which provides for the entry of nephews and nieces under 21.
4. Make specific the term " Persons of exceptional merit."
5. Set up an Immigration Office in a centrally located area of the British West Indies for the handling of prospective immigrants.

Donald Moore, *Donald Moore: An Autobiography.*

Moore gave an impassioned history lesson on blacks in Canada. Central to his comments were the numerous examples of heroic black participation in Canada's wars. The Minister promised to take seriously the delegation's recommendations.

The NCA was determined to truly represent the Canadian black community as a whole and had sent out copies of the brief to black associations across the country. These associations were asked for their input and, in some cases, to attend the Ottawa meeting. In a politically shrewd move, the brief was also circulated to high-profile white groups. These groups were asked for their support, and many, including the United Church and the powerful Canadian Labour Congress, provided it in letters and telephone calls to Ottawa. Twenty-six organizations supported the delegation. It was an all-out campaign demonstrating the capacity, determination, and intelligence of black people.

Don Moore lamented the fact that black churches did not involve themselves in support of the delegation. This break with tradition was curious. Perhaps the churches believed that they could add little to the political sophistication of this campaign? Perhaps they felt that they should not engage in so secular a pursuit? Perhaps the role of black churches in Canada was changing?

Invoking the Commonwealth

Throughout his political career, John Diefenbaker was a proponent of equal rights and freedoms. As Prime Minister in the late 1950s and early 1960s, his calls for an end to apartheid in South Africa rallied black Canadian support behind him. Although Louis St. Laurent, prime minister at the time of the NCA's meeting in Ottawa, was less committed than Diefenbaker to the Commonwealth and Canada's position therein, the delegation's reference to it had a certain impact. In describing the dangers of Canada's Immigration Act, Moore stated:

The NCA's report marked a turning point in black Canadian civil rights activism. Background (left) Don Moore and Dr. Norman Grizzle, foreground Val Armstrong and Lenore Richardson.

> Social and biological sciences have established definitely that there are no superior races. The United Nations Universal Declaration of Human Rights asserts, "All human beings are born free and equal in dignity and rights." And Her Majesty Queen Elizabeth II, as recently as December 25, 1953, pronounced herself as dedicated to the concept of an equal partnership of all Commonwealth nations and races–and urged acceptance of this concept upon all countries of the Commonwealth. *(Donald Moore: An Autobiography.)*

By invoking the Commonwealth and Canada's responsibility to its partners, the delegation presented the Canadian government with a conundrum: How could it continue to treat Commonwealth citizens, especially those in the Caribbean, unequally? The Immigration Act of 1952 stipulated that immigrants could be barred from entering because of their ethnic group affiliation. Did this mean that a white Jamaican could come in, but a black Jamaican could not? How could Canada criticize South African apartheid and at the same time practice apartheid through racist immigration policies?

The new Act maintained the principle that immigration to Canada was not "a fundamental human right" but rather a "privilege." The delegation did not criticize the notion that Canada had the right to choose would-be immigrants. They asked only that this choice be exercised fairly; that it be based not on colour, but on merit.

The 1952 Act was passed specifically to fill Canada's labour shortage needs. The Canadian economy, like the economies of most industrialized nations, was expanding rapidly. Foreign workers were desperately needed. Large surpluses of such workers, both skilled and unskilled, existed in developing countries. And yet, Canada continued to recruit the vast majority of its immigrants from Europe and America.

Canada's Commonwealth partners, principally Britain and politically active West Indian countries, began pressuring it to relax immigration policies so as to include more immigrants of colour. Britain had already done so and, in order to maintain its leadership position within the Commonwealth, it needed to press this case on behalf of the West Indies.

In short, the brilliance of the NCA's presentation was that it added pressure from within to the growing pressure from without. Canada, unless it changed its immigration policies, was in danger of embarrassing itself on the world's stage generally, and before its mother country particularly. Based on post-WW II humanitarian relief efforts, Canada had gained a positive reputation, a reputation it could ill afford to lose.

The West Indian Domestic Scheme

Historically, Canada recruited black immigrants to fill a specific labour need. The West Indian Domestic Scheme followed this pattern. Initiated in 1955, it allowed one hundred women per year from Jamaica and Barbados to enter as domestic servants. This tiny crack rankled many, including newly empowered indigenous black women, in the community. Why open the door, if ever so slightly, to black women only? Were they less threatening? Did the old sexual stereotypes about the black man come into play during policy formation meetings? Were blacks only capable of service-sector employment?

Based on positive reports from white families who benefitted from cheap domestic labour, the program was expanded to include other Caribbean islands. By 1965, 2,700 women had been admitted. Most exercised their option of leaving domestic service after one year, finding the work both demeaning and far more demanding than similar employment back home, to pursue other careers. Many enrolled in schools, joining the only other significant group of West Indian immigrants since the 1920s, university students.

Most of the women were professionals (teachers, nurses, office workers) in their home countries. Their contracts allowed them to become landed immigrants after one year, and to then move about freely and, importantly, sponsor family member immigrants. A year's domestic service seemed "not a bad deal" given the opportunities that followed, and the line-ups at Caribbean islands' recruitment offices were long. After a year's "seasoning" Canada seemed to be offering upward mobility to a class of people who found such movement almost impossible in the caste and colour-based societies of the Caribbean. Still, this was not the type of policy favoured by the majority of blacks.

Separation from family is a constant theme in black history, and, as Austin Clarke describes in *The Meeting Point, Storm of Fortune,* and *The Bigger Light,* the domestics experienced much loneliness and heartache. They were largely a caste unto themselves, finding the politics of skin colour as predominant in Canada as in the status-conscious islands they left. The scheme did nothing to eradicate the underlying principle of Canada's Immigration Act: that there are superior and inferior races of people. In fact, in Canada their "blackness" was accentuated.

The Desire to Emigrate

After WW II, Britain was in desperate need of labour to re-build its economic infrastructure. The Nationality Act of 1948 opened the door to workers, mostly unskilled, from its Caribbean colonies. Though the independence movement was under way in the British colonies of the Caribbean, and many blacks were hopeful of improved social and economic opportunities at home, over 300,000 West Indians emigrated to Britain between 1948 and 1962. The 1950s was a decade of rapid expansion throughout western Europe, and most West Indians did indeed find jobs not available to them on the islands.

180

Colonization In Reverse

What a joyful news, Miss Mattie;
Ah feel like me heart gwine burs–
Jamaica people colonizin
Englan in reverse.

By de hundred, by de tousan,
From country an from town,
By de ship-load, by de plane-load,
Jamaica is Englan boun.

Dem a pour out a Jamaica;
Everybody future plan
Is fi get a big-time job
An settle in de motherlan.

What a islan! What a people!
Man an woman, ole an young
Jussa pack dem bag an baggage
An tun history upside dung!

Some people doan like travel,
But fi show dem loyalty
Dem all open up cheap-fare-
To-Englan agency;

An week by week dem shippin off
Dem countryman like fire
Fi immigrate an populate
De seat a de Empire.

Oonoo se how life is funny,
Oonoo see de tunabout?
Jamaica live fi box bread
Out a English people mout.

For when dem catch a Englan
An start play dem different role
Some will settle down to work
An some will settle fi de dole.

Jane seh de dole is not too bad
Because dey payin she
Two pounds a week fi seek a job
Dat suit her dignity.

Me seh Jane will never fine work
At de rate how she dah look
For all day she stay pon Aunt Fan couch
An read love-story book.

What a devilment a Englan!
Dem face war an brave de worse;
But ah wonderin how dem gwine stan
Colonizin in reverse.

– Louise Bennett, *Selected Poems.*

In Britain this huge influx meant that the community rapidly achieved considerable size, thus mitigating the alienation felt by black immigrants in larger geographic regions like Canada. Letters home were a blend of positive and negative news, but once landed the tendency was to encourage friends and family to follow. In 1962, based primarily on British concerns over having "too many blacks in our midst," the Commonwealth Immigration Act was passed. This Act, a "closed door" immigration policy, severely restricted the flow to Britain. Canada became a second choice destination.

Canada and the West Indies: a Shared Colonial History

How could an enormous geographic region like Canada have anything in common with the small island archipelago of the Caribbean? On the face of it they are so different: one cold, the other hot; one primarily white, the other primarily black; one separated by vast tracts of land, the other separated by water. And yet, from the very beginning their *raison d'être* was the same: to serve the interests of the mother country.

Twentieth Century West Indian Immigration to Canada

Year	West Indians	Percentage of Total Canadian Immigration
1900 – 1909	374	0.03
1910 – 1919	1,133	0.06
1920 – 1929	315	0.02
1930 – 1939	673	0.27
1940 – 1949	2,936	0.68
1950 – 1959	10,682	0.69
1960 – 1969	46,030	3.34
1970 – 1979	159,216	11.02
1980 – 1989	115,753	9.49
Total	337,112	2.84

Note: In 1990, 212,166 immigrants entered Canada. Of these, only 14,420 or 6.8% came from the West Indies. During the 1990s West Indian immigration to Canada appears to be in decline. This table does not reflect the total number of people of West Indian descent in Canada. As Frances Henry maintains in *The Caribbean Diaspora in Toronto* (1994), conservative estimates suggest that there are "455,000 persons of Caribbean birth in the country." This figure includes census-counted Caribbean immigrants, children, and "double-lap" black migrants from Britain.

Source: Immigration Statistics, Ministry of Supply and Services, Ottawa.

Colonies of all kinds exist primarily to enrich home countries. In Canada, the home countries were England and France; in the Caribbean, England, France, Spain, and Holland. The European conquest of regions throughout the world was largely a product of mercantile economics, a sixteenth century doctrine which held that a nation's strength and wealth consisted in the amount of accumulated capital in its treasury. Capital derived

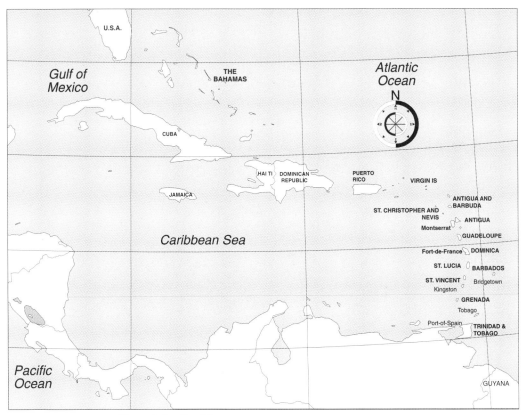

Map of the Caribbean
*Islands, by their geographic nature, tend to develop unique cultural charac-
teristics. Nowhere is this more true than in the West Indies, where, in microcosm, most of the world's population groups are represented.*

from selling exports, and each colony's job was to provide
mother countries with a surplus of export products.

The economics of exploitation determined the existence of
colonies. First the West Indies, and then Canada, were swept up
by the hegemony of mercantilism. Their staple products (in
Canada, fur, fish, and timber, and in the Caribbean, sugar) were
grown, caught, or hewn and sent overseas. As mother countries
become increasingly rich, the colonies become increasingly
poor. The chief mitigating factor to this impoverishment was the
false economy of settlement. In Canada its basis was land grants
to settlers. In the Caribbean it was slavery and the plantations.

During Europe's era of colonial expansion, from the sixteenth to the eighteenth century, all New World colonies were

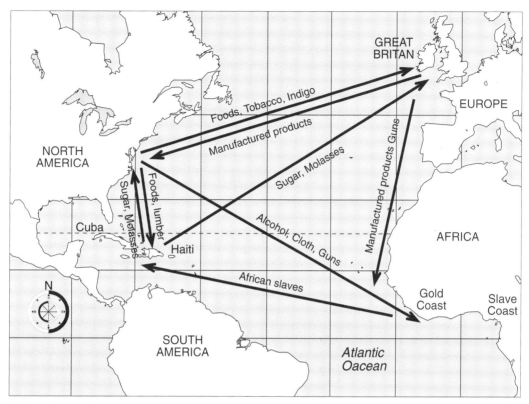

Triangular trade routes

governed by the basic principle of economic exploitation. European countries grew on the backs of their colonies. England, in particular, ensured its imperial growth through a series of merchant, shipping, and transport laws which protected its sources of wealth.

Caribbean rum and tobacco were consumed in Canada and elsewhere. Canadian timber, fish, and other staple products were sent to the Caribbean to meet the needs of plantation owners. Trade between the colonies was an essential component of empire building, and the sale and transportation of black slaves from the Caribbean to Canada became an important part of this support system.

The most efficient form of exploitation was mono-agriculture. Keeping things simple cut down on administrative costs. So, Caribbean islands were turned from multi-agricultural societies into sugar producers. As much land as possible was developed into sugar plantations. Other products necessary for maintaining the plantation economy could be more cheaply sent to the islands. As historian Wolseley Anderson argues in *Caribbean Immigrants: A Socio-Demographic Profile* (1993), this produced a devastating result:

> In Canada...the conditions and possibility existed for small private enterprises or ventures to arise in response to perceived needs in Canadian settlement communities. However, on the sugar cane plantations of the Caribbean, enclaved on the land as they were, entrepreneurship and private enterprise were inhibited, in fact prohibited, thereby accentuating a total authority structure, a rigid dependency syndrome.

Canada's geography and climate did not lend itself to plantation-style agriculture. This fact made West Indian islands more valuable, as colonies, than Canada. Also, Canada's initial settlers, unlike the cargo of black slaves brought from Africa to the West Indies, were, in fact, encouraged to develop companies and associations, and to show personal initiative. Canada's settlers needed to be independent and pioneering. In the West Indies, black slaves were forced into an already existing structure.

As long as a high percentage of accrued profits were sent, either directly or through taxes, to the motherland, Canadian settlers were free to conduct business in their own interest. Black slaves, by far the majority population in the Caribbean, were mere property, wholly dependent on the whim of their masters. "Non-persons," so went the reasoning, cannot engage in private enterprise.

Whereas mercantilism, arguably, mutually benefitted Canadian settlers and England, in the Caribbean it led to unbalanced economic development. The legacy of the "rigid dependency syndrome" established during slavery, reinforced under colonial rule, and entrenched by still existent colour scale prejudice, afflicts blacks more than any other group. "The darker your skin, the lower your position" is still an oft-repeated sentiment in Caribbean societies.

So, why not try to break out of this trap? Why not, for a change, choose to emigrate? Why not move to a land which, at least on the surface, places independence over dependence? When Canadian immigration officials told, and still tell, would-be West Indian immigrants that they "must not be a drain on the state," that they must be "independent or supported by family," it was not interpreted as discouragement. Quite the opposite, it was music to their ears!

The Colour-Class Interconnection

After miscegenation, the main factor responsible for differences in skin colour is melanin, a biochemical pigment which causes darkening. Simply put, the more melanin you have, the darker your skin; the less you have, the lighter your skin. Melanin protects the body from the sun's harmful rays, and people from hot sunny climates, like equatorial Africa, tend to have much more of it than people living in northern environments. (People from such regions tend to have extremely dark eyes, also necessary for protection from the sun.) Thus, skin colour mostly results from an evolutionary adaptation to climatic conditions, and the genetic inheritance of people born to mixed-race unions. These two factors go a long in explaining the many-hued reality which is our world.

There is no connection between skin colour and intelligence. The notion of such a connection, and that dark skin signified inferiority, developed with slavery. Many slavers actually believed that they were doing "negroids" a favour by removing them from their "primitive" surroundings. Bringing black slaves to the New World, teaching them "white" values, and so forth, would "humanize" them, would release them from their prison-house of inferiority. Of course, little "humanizing" occurred and, over time, the equation of dark skin with inferiority became the overriding justification for black mistreatment. The degree to which this equation continues to resonate gives testimony to the power of historical fictions, of how self-serving myths can be turned into widely accepted "truths."

In North America, the term "black" came to replace "negro." The essential difference between the two, however, remains an open question. "Negro" was used by whites, usually in a derogatory manner, as a mark of distinction, separateness, and inferiority. What connotations does "black" evoke? Has society changed, or just made a lateral shift?

We generally refer to people from the Caribbean as black. However, if Canada is a pluralistic society, then the Caribbean is even more so. "Black" there was used as a mark of distinction from Amerindian peoples and mulattoes. (Many light-skinned Caribbean people today are the descendants of black women raped by plantation owners, or women who married outside their race. The same phenomenon occurred in places like Ghana, West Africa where, to this day, many black people have Portuguese names.) The mulattoes, having white blood in their system, were accorded more privileges than blacks. (Interestingly, "one drop of Negro blood" came to have the opposite effect in the US.) Colour lines were established early in Caribbean history.

The term "Caribbean," like the term "black," is a convenient label. It masks a social diversity and a multiculturalism that is one of the world's wonders. Generic terms, however, do apply to common threads. In the Caribbean, such common threads continue to exist. Common to all the regions of the Caribbean is a history of European conquest, plantation economies, and slavery. Colonial administrations ruled each island as an economic satellite. These historical conditions lend credence to the concept of a shared Caribbean culture.

After emancipation in 1834, when many British conservatives wanted to cut colonial ties because the colonies were becoming too expensive to protect and administer, an open-market economy did not replace mercantilism in the Caribbean. European powers attempted to maintain their monopolies on Caribbean products by replacing black slaves with indentured labourers. The effect of this immigration supplanted the simple white-black social order with a stratification based on many hues.

Nineteenth century immigration to the Caribbean included cosmopolitan thousands from Portugal and Madeira, China and Hong Kong, India and the Middle East–all superimposed on the freed African and Amerindian population where, as in the case of Guyana, they still existed. The result of this stream of immigration on Caribbean societies, especially those with considerable land space like Guyana, Trinidad and Jamaica, was to provide the basis for a cultural inflorescence in which race, colour, language, religion, folkways and ethnicity all mixed and mingled beneath the influence of the sovereign values of the British colonizer. (Anderson, 1993.)

Emancipation freed black slaves in Canada and the British West Indies in 1834, and in other European holdings in the years following. Plantation owners began importing indentured labourers from India, China, Portugal, and Africa to work the plantations. Over 400,000 Indians came to the Caribbean during this period of mass immigration. Though many of the conditions of indenture resembled slavery, a new social order was erected which threatened the concept of a shared culture. Many of the indentured labourers came with their families. They were free to develop their own social structures, an opportunity denied to blacks under slavery. Blacks, displaced from most available jobs by this wave of lighter-skinned immigrants, were placed at the bottom of a hierarchy of colour. Resentment grew in lockstep with denial of opportunity.

The colonial strategy was simple, but ingenious: help certain groups in education, employment, and other services by denying equivalent opportunities to others, and, in so doing, sow strife among the coloured populations so as to make necessary continued control. In time, the polarization of white-black relations was replaced by a many-hued stratification, with whites standing "innocent" at the top.

The post-emancipation era was also the time of nineteenth century race science. Under colonial occupation colour scale theories affected every aspect of life in the West Indies. Divide and conquer policies of colonial administrations worked their vicious magic. In time, resentment was compounded in many blacks by an intense self-loathing and a determination to dis-

The colour continuum which associated blackness with disadvantage and whiteness with power and privilege was maintained, and European standards were the ideal. To rise in the social scale implied the adoption of European behaviour patterns, and the ambitious individual sought not to replace the ruling elite but to join it. Correspondingly, black features and behaviour were considered undesirable. Status, colour and culture were highly co-related during the colonial period, and were the direct legacy of slavery. To determine a person's place in society it was necessary only to look at the colour of his skin.

James Walker, *The West Indians In Canada.*

tance self from culture, a phenomenon Frantz Fanon would later describe in his book *Black Skin, White Masks.*

Fortunately, black pride movements established themselves in the Caribbean. Black West Indians, through sheer guts and determination, created their own agendas and pushed towards independence. Achieving independence did much to overcome the powerful legacy of racism. This need for independence and starting life afresh, however, also caused many to emigrate. Canada became a beneficiary of the post-WW II Caribbean diaspora.

The notion of multiculturalism makes inherent sense to West Indians. In the 1960s, when Canada began making positive statements about "respecting diversity," it attracted the attention of many. Perhaps the rallying call of West Indian culture, "Unity In Diversity: Out Of Many, One: One People, One Nation, One Destiny," could be realized in a new land? For, in truth, the stratified colour-class dominated West Indies served black interests least.

Most of the Caribbean immigrants to Canada come from Jamaica, Trinidad, Guyana, Haiti, and Barbados. Perhaps they come here for Canada's pluralism, having experienced something similar in their home countries. Is it not time that Canada recognize the Caribbean as a mosaic?

Much has been written about the indigenous black population, those born in Canada, not "getting along with" West Indian immigrants. Yet the indigenous black population fought hard to open the doors to West Indian immigrants. These blacks knew well the trials and tribulations facing blacks in the West Indies.

Rifts between the two communities were partly a result of the success of black activism in the 1950s and 1960s. The crowning achievement of this activism was the opening of immigration doors. West Indians, however, brought new concerns to the table, and many indigenous blacks felt that their impact was being overshadowed, and contributions diminished or not fully appreciated. History will show that such divisions were temporary phenomena, part of a natural period of adjustment. The destiny of all black people in Canada continues to be determined by the total community's success in overcoming racist barriers. In Canada, the ties that bind black people from

Africa, the Caribbean, Europe, and North America, are producing a community of shared interests. More so than in perhaps any other country blacks in Canada are learning from each other and, in so doing, recognizing the potential strength of black diversity.

11

A Context for Change

The 1911 census revealed that Canada's black population had dropped to 16,174 persons. Most blacks had left the Dominion, following a pattern of short-duration settlement which began in 1792 with the black Nova Scotian exodus to Sierra Leone. In 1870, push and pull factors led the once proud Elgin Settlement to close its doors. Most of the settlers had already left.

Some exceptions to this rule of departure did exist. Blacks moved to the cities and set down roots. This was especially true in Toronto and Montreal. In Nova Scotia, blacks saw the period leading up to the twentieth century as one of "consolidation during which many challenges had to be met. It was time to settle down and produce results, whatever the odds" (Bridglal Pachai, *Beneath the Clouds of the Promised Land*, 1990). Blacks in British Columbia and southwestern Ontario established viable communities. The building blocks for the future were laid by small black communities. With black immigration at a standstill, they had only themselves to rely on.

Climate was the most often cited reason for blacks leaving. In the early twentieth century, with the attempt by black Oklahomans to settle the Canadian Prairies, it became a centrepiece of Canada's immigration policies. It was clear that blacks, "being tropical people not accustomed to the cold," were specifically targeted by this provision. As Dr. Sheldon Taylor explains in his ground-breaking study *Darkening The Complexion of Canadian Society* (1995), under Prime Minister Laurier (1896–1911):

> Canadian politicians and bureaucrats began viewing the black immigrant as anathema to their nation-building plans. Instead, they cast the sturdy European immigrant–honed by generations of life on the farm–in the

role of ideal settler. Clifford Sifton, Minister of the Interior…placed every conceivable stumbling block in the way of sizeable black immigration to Canada, and in particular to the Canadian West. Frank Oliver, Sifton's successor, maintained "a no blacks wanted here" immigration policy from 1905 until the end of Laurier's administration. The Laurier government's rationalization…was based upon the myth of black people's inability to tolerate the Canadian climate. Sadly, this racist policy and the popular attitudes behind it became entrenched and so, remained crucial to Canada's official response to black immigration for nearly two decades after the end of the Second World War.

It is quite possible to shrink a community out of existence. Taylor's 1995 study reveals that immigration was part of a "systemic pattern" of differential treatment towards blacks. As such, the whites-only, except in specific cases of labour need, immigration policies of post-Confederation Canada were significant push factors leading to black depopulation.

The 1923 Immigration Act essentially defined British subjects, the most preferred immigrants, as whites only. Dark-skinned people living in the many British colonies of the time were excluded, stamping a new definition on the term "Commonwealth." Obviously, Canada wanted to prevent the formation of a multicultural mosaic like those which existed on most Caribbean islands.

The sub-title of Taylor's work, *Black Activism, Policy-Making And Black Immigration From The Caribbean To Canada, 1940s–1960s,* denotes a phenomenon of enormous historical and contemporary importance. Black communities, especially in urban centres, understood the dynamic interchange between discrimination from within (racism and segregation) and discrimination from without (restrictive immigration policies).

Black activists also understood that they were not alone. Through progressive immigration policies, Canada's Jewish community had grown substantially in the decades preceding the Depression. Then, in 1930, the doors were slammed shut to would-be Jewish immigrants suffering persecution overseas.

Irving Abella and Harold Troper's *None is Too Many* (1982) describes the growth of anti-Semitic hate propaganda throughout Canada. Forced into their own protective enclaves, similar feelings of discrimination from within and without drew Jewish and black community members together as friends and political reformers.

Canadian Negro Women's Association (CANEWA) members attending the "Awards of Merit" Banquet and Ball, October, 1961

In describing his book, Women of Vision: The Story of the Canadian Negro Women's Association 1951-1976, *(1996), Lawrence Hill writes, "Few people could name the Black community group that, for a quarter of this century, set up student scholarships, led protests against media and the police, initiated the celebration of Black history in Ontario, created the precursor to Caribana, organized the first National Congress of Black Women, and raised thousands of dollars for community projects." In so doing, Hill relates some of the many exceptional contributions the CANEWA made to the black and women's struggles for freedom, justice, peace, and equality in Canada.*

They worked in concert to bring about legislation like the 1944 Racial Discrimination Act. While "No Dogs, No Jews" signs became an embarrassment to Toronto residents, equally embarrassing were the signs which read "No Dogs, No Jews, No Niggers." The Act did away with such racist hate propaganda, or at least forced racist perpetrators into hiding. Black and Jewish activists allied on many of the campaigns to entrench human rights legislation in Canada. These alliances spread to include other ethnic groups. Black Canadian activists, modelling some of their protest strategies on American initiatives, were on the vanguard of change.

Shifting Values

In the late 1950s and early 1960s, Caribbean and African countries threw off the cloak of colonial rule and achieved political independence. Such independence stated to the world that blacks were finally free, could handle the responsibilities of statehood, and did not want or require white overlordship. The newly independent states of the developing world would now negotiate on their own terms with the industrialized west.

While the spectre of black "over-representation" in international bodies like the Commonwealth and United Nations concerned many, Canada was increasingly supportive of these developments. Black leaders used these forums to criticize all forms of racial discrimination. Apartheid in South Africa, segregation in the South, and restrictive immigration policies became principal targets. An international black voice was emerging.

The Canadian press showed a marked up-turn of reporting on black issues. While the successes and setbacks of the American civil rights movement and stories about emergent independent black states stole many of the headlines, numerous articles and editorials about black Canada began to appear. The black press became more politically involved, fostering the development of black pride and world black consciousness by publishing articles on local heroes, independence movements, and open critiques of Canada's "Jim Crow Iron Curtain."

In 1960, active protest pushed the Diefenbaker government into passing a new Bill of Rights. The Bill rejected discrimination based on race, colour, religion, sex, and national origin. It contrasted sharply with existing immigration regulations. Change was inevitable.

Television was acting as a democratizing force, sending graphic images of apartheid-inspired violence around the world. In March of 1960, South African police attacked peaceful demonstrators at Sharpeville. Sixty-seven blacks were massacred. Press reports described the scene in horrifying detail; television showed it. A sense of guilt swept across the nation as Canadians learned that jets built in Montreal had fired on the crowd. After Sharpeville, three thousand people turned up for a Toronto rally, organized by the Committee of Concern for South Africa, calling for an immediate end to Canadian-South African trade, and pressing the case for South Africa's expulsion from the Commonwealth.

At a meeting of Commonwealth prime ministers (March, 1961) in London, Diefenbaker and Prime Minister Jawaharlal Nehru of India, with the support of black African leaders, "proposed a general resolution condemning racial discrimination in terms that would be unacceptable to South Africa's Prime Minister H. F. Verwoerd, and that nation accordingly withdrew its application for continued membership and resigned from the

Commonwealth" (Winks, 1971). Diefenbaker returned home to a hero's welcome. Blacks and whites praised him for befriending Africa and bridging the continents.

Diefenbaker was the only white prime minister to challenge South Africa. To Africans he represented freedom from colonial status. His bold moves embarrassed Britain, which could have solidified its leadership role in the Commonwealth by supporting initiatives to isolate South Africa. Britain refrained from gestures of support for fear of offending the large white English population of South Africa, and because its investments and trade with that country were vital to its national economic interests. From all corners, Canada looked like a nation determined to chart its own course.

The Divergent Paths of Britain, Canada, and South Africa

Britain's 1948 open door immigration policy was meant to firm up relations between the mother country and her "Commonwealth dependencies." On paper, this policy was an example of Commonwealth nations being linked by shared objectives and interests. Arguably, Britain was simply filling an essential need for immigrant labour. As the 1950s wore on, and blacks were increasingly clustered in their own communities, it became evident that whites had little in "common" with them and were not interested in sharing "wealth." Colour barriers became more entrenched and black upward mobility more restricted.

> The influx of West Indians to Britain grew rapidly, and, as was demonstrated by the Notting Hill Riots of 1956, race relations tensions began to surface in urban and industrial areas where settlement of West Indian and other visible minority newcomers was most dense. In the face of these domestic British circumstances and the continuing political winds of change that blustered over the British Commonwealth and Empire, the Commonwealth Immigrants Act was passed in 1962. The effect of this Act was to remove from West Indians the "right" to enter, work in and settle in Britain and to replace it with a "privilege" underwritten by a Ministry of Labour employment voucher. (Anderson, 1993.)

As Britain invoked this new "privileged" access, Canada opened its doors. With Britain closed and the US in turmoil, Canada became the preferred destination for West Indians. The 1962 Regulations of the Canadian Immigration Act stipulated that skill, merit, and the ability to fill occupational needs were to be the main criteria used in the selection of unsponsored immigrants. It rejected, bringing it in line with the Bill of Rights, racial discrimination or country of origin as criteria.

The result of this opening was a doubling of the West Indian population. Between 1962 and 1966 roughly 10,000 West Indian blacks entered Canada, most of them settling in Ontario, and many filling important jobs in nursing and teaching. The availability of these and other jobs was a significant pull factor. Uncertainty over the economic and social status of newly independent Caribbean countries was an equally significant push factor.

A number of components made these changes possible, not the least of which was black activism. The essential thinking behind the 1950s changes in provincial human rights policies was transposed from the domestic arena onto foreign affairs and immigration. Blacks had fought hard to rid Canada of its segregation and policies of exclusion. As a natural development and good example of the community's evolution and cohesiveness, they turned their attention to bringing down Canada's "Jim Crow Iron Curtain."

Signs were beginning to appear that blacks were penetrating the glass ceiling of racism which prevented upward mobility for ethno-racial groups. The work of Dan Hill and the investigations of the Ontario Human Rights Commission (OHRC) were having a chilling effect on racist employers and landlords. Increasingly, public institutions (hotels, restaurants, sports clubs) practicing segregation were being drawn out of the closet and exposed as racist by revitalized black organizations like the provincial branches of the Association for the Advancement of Coloured People.

A growing number of white organizations supported city black activists. Labour unions, who for many years practiced their own policies of exclusion for fear of losing jobs to blacks working for less pay, were admitting blacks and supporting the cause. University campuses, in Canada and the US, became are-

*Prominent blacks like Calvin Best and **Leonard Braith-**
waite broke new ground for all ethnic groups.*

nas of protest. By 1965, 3,000 West Indian blacks were attending Canadian universities on student visas, up from only 400 a decade earlier. Jewish groups, with members who had family and friends murdered in the Nazi death camps, continued to support black causes, following a pattern in the US where many Jews viewed KKK lynchings as an attempt at ethnic cleansing.

Perhaps most importantly, blacks were penetrating the echelons of power. In 1961, Nova Scotian Calvin Best was appointed president of the Civil Service Association of Canada. Also in 1961, Dan Hill was named director of the OHRC. These, and other meritorious blacks serving on school boards, union executives, etc., were making decisions affecting all Canadians. They were also laying the groundwork for upward mobility by people from other ethnic groups.

In 1963, Canadian-born Leonard Braithwaite was voted into the Ontario Legislature. A Liberal, he represented the Etobicoke riding, whose population was comprised mostly of upper and middle-class whites. His election suggested that merit and not colour could be the determining factor in future elections.

While liberalism, integration, and high profile black role models were gaining a foothold in Canada, South African whites were "circling the wagons." In 1948, the same year that Britain's Labour government opened its doors, the government of South Africa established apartheid as an official policy. Blacks, who made up eighty to eighty-five percent of the population, were disenfranchised and denied any say in the nation's affairs.The African National Congress (ANC), established in 1912 to defend the rights of blacks, organized strikes, boycotts, and mass marches to overthrow apartheid and gain equality in civic, social, economic and educational opportunities. Time and again these actions were met with brutal violence, perpetrated by South African police forces. Thousands were killed, but the protests continued. Feeding on the Cold War sensibilities of western nations, the government insisted that the ANC was a Communist-led conspiracy, a tactic also used in America to quell black activism. In 1962, ANC leader Nelson Mandela was arrested for treason. He spent the next 27 years in prison.

After Mandela's imprisonment the protest movement intensified. His wife, Winnie Mandela, assumed a leadership position in the ANC and ensured that his philosophies and protest strategies continued to resonate with South African blacks. At numerous times Mandela was accused of inciting race riots from his prison cell. Much of his jail sentence was spent in solitary confinement.

The plight of South African blacks touched a raw nerve among blacks around the world. Freeing Mandela and ending apartheid became essential components of a world movement. Civil rights organizations in Canada and the US looked beyond their own agendas and marched in support of the dispossessed of South Africa. "Apartheid" was becoming a synonym for all forms of segregation. South Africa had successfully turned Mandela into a martyr. He came to represent the struggle for freedom everywhere.

Nelson Mandela is the son of a Tempu chief. As a Johannesburg lawyer, he joined the ANC in 1944 and quickly assumed a leadership role. From 1962 to 1989, the state tried to break his spirit and crush resistance to apartheid by holding the ANC leader in prison. His determination never waned. Finally, due mostly to intense international pressure, South Africa released him. The government believed that at the age of 71, Mandela would be unable to rally his people. Mandela is now the President of a free South Africa.

Dresden, Amherstburg, Africville, and North Preston

By the mid-1960s, Canadian examples of discrimination and segregation became intolerable for a growing number of blacks. Activists like Bromley Armstrong and Howard McCurdy, in keeping with their American counterparts, felt that they must test human rights legislation. It was important to discover whether the onus for bringing about change still rested with the victims of racism, or if legislation resulted in real protection.

In 1954, two blacks from Toronto visited Dresden, a small town in rural Ontario. In direct violation of the Fair Accommodations Practices Act, they were refused service in two restaurants. The *Toronto Telegram* was contacted immediately and sent black "testers" of their own. They too were refused service. Dresden suddenly became a focal point of world-wide attention.

Influential social activist and politician,
Howard McCurdy

In international, national, and black newspaper articles, television reports, and in public hearings, Dresden was described as a Jim Crow segregationist enclave. These open comparisons with US-style racism embarrassed Canadians from coast to coast, especially since blacks continued to be refused service! The OHRC launched an intensive antiracist educational campaign in the community and numerous inquiries were held. Nevertheless, even with all this negative publicity, it took ten years before blacks living in or visiting Dresden could move about freely. To many blacks, this suggested that Canada's paper regulations were toothless.

The recalcitrance of the Dresden restaurant owners was based on the entrenched racism of the community. Without widespread community support they could not have held out for so long. It seemed that concern over human rights abuses could not negate the rights of freedom of commerce. Perhaps most importantly, it exposed a gulf between urban and rural life in terms of race relations. Following a pattern established across North America, residents of Dresden came to resent the imposition of "city values" on their town.

Chapel at Uncle Tom's Cabin Site, Dresden, Ontario.

Dramatic events also occurred in 1965 at Amherstburg, Ontario. A cross was burned in the town centre, threatening phone calls were made to black residents, the black Baptist Church was defaced, and the sign welcoming visitors to the town was spray-painted "Amherstburg Home of the KKK."

Amherstburg, whose population was roughly equal between whites and blacks, held a special historical significance for black Canadians. The Baptist church was built in 1849 and, in Harriet Beecher Stowe's famous novel *Uncle Tom's Cabin,* it was the meeting-point where Eliza and her husband were re-united. The character of Uncle Tom was, and still is, widely believed to be modelled on the life of Josiah Henson, founder of the Dawn Settlement and "the most famous and most controversial slave ever to make his way to freedom in Upper Canada" (Hill, 1981). Defacing such a shrine with racist graffiti provoked intense anger among Amherstburg blacks.

Five days of racial incidents began when three black teenagers were barred from a local raceway. When two of them returned, they were arrested. Amid calls for mass marches,

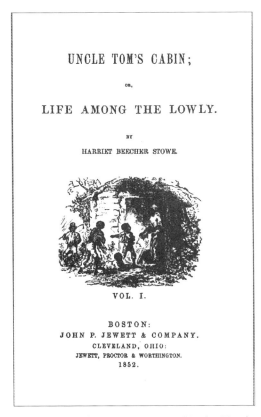

Harriet Beecher Stowe wrote Uncle Tom's Cabin *to expose the horrors of slavery. The novel told dramatically how Uncle Tom and his family tried to escape from a tyrannical overseer, Simon Legree. It vividly described Uncle Tom's daughter, Eliza, making her way across ice floes, pursued by baying hounds and a crazed Legree with his rawhide whip. The book, published serially (circa 1851), electrified the American public and caused a stir in Canada and Europe. It sold millions of copies, was translated into 37 languages, and has been credited with inspiring President Abraham Lincoln to end slavery.*
Dan Hill, The Freedom Seekers.

black unrest grew. Though no one claimed responsibility for the cross-burning, the classic symbol of KKK intimidation, Professor Howard McCurdy contended it was Klan work. Given the growing presence of the KKK in Canada, his contention was not unreasonable.

As news of the situation spread across Canada, there was a rising fear of open racial violence. In the end, however, moderate voices prevailed, and most blacks were satisfied with a full-scale investigation by Dan Hill and the OHRC, an investigation which led to greatly increased integration in the town. As in the Dresden situation, no arrests were made.

In Nova Scotia two areas of black settlement, Africville and North Preston, began attracting widespread attention. Most press coverage focused on Africville, increasingly portraying it as an uninhabitable rat-infested slum. The proud traditions and legacies of Africvilleans were swept under a sea of outrage over an "American-style ghetto" north of the border. For many years the Halifax City Planning Commission proposed razing the community and relocating its residents. For many years Africvilleans resisted.

Debate swirled inside and outside the black community. Africville became a subject of sociological study, with experts from across Canada making pronouncements about what should be done. Many non-Africvillean blacks supported razing the settlement and relocating its residents in integrated communities. To these blacks Africville, with its high rate of illiteracy, malnutrition, and poor housing, stood as too strong a symbol of black disadvantage. In the end, even though "Africvilleans strongly rejected relocation and urged that they be allowed to stay in Africville and develop it according to City specifications" (Donald Clairmont, *The Spirit of Africville*, 1992), Halifax city officials sided with the experts. They had the support of most of Canada.

By 1967, all the residents were relocated and the community demolished. In its place now stands an under-utilized park, and the bitter memory of many who were ill-compensated during the relocation process.

With the benefit of hindsight, we might question the urban renewal strategy implemented at Africville. The building of the South Bronx Expressway in New York pushed that community to the edge of destruction. It is now being revitalized by proud local residents and business people. Perhaps the money spent to raze Africville and relocate its residents should have been granted to Africvilleans, as they themselves suggested, to re-develop the community themselves? As Donald Clairmont con-cludes:

> Africville lives on as an indictment against racism, as a cri-tique of technocratic, imposed approaches to social change, and as a celebration of community and the human spirit. Twenty-five years ago, the local newspaper proclaimed, "Soon Africville will be but a name. And in the not too dis-tant future that too, mercifully, will be forgotten." It hasn't been. It shouldn't be. It won't be.

North Preston came under media scrutiny during the 1950s and 1960s. Located in the country, it was described as a rural blight, in contrast to the urban blight of Africville, which it was otherwise compared to. Nova Scotia was gaining a reputation for segregating its blacks in slave-status homelands with ser-vices befitting animals, poor or non-existent educational facili-ties, and dilapidated housing. Constant comparisons were made between these settlements and black ghettoes in the US, which were reaching boiling point.

Through statements of outrage, and in its zeal for reform, the popular press effectively negated the proud tradition of

Burnley "Rocky" Jones

In some respects, the Jones family embodies a century of black Nova Scotian history. Best known among the many distinguished Jones' (past and present), is Burnley "Rocky" Jones. Raised with his brothers and sisters in the segregated town of Truro, "Rocky" has dedicated his life to the black struggle for freedom and equality. Dubbed "Canada's Stokely Carmichael" –by a press eager to make such comparisons–for his work in Toronto during the civil rights movement, Jones graduated from the Dalhousie University law school in 1992. He continues to work on behalf of black and other Halifax communities as a lawyer with the Dalhousie Legal Aid Service.

"I accept the Nobel Prize for peace at a moment when 22 million Negroes of the United States are engaged in a creative battle to end the long night of racial injustice. I accept this award on behalf of a civil rights movement which is moving with determination and a majestic scorn for risk and danger to establish a reign of freedom and a rule of justice."

Martin Luther King, Jr.,
Nobel Prize for Peace
Acceptance Speech,
December 10, 1964.

North Preston blacks. Fortunately, in this case community activists Calvin Ruck, Burnley Jones, William Oliver, and others were able to stall the bulldozer and wrecking ball, and North Preston still stands today.

A New Mood in Black America

Mississippi Burning, the box office hit movie, tells the story of the murders of one black and two Jewish civil rights workers who went to that state to register blacks for the 1964 election. These three young men were among thousands of voter registration activists who entered the deep South during "Freedom Summer." As determined as activists were to get blacks the franchise, white southerners, led by the KKK, were equally determined to keep blacks "in their place." The fight for Dixie was on, and violence erupted everywhere.

Violence in the South was matched by an explosion of race riots in the northern cities of New York, Chicago, Philadelphia, and others. Ghetto conditions in these cities had reached crisis proportions. When a teenage black student was left for dead by white police officers in Harlem a riot began which exhibited for all of America black anger in bold face. Many black and some white civil rights activists were killed or injured in what became known as the "long hot summer."

Anger over differential treatment in housing, employment, education, and virtually every other aspect of life, caused a renewed appreciation for the voice of a different kind of civil rights advocacy, black nationalism. In 1964, the Mississippi Freedom Democratic Party (MFDP) was shut out of the Democratic Party Convention. As a result, many of its members, and others from the Student Nonviolent Coordinating Committee (SNCC) began to re-think their allegiance to Martin Luther King, Jr. and the strategy of non-violent resistance. The black nationalist movement, begun in the 1930s under Elijah Muhammad, leader of the black Muslims and the Nation of Islam (NOI), offered a strategy based on black self-help and white exclusion. It harkened back to Garveyism, "back to Africa," and self-reliance.

Malcolm X and the Nation Of Islam

To the Nation Of Islam there could be no true integration until blacks came to the negotiating table as equals. In the ghettoes of most northern cities black Muslim enclaves looked like pillars of prosperity and clean living, standing proudly in direct contrast to their immediate surroundings. The success of these enclaves, and the dynamic nature of NOI religious services, brought many into its ranks. In northern US cities, where the civil rights movement was making few inroads, and in Halifax, Montreal, and Toronto, more and more disenfranchised blacks were turning to the NOI.

At the same time, total reliance on black self-help made many whites fearful that the NOI favoured complete segregation. This, combined with statements about whites as "blue-eyed devils" and overtly pro-Africa political platforms, caused the added concern that the NOI was fostering hatred of whites and, ironically, a new brand of black racism. Some press reports labelled the NOI "fascist," thus alienating white civil rights activists.

The fiery rhetoric of Malcolm X, who became the NOI's leading spokesman, was set against the more palatable philosophies of King, who was widely revered in northern liberal circles. Malcolm X implored blacks to consider themselves part of an African majority. He argued that the black diaspora was part of a white conspiracy to divide and conquer, and that little real change had occurred because blacks still retained a "slave mentality," the result of 400 years of oppression.

Malcolm X maintained that there would be a black revolution, and whether it was peaceful or violent was up to white society. Urban blacks began marching to a new prophet, one whose power over the community caused the Federal Bureau of Investigation (FBI) to launch a secret campaign to dethrone him. Malcolm X's words did represent a significant departure in civil rights activism.

Martin Luther King, Jr., and Malcolm X had their only meeting in Washington, March, 1964. Though this picture suggests otherwise, the meeting occurred by chance, and the two men were in Washington for different purposes. Interestingly, this photograph has become one of the most widely distributed pictures of the civil rights era. To at least some degree, it has been used as a propaganda vehicle in the name of black unity. Both Malcolm X and King realized that white society's focus on their differences served the interests of the status quo. A close reading of their collected writings reveals that though they shared much in common, they also had considerable differences.

In 1963, the Canadian Broadcasting Corporation (CBC) commissioned black Canadian writer Austin Clarke to interview Malcolm X. At the time the interview, conducted in New York, was one of the most extensive ever with the leader of the "Muslims of America." The interview did indeed reveal that Malcolm X rejected King's "pacifism." Malcolm X also displayed an awareness of the black situation in Canada, where he was gaining a considerable following.

In 1964, Malcolm X took his pilgrimage to Mecca and Africa. The trip caused a dramatic change in his political philosophy. He changed his name to Al Hajj Malik al-Shabazz, disassociated himself from Elijah Muhammad and the NOI, became more openly conciliatory to whites supporting the black cause, and began building a movement based on Pan-African American pride.

Al-Shabazz grew increasingly supportive of cooperation between civil rights organizations. "If white people realize what the alternative is, perhaps they will be more willing to listen to Dr. King," he stated. Sadly, he would never see his dream of black empowerment materialize. On February 21, 1965, al-Shabazz was gunned down while delivering a speech at the Audubon Ballroom in Harlem. His assassins, widely believed to be NOI members (and unwitting tools of the FBI), were never brought to justice. He was only 39 years old.

"By Any Means Necessary"

Whether Malcolm X's famous slogan was a call for revolution or a statement about black self-defence and empowerment, remains an open question. In the last of his Harvard University speeches (December 16, 1964) al-Shabazz said:

> In order to get any kind of point across our people must speak whatever language the racist speaks. The government can't protect us. The government has not protected us. It is time for us to do whatever is necessary by any means necessary to protect ourselves.

Such arguments, when combined with his earlier notion that only a separate black state would be just compensation for 400 years of servitude, gave the impression that Malcolm X was a strict black nationalist. And yet, his message to black Americans was also one of hope and inspiration:

> Once our people are taught about the glorious civilization that existed on the African continent, they won't any longer be ashamed of who they are. We will reach back and link ourselves to those roots, and this will make the feeling of dignity come into us; we will feel that as we lived in times gone by, we can in like manner today. If we had civilizations, cultures, societies, and nations hundreds of years ago, before you came and kidnapped us and brought us here, so we can have the same today. The restoration of our cultural roots and history will restore dignity to the black people in this country.

For Malcolm X/al-Shabazz, power was equated with knowledge, education, and cultural awareness. His autobiography is a testament to the richness of this message.

Shifting Focus: America in Vietnam

Concerns over communism and communist infiltrators dominated America in the 1960s. Agitators of all kinds were branded as communists. FBI files were kept on thousands of Americans, including King and Malcolm X.

In 1965, the first US soldier set foot in Vietnam. Over 58,000 American soldiers were to die before the government pulled out of the war in 1973. The total number of Vietnamese, Laotian, and Cambodian casualties will never be truly known. The distinction between enemy soldiers and civilians broke down, as the American military strafed villages and unleashed a bombing campaign of epic proportions to destroy Vietcong supply routes.

At home, race relations hardened as civil rights organizations openly supported anti-Vietnam War protests. Some peaceful marches broke down and demonstrators were jailed. Many Americans, including King and Malcolm X, believed that the US was willing to suffer such enormous casualties in Vietnam because of the over-representation of blacks and "poor southern crackers" in the armed forces. To many Americans, black and white, Vietnam became a class war.

As part of its Cold War strategy, America demanded support for its international campaign to root out communism in Vietnam. Some Canadians volunteered and saw active duty. Thousands of draft-age young men, however, burned their draft cards and fled to Canada.

In 1964, Cassius Clay, after defeating Sonny Liston for the world heavyweight boxing title, changed his name to Muhammad Ali and joined the NOI. He became a personal friend and political associate of Malcolm X. In 1967, Ali was drafted, but refused to serve, arguing that America had no business perpetrating violence overseas when racial violence was the order of the day in its own streets. Others maintained that he was hiding behind the Muslim faith and trumped-up claims of pacifism. Fined and imprisoned, Ali served three years of a five-year term before the Supreme Court overturned his conviction. After 1966, the Johnson administration became obsessed with winning the war in Vietnam. This myopia, followed by that of President Richard Nixon, led to greatly increased black frustration at home. As the cities burned, American Presidents turned a blind eye.

Voter Registration, "Let the Cities Burn," and Black Power

In 1965, the civil rights movement turned its attention again to voter registration. That year less than one percent of blacks in Selma, Alabama registered to vote. Protesting the police murder of a young black activist and intimidation tactics designed to keep blacks disenfranchised, King, the SCLC, and the SNCC began a five-day march from Selma to Montgomery, the state capital. This 50-mile odyssey became known as the "We Shall Overcome" campaign.

After ten years of struggle, the right of blacks to vote was still being denied. The freedom marchers wanted the Alabama government to provide protection for black voters. The Alabama government responded by tearing into the demonstrators. Black blood poured onto the streets, and the march was postponed. The nation watched in horror.

One week later President Lyndon B. Johnson, shaken by the highway murder of Viola Liuzzo (a white woman), announced his support for a new voting rights law. No doubt he had in the back of his mind Malcolm X's "ballots or bullets" threat. The protesters were allowed to complete their demonstration, this time under federal army protection. They were joined by thousands from across America. On March 25, 25,000 marchers, many waving American flags, stood before the Montgomery capital.

Black activists were working on a state-by-state basis and the biggest hurdle, Mississippi, was still ahead of them. After Selma, many believed they had the support of the Johnson administration. Johnson himself had said "We Shall Overcome" before a live television audience in his statement supporting the Selma protest.

James Meredith, who in 1962 was escorted from class to class by federal army troops when he broke the colour barrier at the University of Mississippi, led the march on "Ole Miss." Half a million blacks lived in Mississippi and only a minuscule percentage of them had dared registering to vote. On June 6, 1966, just the second day of a 220-mile march for freedom from Memphis, Tennessee, to Jackson, Mississippi, Meredith was shot and wounded.

This shooting spurred the development of the Black Power Movement. King and Stokely Carmichael, then chairman of the

SNCC, resumed Meredith's march through Mississippi. They split, however, over the philosophic orientation of the march. To King it was still "Freedom Now," but to Carmichael the appropriate rallying slogan was "Black Power."

A schism developed within the civil rights movement when Carmichael, based on the support of a growing number of blacks, refused to moderate his message. Black Power had a special appeal to urban blacks who suffered daily in over-crowded and over-run ghettoes. The week-long Watts, Los Angeles, riot of 1965, one of the most violent in the nation's history, displayed a new level of desperation among

Outline of the most dramatic growth in black voter registration in the southern States			
State	**1960**	**1966**	**Percent Increase**
Alabama	66,000	250,000	278.8
Mississippi	22,000	175,000	695.4
South Carolina	58,000	191,000	229.3
Texas	227,000	400,000	76.2
Virginia	100,000	205,000	105.0

Source: US Department of Commerce, Bureau of the Census.

black people. There, and in the other city riots which followed, blacks had grown tired of slow incremental change. In acts of blatant hostility, Watts suffered $45 million of property damage.

For many blacks the Watts riot sent a necessary message to whites. In the years that followed other cities, particularly Chicago, Detroit, and New York, would witness intense rioting. In the summer of 1967, over 100 American cities experienced racial violence. America had become a nation of two societies.

On April 4, 1968, James Earl Ray, a white man, assassinated Martin Luther King, Jr. Another string of race riots, resulting in 45 deaths, followed King's murder. An assassin's bullet had felled the godfather of peace and non-violent protest, leaving America, once again, a nation divided. More and more blacks saw direct violent action as the only response to racist discrimination. Such feelings had become bred in the bone.

Black Canadians Respond

Canadian blacks mourned the death of King, as great a hero north of the border as elsewhere. His assassination led to a new militancy in Canada. On "November 30, 1968 an interim committee was struck at a Black Panthers' meeting in Halifax, under the chairmanship of Dr. Oliver, to design the structure of a political organization to represent black interests and aspirations in Nova Scotia.

*The Black Panther Party was founded in 1966 by Huey Newton and **Bobby Seale** (above). Its political platform, a ten-point program emphasizing freedom, employment, education, housing, and justice, incorporated different aspects of Garveyism ("black is beautiful"), the NOI, and the civil rights movement. The Panthers demanded that the government rebuild shattered ghetto communities in compensation for slavery. Their stark dress code and public brandishing of guns sent a chill through white America. There was a growing fear that the Panthers would start a black revolution using "any means necessary."*

The result was the formation of the Black United Front in 1969 to bring Blacks closer to the realization of their objectives: to reach economic, political and social power" (Pachai, 1993).

The Canadian establishment now wondered aloud what blacks might do "to get their share of the pie." Could claims equating discrimination against blacks in Canada with discrimination in the US really be justified? What would the future hold? Though talk of self-segregation and never "fraternizing with the white devil" did arise in Nova Scotia and other Canadian sites of black unrest, enough significant changes were occurring to prevent black nationalism from gaining a real foothold. These changes were the result of progressive black activism and a new liberalism taking root in Canadian society.

When Detroit was "set on fire" in the summer of 1967, from across the river Windsor residents watched with fear and trepidation. Black Canadians were not passive observers of this or other American race relations dramas. Many actively supported the civil rights movement by becoming directly involved or by sending money in support. Most importantly, black Canadians sought to solidify gains already made.

The black Canadian drama had, arguably, unfolded earlier. During the 1950s, the intensive lobbying of Don Moore, Director of the Negro Citizenship Association, Sydney Williams of the Canadian Association for the Advancement of Coloured People, and many others had resulted in tangible gains. The success of the black civil rights movement in Canada had much to do with black activists' ability to form alliances with other persecuted populations and an understanding of Canada's immigration needs. They formed "rainbow coalitions," to use Jesse Jackson's terminology, long before Jackson and the American civil rights movement understood the power of such unions. Without the numbers to effect change themselves, blacks extended the invitation to others.

The clever manner in which activists like Don Moore informed Canadian immigration authorities about, for example, a surplus of qualified nurses in the West Indies, led to the opening of doors for specific forms of employment. More generally, by invoking the Commonwealth and Canada's commitment to it, the NCA brought forward an issue with broad-based implications. These, and numerous other examples of black activists working within both to manipulate the system and appealing to a wide consensus, are described in Dr. Sheldon Taylor's *Darkening The Complexion Of Canadian Society.*

Changes to the Immigration Act: the 1967 "Points System"

For indigenous blacks the 1967 immigration regulations represented victory in a battle begun shortly after World War II. What has become known as the "points system" stipulated that all immigrants, irrespective of their country of origin, were to be assessed on the following factors:

> education and training; personal assessment by an Immigration Officer; occupational demands; occupational skills; arranged employment (or designated occupation); knowledge of English and French; relative in Canada; employment opportunities in the area of destination.

Major Sources of Caribbean Immigrants, 1965 – 1979

Date	Jamaica	Trinidad	Guyana	Haiti	Barbados
1965	214	780	609	98	560
1966	1,407	1,127	628	126	699
1967	3,459	2,340	736	378	1,181
1968	2,886	2,419	823	444	821
1969	3,889	5,631	1,865	550	1,242
1970	4,659	4,790	2,090	840	853
1971	3,903	4,149	2,384	989	677
1972	3,092	2,739	1,976	936	534
1973	9,363	5,138	4,808	2,178	800
1974	11,286	4,802	4,030	4,857	790
1975	8,211	3,817	4,394	3,431	782
1976	7,282	2,359	3,430	3,061	544
1977	6,291	1,552	2,472	2,026	634
1978	3,858	1,190	2,253	1,702	455
1979	3,213	786	2,473	1,268	293
Totals:	74,013	43,619	3,4971	22,884	10,865

Source: Immigration Statistics, Ministry of Supply and Services, Ottawa.

The basic framework, a system based on merit, had been established in the 1962 Immigration Act. The 1967 changes represented a fine-tuning and further liberalization. With the playing field now levelled, meritorious black West Indians began flocking to Canada. During the 1960s Canada's black population more than doubled. The rapid influx of West Indians presented new challenges for the community. Racism became more evident as their numbers grew. The capacity of Montreal's Little Burgundy and similar communities across Canada to serve as acclimatizing filters was being strained. Indigenous blacks were growing older, and some felt threatened as West Indian populations came to dominate in Canada's cities. The new immigrants strove to retain much of their Caribbean culture. Some, imbued with a strong sense of independence and island identity, disassociated themselves from disadvantaged Canadian-born blacks. Only in the Maritimes does the Canadian-born contingent still outnumber immigrant blacks. In a 1995 interview, black activist and educator Robert Upshaw drew this comparison between Halifax and Toronto:

> The greater Toronto area–its schools, places of work, municipal governments, community organizations, etc.–must deal with the entire black diaspora. Toronto has substantial numbers of Africans. What do the tens of thousands of people from Somalia, Ghana, Nigeria, and other African nations have in common with recent West Indian immigrants or the indigenous black community? Of course, there can be real strength in such diversity. But, in the struggle to survive it is often difficult to build coalitions. In Halifax, the black community is comparatively homogenous. Most people have a shared cultural frame of reference. Here, a community of shared interests exists. It has developed out of the need to break down racist barriers to black achievement. I sense the same thing developing in Toronto and other Canadian cities. The key is historical knowledge. Such knowledge shows black people the world over that their commonalities far outweigh their differences.

Upshaw also commented on the adjustment process of West Indians living side-by-side with blacks from neighbouring islands. At first, to some the coincidence of skin colour was the only tie that bound. Increasingly, however, black Canadians of all backgrounds are uniting behind common causes and using their new urban visibility to press for changes beneficial to the entire community.

Examples of black groups with broad social-service mandates can be found across Canada. Following the leadership of Eleanor Rodney, Hamilton, Ontario's African Caribbean Cultural Potpourri Inc. (ACCPI) provides support through charitable donations, hospital grants, academic scholarships, youth job placements, and education programs. ACCPI initiatives clearly illustrate a willingness to integrate, and that the "black tile in the mosaic" benefits all of Canada. Similarly, the work of Abdi Mohamoud, formerly a star on Somalia's Olympic basketball team and a refugee from the horrors of civil war, demonstrates the determination to adjust and contribute. With his associate Said Ali-Korshel, Mohamoud established the Somali Canadian Sports and Arts Centre, a Toronto-based volunteer agency providing sports, cultural, and social opportunities in mainstream society to over 1,000 Somali-Canadian youth.

An honest investigation into social history would uncover a vast reserve of black groups and individuals who have dedicated themselves to the well-being of all. Clearly, Canadian society has something to learn from the magnanimous colour-blindness of Eleanor Rodney, Abdi Mohamoud, and the legions of others who quietly "do the right thing."

12

New Black Voices

Before the American Civil War Canada's black population stood at roughly 60,000, the majority living in individual settlements. The achievements of many of these settlements could have served as building blocks for a more integrated future. Unfortunately, their record of success went largely unnoticed. Arguably, in the wider context of Canadian society and the thrust for nation-building after Confederation, these settlements were a double-edged sword. By and large, they were unable to sustain themselves during the fifty-year period following 1861. Canada's black community sank from its apogee to its nadir.

Essentially, Canada's post-Confederation immigration policies followed a pattern of allowing entry to coloured people only when short-term labour demands required it. After the job was done or when white workers became available, restrictive measures were used to drive out ethno-racial people and to discourage any future growth. Blacks, Chinese, Japanese, and South Asians particularly felt the brunt of such practices. This pattern continued into the 1950s.

The case histories of white backlash against increasingly populous ethnic groups is part of Canada's historical record. In 1907, the Vancouver-based Asiatic Exclusion League was formed. A significant number of Japanese, Chinese, and East Indian people had settled in Vancouver, and the "darkening complexion" of the city concerned many whites. The League was established to stem the tide. Years later, it launched a demonstration protesting the arrival of a ship carrying over a thousand Japanese and Sikh immigrants. This protest erupted into the most destructive race riot in B. C. history.

Race riots, the treatment of the black Oklahomans, immigrant disenfranchisement, the disproportionately high numbers of coloured workers killed in massive construction projects, and numerous other examples, point to the fact that colour discrimination was fundamental to Canadian history. Race thinking affected everything from strict quotas placed on women of colour (in an attempt to restrict the total numbers of such immigrants born in Canada), to the treatment of landed ethnic groups. Of the 4,995 Oriental people who came to Canada between 1906 and 1925, 4,909 of them were men, a ratio of 40:1! Oriental men were simply part of a labour exploitation scheme. There was never any intention of providing them with long-term settlement opportunities.

The 1920s and 1930s saw a dramatic growth in the number and political profile of hate groups such as the KKK. Though many of these groups had their origins in the US, their propaganda was consistent with made-in-Canada notions of white supremacy. The social and political climate between the world wars, especially during the Depression, provided fertile ground for the peddling of hate propaganda. Religious, political, business, and educational leaders either directly supported initiatives to preserve Canada for the established white community, or turned a blind eye to racist activities.

In terms of immigration, successive Canadian governments maintained their "innocence" by not adopting formal policies that openly restricted certain peoples. Rather, they allowed authorities to act "with discretion." The whites-only agenda, however, was plain to see for anyone who cared to look. It was expanded to include Jewish immigrants during the 1930s and through WW II. It was not seriously compromised by post-WW II immigration policies which, on paper at least, insisted that Canada must be pro-active in its pursuit of immigrants to expand the economy.

It is against this background that we must understand the radical changes in immigration policies during the 1960s. These changes were the result of world events and the determined efforts of blacks and others to win victories at home and then challenge Canada to open its doors.

Immigration and the Test of Multiculturalism

By reducing the emphasis on "preferred nationalities" and matching immigration to education, skills, and Canada's economic needs, the 1962 Immigration Act attempted to address the criticisms of West Indian leaders, some of whom had personal experiences with Canadian racism.

> As a young man Sir Alexander Bustamante, the prime minister of Jamaica from 1962 until 1967, had lived briefly in Canada, which he had not liked. In 1961 the Jamaican premier, Norman Manley, openly attacked the Canadian color bar, as he saw it; and two years later, while speaking at the University of New Brunswick, the new Prime Minister of Barbados, Earl Barrow, charged Canadians with discriminating against West Indians in trade as well as in immigration. Eric Williams, Prime Minister of Trinidad and Tobago, was even more forthright in his condemnation of the "color-bar." (Winks, 1971.)

Given its statements at Commonwealth conferences and in other international forums, Canada could not ignore these criticisms. It was compelled to act. The 1962 Act allowed unsponsored or independent Caribbean immigrants to enter Canada for the first time.

Implicit in the new immigration regulations was the recognition that immigrants contribute enormously to the economy. Historically, economic growth and high immigration have, in Canada, gone hand in hand. And, indeed, most Caribbean immigrants arriving after 1962 acquired jobs suitable to their skills. Just the same, adapting to a new country was difficult, especially for immigrants separated from family. There is considerably more to life and community-building than work, a fact not fully recognized by Canadian authorities.

Pivotal to the black agenda for change were the Black United Front; the British Columbia Association for the Advancement of Coloured People (BCAACP), where Bill Brown, Rosemary Brown, and Norman Alexander developed their social activist philosophies and skills; Toronto's West Indian Federation Club, the venue used to launch Austin Clarke's early novels; and, Halifax's Kwacha House, where, led by "Rocky" Jones and others, numerous once disenfranchised blacks gained political consciousness. These, and other organizations, were dedicated to solving issues of adjustment, fighting discriminatory immigration policies, and fostering black racial uplift. They were critical to black advancement in Canada.

Following the White Paper Recommendations of 1966, the 1967 immigration regulations focused on the moral issues of family unification and assistance to refugees. The black community campaigned hard for this type of recognition. Many of its

Caribbean Immigration to Canada, 1967 – 1990

Year	Total Canadian Immigration	Caribbean Inflow	Percentage
1967	222,876	8,403	3.8
1968	183,974	7,533	4.1
1969	161,531	12,003	7.4
1970	147,713	11,932	8.4
1971	121,900	10,843	8.9
1972	122,006	10,209	8.4
1973	184,200	24,404	13.2
1974	218,465	27,915	12.8
1975	187,881	22,367	11.9
1976	149,429	18,172	12.2
1977	114,914	14,383	12.5
1978	86,313	10,581	12.3
1979	112,096	8,839	7.9
1980	143,117	9,639	6.7
1981	128,618	11,470	8.9
1982	121,147	11,855	9.8
1983	89,177	9,982	1.2
1984	88,239	7,571	8.6
1985	84,302	8,479	10.1
1986	99,219	12,820	13.0
1987	152,098	17,445	11.5
1988	161,929	12,393	7.7
1989	189,956	14,099	7.4
1990	212,166	14,420	6.8
Totals	3,483,266	315,781	9.1

Source: Immigration Statistics, Ministry of Supply and Services, Ottawa.

members understood, through agonizing personal experience, the impact of separation from family. The constant theme of separation in world black history played a strong role in their lobbying efforts.

However liberal in intent, the 1967 Act was flawed in that it did not provide for assistance in integrating new arrivals into Canadian society. Chief among these needs was English or French language training, a service generally left to unprepared and somewhat beleaguered school systems. The adjustment process became the ultimate test for Canadian multiculturalism.

Largely speaking, growing immigrant communities had to rely on their own people through often painful periods of settlement. Initially, this process led to a breaking down of alliances between groups as adjustment to a new society (language, work, housing, education, and, in general, learning the system) took precedence. (Some critics maintained that federal and provincial government policies promoted "islandism" which militated against black unity and power.) As a result, special-interest groups, like the Jamaican Canadian Association (JCA), were founded to address the specific needs of immigrants from particular Caribbean islands. Later such groups as the JCA adopted a broad mandate and work, in many instances, on behalf of all blacks in Canada.

The success of multiculturalism would ultimately depend on the equal sharing of the Canadian pie and meaningful contact between races. Would Canada develop along the lines of the US which preaches melting pot and equality for all, but which in reality has "ethnic boxes" and treats minority communities unequally? Or would a multicultural mosaic, with immigrant groups retaining their cultural heritage in a new context and experiencing equal opportunities, become a reality?

Trudeaumania vs. Nixon

On June 25, 1968, the federal Liberal party, on a tidal wave of support for its leader Pierre Elliott Trudeau, swept to power in an election that changed the nation. Canadians saw Trudeau as a man who would shatter the stereotypes of political leadership. Many blacks joined in the euphoria. This "socialist dressed up as a liberal" would help their cause. Trudeau was brash, elegant, cool, and nonconvential. Most importantly, he distained white conservatism.

"Trudeaumania" stood in sharp contrast to events in the US where, also in 1968, Richard Nixon was elected President. He rose to power by way of a "silent majority." In general, these were whites opposed to 1960s social developments, especially the re-defined place of black Americans, but did not voice their opposition. Nixon's campaign called for a reduced role of the federal government in domestic affairs, and an expanded one for state and municipal governments. This struck fear in the hearts of blacks, particularly in the South. In power, Nixon slashed the budgets of Johnson's Great Society programs and cracked down on all protest movements. He was determined to win the war in Vietnam at a time when black Americans were marching to the tune of "No Vietcong Ever Called Me A Nigger," (i.e. "What am I doing fighting this non-enemy?").

Using the Black Power salute, US athletes **Tommie Smith** *and* **John Carlos** *at the Mexico City 1968 Olympics graphically demonstrate America's two societies.*

Many black Canadian and West Indian intellectuals were optimistic about Prime Minister Trudeau. Some likened him to Prime Minister Eric Williams of Trinidad and Tobago. Both were activist scholars. (Given Trudeau's history and political interests, there was a good chance he had read William's seminal work *Capitalism and Slavery* (1964), the bible of West Indian activism and independence.) In time, immigrant circles would credit Trudeau with opening the doors to people of colour, for he viewed Canada as "bilingual in a multicultural context."

Canada and the US seemed to be on divergent paths in terms of race relations. Events in Montreal, however, would soon suggest otherwise.

The Sir George Williams Incident

The uprising at Sir George Williams University was a source of considerable controversy among blacks. To some historians, the incident represented a schism in the black community. Robin Winks (1971) wrote:

> Many of the young, who read Baldwin, Genet, Malcolm X, and Frantz Fanon, would by 1970 reject the delicate world of reprobation, the NAACP–"for elderly Negroes, those 35 and up"–and accommodationist values, and would begin to speak of Black Power. That the turning point may have come in February of 1969 in the thoughtless, needless, and frustrated destruction of the twentieth century's symbol of quantification, the ultimate equality–Sir George Williams University's computer centre–provides an ironic caesura to our story. The conviction in Montreal of Trinidadians involved in the damage to the center would, in 1970, set off extensive Black Power rioting in Trinidad.

Some black elders' criticism of the students for their destructive act suggested a growing division between old and new, between blacks who lobbied quietly behind closed doors and new arrivals predisposed to American-style direct action. Other black elders understood too well this act of frustration. They understood also that the new arrivals could not be blamed for ignorance of the long black struggle for equality in Canada. How could they be blamed? This struggle existed mostly in an oral tradition, in the hearts and minds of those who had suffered. It had not yet been truly documented.

For hundreds of years blacks in Canada helped shape the complex social, cultural, political, and economic relationship between Canada and the US. White Canadians grew accustomed to blaming "American contamination" whenever anti-black racism reared its ugly head north of the border. A sense of superiority pervaded the Canadian consciousness. This superiority, based on "not lynching blacks here" and the like, was in some ways legitimate, especially given the open immigration policies of the 1960s. Nonetheless, it was severely tested on that fateful night in February of 1969.

The destruction and riot at Sir George Williams were reactions to home-bred racism. That this act of outrage took place at an educational institution was not by accident, and should have sent a warning signal to all Canadians. For West Indian immigrants, and their children who followed them, education was the avenue of upward mobility. For indigenous blacks it was, following Malcolm X and many others, the only means through which slave-status could be permanently eradicated. Education would become a critical battleground for Canadian blacks. It would also become a vital test of Canadian multiculturalism.

After an active career in social work and as a university instructor, Barbados–born **Anne Cools** *entered politics in 1980. In 1984, she became the first black appointed to the Canadian Senate. In 1969, Anne Cools was one of the leaders behind the Sir George Williams protest.*

Speaking with One Voice

In 1969 the National Black Coalition of Canada was established in Toronto. That year over 12,000 Caribbean immigrants entered Canada. Most came to Ontario, establishing a pattern which has continued to this day. Despite the federal government's articulated commitment to multiculturalism (1971), black leaders recognized the political importance of cohesion among blacks, old and new. As James Walker (*Racial Discrimination In Canada: The Black Experience*, 1985) explains:

> The Black Coalition of Canada was founded...to coordinate the efforts of black organizations across the country for concentrated effect and mutual support. Although the flood of blacks from overseas temporarily diverted attention away from black issues per se to the adjustment problems of the immigrants, repeated experience with discrimination united indigenous and immigrant black Canadians in a common interest. Aided by an expanding

economy which needed skilled workers, and utilizing
human rights legislation with considerable effect, blacks
penetrated economic and social situations beyond their tra-
ditionally defined "place."

Adjustment meant negotiating the colour line which, against
the good intentions of government documents, was still very
much in place. Trudeau, preoccupied with the French-English
divide and the growing militancy of Quebec separatists, and the

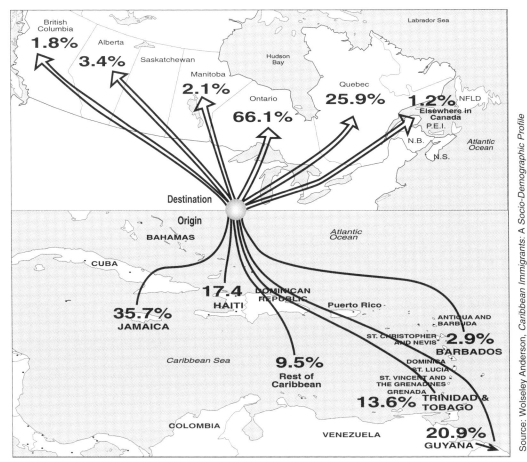

Immigration patterns from the Caribbean to Canada, 1967–1990

federal government, were relatively silent about black community needs, suggesting to blacks that they were on their own.
   In 1973, to clear an enormous backlog at immigration
offices, a general amnesty was granted to all non-status immi-

grants in Canada. Combined with this was the highest number of West Indian immigrants–24,404 people–admitted to Canada in history. Black lobbying for expansionist and universal immigration policies had borne fruit. Blacks were getting quality jobs and their families were being re-united on Canadian soil. The future looked bright. But that same year the economy slumped and job losses in many sectors were heavy. Immigrants became a convenient scapegoat for displaced white workers who erroneously believed that the "darkening complexion of Canadian society" was responsible for rising unemployment, rising taxes, rising deficits, and decreased services. These beliefs were supported by a spate of anti-immigrant reporting in the press.

During the mid-1970s a wave of violent racist attacks struck Canadian cities from coast to coast... "Prime Minister Pierre Trudeau was led to declare, in a Montreal speech in 1975, that 'racism is evident in this country and violence is coming to our land.' An American television program in 1977 described Toronto as a 'racial time-bomb'" (Walker, 1985). In 1975, 1,500 Haitians were deported after Canadian authorities rejected their claims for refugee status. Anger grew in the black community, especially in Montreal and Toronto, over perceptions of differential treatment of black refugee claimants. Once again, Canada was being polarized along racial lines, only this time the lines were multi-racial.

An Emerging Black Presence:
the Cultural Politics of Caribana

Approximately two-thirds of Canada's West Indian population reside in the greater Toronto area. Since the 1960s, this community has grown into one of the area's most substantial and politically active groups. In 1967 the Caribana festival–expanding on the Calypso Carnival program previously established by the Canadian Negro Women's Association–was founded. Canada was celebrating its Centennial, and Caribana represented black participation in the festivities. From relatively small beginnings, it now attracts upwards of a million participants from across North America to its annual August parade.

Caribana illustrates an attempt to unify sometimes fractious Caribbean peoples and a method of portraying island culture in

Caribana's ultimate goal is to foster unity. Though press coverage often focuses on the negative, historically it has done much to achieve this goal and to put Toronto on the international map.

an aesthetically pleasing fashion. "Carnival," a rich blend of African rhythms, Caribbean folklore, masquerading, and European pageantry, is celebrated on all Caribbean islands. Historically, it evolved to include non-black Caribbean populations, particularly East Indians and Chinese. A street festival celebrating this rich tradition on Canadian soil would prove that Caribbean peoples were pre-disposed to making multiculturalism work. As Cecil Foster writes in *Caribana: The Greatest Celebration* (1995):

> The Caribbean Cultural Committee decided to call the street festival Caribana–coining a word with no specific meaning, but capturing the notions of Canada, the Caribbean, bacchanal and merrymaking.

The work of Caribana organizers has resulted in positive multiculturalism. The steel pans of calypso musicians fuse with pulsating reggae rhythms, as costumed revellers turn everyday life upside down. Year in and year out, black, white, and brown peoples all celebrate the West Indian presence in Canada. They are celebrating the determination of black people to unite and to overcome–through parody, music, and dance–racism and other societal constraints. Though Caribana festivities last but two weeks and culminate in the grand parade, black participants work year-round in preparation. Caribana, like "Carnival" on the islands, Brazil, and elsewhere, is about cultural pride and cultural retention. In short, Caribana is much more than an extravagant "jump-up." It represents a struggle for recognition. Dogged by government underfunding, a perception of mismanagement, and an under-appreciation of the huge revenues it brings to Toronto, its organizers continue to press forward. Their resilience is a testament to the persistent struggle to make black causes visible.

Political Activism and Setting Down Roots

Black cultural and political associations experienced an enormous membership growth throughout the 1970s. Whereas a weary black American community seemed to be splitting along class lines (except in cases where activist black mayors took up the cause of ghetto communities), Canadian blacks were forming coalitions and working towards consensus on key issues. Emergent associations drew together highly skilled professionals, service sector employees, black educators, and those still marginalized.

By the mid-1970s all major Canadian cities had active black groups. They served as filters for incoming immigrants, helping them adjust to their new context. West Indian sports clubs brought cricket and soccer to Canadian cities. Black businesses, like the Third World Bookstore in Toronto and numerous restaurants, food stores, and hair-styling salons, catered to a new clientele. The black tile in the Canadian mosaic was becoming increasingly visible.

Black women's groups formed to help address the double burden of racism and sexism. At a 1973 conference, hosted by the Canadian Negro Women's Association (CNWA) of Toronto, a motion was passed to form the Congress of Black Women of Canada (CBWC). Chapters of this national organization were formed in Montreal (1974), Windsor (1975), and Nova Scotia (1976). Aileen Williams, of the Ontario Black History Society, argues that "this increased politicization was necessary because the feminist movement was not addressing the needs of black women." In the US, black women were also finding a new voice, a phenomenon which critics like bell hooks (*Killing Rage*, 1995) attrib-

> ### Congress of Black Women of Canada
>
> *In Toronto (April, 1973), 200 participants attended the inaugral meeting of the National Congress of Black Women (NCBW). The NCBW, founded by the CANEWA, became (Winnipeg, 1980) the Congress of Black Women of Canada. In education, health, immigration, police-community relations, and child development, the Congress' many chapters represent black women from coast to coast. Inspired by Kay Livingstone's gritty determination, leaders like Fay Cole and 1995 director Patsy Jordan ensure the Congress fulfills its mandate of twinning women's equality rights with black liberation struggles.*

utes to their strength, being excluded from white feminist discourse, and to the need to come out from the shadows of a male-dominated civil rights movement.

In the late 1960s education lobbies, like the Nova Scotia Black Educators Association, began to identify specific problems with public education systems. These groups served as liaisons between black students, parents, teachers, and governments. Their achievements and setbacks represent, in microcosm, the post-1967 black struggle for equality.

Since the early 1970s, election candidates have paid special attention to black newspapers and magazines during political campaigns in urban ridings. There was a growing roster of black newspapers, television programs, and radio shows. Newspapers such as *Contrast, Share, Provincial Monitor, Afro-Canadian,* and *Caribe* (published by the late Dr. Ralph Eric James, whose intellectual and humanitarian contributions to Manitoba are legend), covered issues of both local and national concern not examined in the mainstream media.

In 1970, Nova Scotian Winston Ruck was elected president of the United Steel Workers of America, Local 1604. Ruck had worked in the Sydney Steel Plant for 37 years. His election symbolized the new place of black workers in the union movement. A dedicated activist, Ruck later served as Executive Director of the Black United Front of Nova Scotia. In 1990, upon receiving the Tom Miller Human Rights Award, he said: "Those in authority have to reach out to all minorities and bring them into the fold. There must be political will. We're all brothers and sisters, we have more in common than not in common. Our differences are small" (Pachai, 1993).

The Blacks in Canada: A History was published in 1971, and still stands as the most authoritative history of the black experience in Canada up to 1967. It is an essential source for scholarly, educational, and trade book publishing. Much of the information accumulated by its author, Robin Winks, might have been lost had this book not been published. Winks teaches at Yale University and has a continuing interest in Canadian black history.

Also in 1971, sprinter Harry Jerome was awarded the Order of Canada medal for "excellence in all fields of Canadian life." Jerome, born in Prince Albert, Saskatchewan, proudly represented Canada in three Olympic Games, winning bronze at Tokyo in 1964. The Harry Jerome Scholarships–organized by the Black Business and Professional Association–recognize black academic achievement, leadership, and community volunteerism. They carry on his legacy of commitment.

*In 1972, **Rosemary Brown** and **Emery Barnes** were elected to the B. C. legislature, marking the beginning of distinguished political careers.*

In addition to the personal and professional triumphs of these and numerous others, one must remember the growing list who toiled outside of popular recognition. Blacks, in the early 1970s were setting down strong roots in Canadian society. They were appearing in places (government, the media, university faculties, medicine, and the law) which had been, with the odd exception, all-white preserves. They were changing the social, cultural, economic, and political landscape of Canada. The barriers to integration were collapsing.

"Who Gets In and Who Doesn't"

The world oil crisis of 1973, statistics indicating a significant birth rate decline, and fears of a serious economic recession, caused the federal government, in 1974, to re-open the immigration question. The public was asked to participate in a national discussion on the future of Canada's population, particularly the number and type of immigrants and the policies governing their integration. The result of this probe was the *Green Paper on Immigration,* tabled in Parliament in 1976. Despite the vocal protests of black activists, its recommendations were proclaimed in 1978. The result was a dramatic decrease in the total number of immigrants. West Indian immigration dropped from a high of 27,915 in 1974, to a low of 8,839 in 1979.

Significantly, the percentage of West Indian immigrants in the total Canadian immigration flow also dropped precipitously, from 13.2% in 1973 to 7.9% in 1979. This prompted charges from activists that a new colour line had been imposed, and its principal target was blacks.

Was the government listening to voices opposing black immigration? Did this dramatic percentage decrease suggest that Canadian society felt that blacks were less able to assimilate than other ethnic groups? If the government really believed that immigration creates employment and wealth, why was it clamping down so drastically at a time of economic recession?

The 1978 regulations stipulated a shift away from family-class immigrants towards independents and refugees. This distressed many blacks who had come to Canada, established themselves, and hoped to sponsor family and relatives. It also spread dissension as some ethnic groups were perceived as being favoured and others disadvantaged by the new regulations.

Lobbying for Change and the Wisdom of the Early Black Canadian Civil Rights Strategy

To many contemporary critics the drive for total inclusion is hampered by "group identity politics." They argue that a single-minded pursuit of issues only relevant to particular groups, however isolated and disadvantaged these groups may be, serves the interest of the status quo, or at least slows down the process of reform. In short, issues of concern to a relatively small group are easily dismissed by the majority.

The wisdom of the post-WW II black Canadian reformers was that they emphasized human rights, joined forces with other marginalized groups, and successfully challenged racist misconceptions by pointing out the advantages of cultural pluralism to Canadian society at large. Encoded in history, these advantages (e.g. the correlation between economic growth and liberal immigration policies) speak to the notion that enlightened self-interest should dictate policy.

Canada, always a pluralistic society, was beginning to recognize the source of its own vitality. Though change was slow in coming, by clearly delineating internal contradictions which slowed Canada's growth and prosperity, black activists from the 1940s through the 1960s helped change the course of Canadian democracy.

The late Wilson Head brought a lifetime of experience in civil rights activism when he moved from the US to Canada in 1959. Among his numerous accomplishments was the creation, in 1975, of the Urban Alliance On Race Relations, an organization still dedicated to fighting discrimination against all ethno-racial groups. In many ways, the mandate of

Wilson Head

the Alliance harkens back to the successful campaigns of the 1940s and 1950s. It represents an effort to bring together groups, black and otherwise, who, given the pressures of adjustment, are often forced into a restricted posture vis-à-vis the struggle for equality.

During the 1970s, especially after the Royal Commission on Bilingualism and Biculturalism, a new vocabulary began to take root in Canada. In recognition of the fact that over a third of Canadians came from backgrounds other than English or French, Liberal Norman Cafik, Minister of State for Multiculturalism, reaffirmed his government's policy on *The Nation's Business* (January 8, 1978):

> ... that every policy of government takes into account the cultural diversity of our country. In matters of external

affairs…in the question of immigration…in the subject of reunification of families; or in citizenship–that those very legitimate concerns of a third of our people, are taken into account by the cabinet when they make their decisions.

Though many people of colour (especially recent immigrants) took heart in such pronouncements, there seemed to be little consensus in the body politic about such matters. As Professor Vincent D'Oyley (University of British Columbia) avers in "Beyond the English and French realities in Canada: The politics of empowerment of minorities" (*Bilingual and Multicultural Education: Canadian Perspectives*, 1984), though this "vision of Canadian multiculturalism reached its apogee…in 1977-1978," it no doubt contributed to the 1979 Conservative federal election victory. In other words, Canadians were at odds about the "darkening complexion" of their society.

Following the Liberal government's commitment to multiculturalism in 1971, terms such as "visible minority," "ethnic minority," etc. gained considerable currency. As early as the 1960s concerned critics, sensing a disjunction between multiculturalism and cultural pluralism–that is, between protests launched in the name of specific ethnic grievances and a more holistic embrace of cultural pluralism, welcoming difference, and universal struggles–and worrying about the balkanization of Canadian society along "tribal" lines, began to question both the appropriateness and the usefulness of such terms. They worried specifically about groups splintering off into factions and, in so doing, negating their bargaining power with the state, and losing whatever acceptance ethnic groups had gained from the still dominant English and French communities.

Contemporary observers like Donald K. Gordon ("Bigotry visible in 'visible minority,'" *Toronto Star,* Feb. 23, 1993) maintain that such terms should be eliminated. In a 1996 interview he stated that, "They are presumptuous paternalistic descriptions meant to preserve the hegemony of white superiority while psychologically instilling a sense of inferiority in others." In this context, it is well to remember that Stokely Carmichael and others have similarly criticized such descriptions. After all, people of colour are the overwhelming majority in the world: a fact which North America, and perhaps especially Canada, tends to ignore, preferring, in Gordon's words, "to create its own narrow context."

Essentially, the issue as per strategy is still with ethnic communities. They face a difficult "Catch-22" situation, needing to bring their concerns to the fore, and yet avoiding pernicious labeling–whether it be externally or internally imposed–of all sorts. Being designated a "special interest group" can be extremely injurious. In short, they need to follow the example of reformers like Don Moore, Ralph Eric James, Kay Livingstone, the Olivers, Wilson Head, Rosemary Brown, and Carrie Best by presenting their issues in a manner that reflects the interests of all Canadians. Creating a "narrow context" makes little sense in the global village which is our world. The challenge facing ethnic communities is to contribute to the broadening of understanding of all Canadians.

This challenge was, and perhaps still is, especially difficult for the black community. The people who had successfully fought the battles in the early years were growing old, and many were in need of a well-deserved rest. This did not prevent them from sharing their wisdom and experience with the emergent groups from the Caribbean. However, "allegiance to island"–forged over centuries of overcoming the particular dicta of slavery and specific colonial administrations, and through the development of unique cultures–was strong, and the possibility of fragmentation real. Cooperation between different black immigrant groups, and listening to the learned voices of those responsible for, among other things, the immigration doors being opened, would prove essential in the years to come.

*The life and career of **Dr. Carrie Best** (Order of Canada recipient, author, historian, journalist, philanthropist, community activist, founder–in 1985, at the age of 82–of the Harambee Centres, Canada, President of the Kay Livingstone Visible Minority Women's Society of Nova Scotia) stands as a hallmark of extraordinary black achievement in Canada. Born in 1903 and raised in New Glasgow, Nova Scotia, Carrie Best continues to work on behalf of all people. Her ultimate goal: a more tolerant society for all, regardless of race, colour, creed, or gender. She embodies the very best of Canada's twentieth century struggle for a humane democracy.*

More Talk about Cultural Diversity and Race Relations

Mid-1970s protests against systemic racism led to considerable soul-searching in Canada. Black Canadians looked south of the border and saw real advances. The number of black elected officials grew by 88 percent between 1970 and 1975. Black mayors in Atlanta, Detroit, Newark, and Los Angeles were re-shaping city politics and implementing programs designed specifically for blacks and other persecuted minorities. Black Canadians began agitating for similar progress.

Between 1975 and 1985, dozens of official inquiries were launched on ethnic group issues. There was a growing recognition that the Canadian pie was not being carved up equally, and that large sectors of the population were falling through the cracks. Black community organizations made presentations and filed report after report to federal, provisional, and municipal government commissions. An increasing number of blacks claimed they were experiencing discrimination in housing, employment, education, and at the hands of the justice system–the police, the courts, and prisons. Objective data supported these assertions. More and more blacks were being locked into low-paying service sector jobs with little opportunity for upward mobility. Depressingly, race relations seemed to be hardening. As Walker (1985) explains:

> A majority of white Canadians admitted to some degree of racial bias, and about one-third reported that they might move if many black people moved into their neighbourhood. Specific characteristics were also attributed to blacks by some white persons surveyed, showing that stereotypes derived from slavery still persisted...Despite the variety of backgrounds and skills possessed by the blacks in Canada, there remained a tendency to ignore actual experience and to simplify the complexities in terms of traditional images.

Recommendations proposed by immigrant groups to address discrimination and race relations problems suggested two things: that multiculturalism was not working and would not work on its own; and, if Canadian society wanted it to work, it would cost money, lots of money. Governmental authorities faced with such a mass of information, but with the choices clear, had the option of either 'doing as little as possible and hoping for the best,' or, implementing real programs to address real needs. The black community's aspirations were left in the balance.

The 1982 Canadian Charter of Rights and Freedoms

What were blacks and other ethnic minorities entitled to in Canada? This was the question as the country moved into the 1980s. The question was answered, substantially, in 1982 when the Trudeau government "brought the Constitution home," gave it a "made-in-Canada" amending formula, and adopted a charter of basic rights and freedoms for all Canadians.

To black Canadians the Charter, which reflected Canada's United Nations commitments in the area of human rights, brought a new sense of hope and opportunity. Section 27 instructs that the Charter is to be interpreted by courts in a manner consistent with both the preservation and enhancement of Canadian multiculturalism. Black Canadians had witnessed the American NAACP successfully challenge racism and segregation through the Supreme Court. It seemed that the same opportunity would now be available to them and other groups experiencing discrimination.

The Charter also allows groups to seek positive measures to ameliorate conditions of disadvantage, and enshrines the concept of affirmative action as a means to achieve this desirable end. When the Court Challenges Program was adopted, blacks gained the opportunity to receive financial assistance in legal challenges against specific laws or government programs thought to be discriminatory. As a result of this legislative activity governmental authorities were compelled to take seriously the complaints levied during the ten-year period from 1975 to 1985. (This programme was stripped of funds during the Mulroney years.)

> **Section 15 of the**
> *Charter of Rights and Freedoms:*
>
> 15 (1) Every individual is equal before and under the law and has the right to the equal protection and equal benefit of the law without discrimination and, in particular, without discrimination based on race, national or ethnic origin, colour, religion, sex, age or mental or physical disability.
>
> 15 (2) Subsection (1) does not preclude any law, program or activity that has as its object the amelioration of conditions of disadvantaged individuals or groups including those that are disadvantaged because of race, national or ethnic origin, colour, religion, sex, age or mental or physical disability.

In short, the Charter, combined with provincial human rights legislation protecting against racism by private agencies and the Canadian Multiculturalism Act, suggested that blacks would be aided in their quest to re-define their place in the Canadian mosaic. The Charter was seen as pro-active legislation which would level the playing field.

Whether the Charter has provided the disenfranchised with an effective tool for widespread change is debatable. After it came into force some interest groups formally organized to initiate Charter challenges, e.g. ARCH (the Advocacy and Resource Centre for the Handicapped), and LEAF (the Women's Legal Education and Action Fund). Initially black advocates did not organize around expensive and slow Charter litigation. Perhaps the court was not viewed as fertile ground for real change in the

On March 19, 1988, 1,200 people marched in protest against the Montreal police shooting of an unarmed black youth. Similar anti-racist demonstrations, many targeted directly at police forces, occurred with increasing frequency in cities across Canada during these troubled years.

black community, despite the Charter's initial raising of hopes? Perhaps the perception of racism in the justice system was too strong?

This changed in 1994 when the Toronto-based African Canadian Legal Clinic (ACLC) opened its doors to a rush of hope and expectations. The ACLC's mandate is to challenge Ontario's "racially biased justice system" through test-case litigation, some of which relies on the Charter.

Post-1967 Black Education in Canada

Perhaps no other issue pertaining to the black experience in Canada has been more thoroughly researched, documented, written about, and hotly debated, than that of education. In perhaps no other arena has black activism been so consistent in its message. In perhaps no other area have black activists been so frustrated.

Nova Scotia continued to have segregated schools into the 1960s. In Ontario, legislation allowing for segregated schools remained on the statute books until 1964. That year, due to the efforts of Leonard Braithwaite and others, an act to amend this legislation was finally passed. In 1965, the last segregated school in Ontario closed its doors.

Scarcity of educational opportunity in countries like Jamaica is often cited as the primary reason for the high value placed on education throughout the West Indies. One of the main reasons black West Indians emigrated to Canada from the 1960s onwards was for equal opportunity to quality education. In the Caribbean, these opportunities were restricted by high costs and the colour line.

In Canada, where all teenage students have the opportunity to attend high school, one would predict that black students would take immediate advantage of their legislated right to pursue upward mobility through education. And yet, as Patrick Solomon in *Black Resistance in High School: Forging a Separatist Culture* (1992) points out, we have the paradoxical situation of "high educational aspiration and low school performance."

Relatively progressive provincial Education Acts require that schools provide education in accordance with students' needs. Furthermore, there is a tradition of legislative recognition of education as an equality issue. For example, the BNA Act enshrined publicly funded separate schooling for Catholics. Provincial Human Rights Codes and the Charter protect against discrimination in the delivery of services, including education.

Establishing equality rights in education using such legislation is, however, a difficult process. Generally, schools are left to determine students' needs and cultural bias often influences assessment. The historical "streaming" of black students into vocational programs reflects a form of racism through discriminatory placement. From the perspective of many black educational activists, the legacy of race science in Canadian education systems encouraged low teacher expectations and misplacement of black students. Research concerning this pattern suggests that in thousands of cases black parents were unaware that their children, especially the boys, were being placed in courses which severely restricted their life opportunities. This research also suggests that to a considerable degree such streaming was a self-fulfilling prophecy on the part of schools, many of which did not know what to do with this influx of black students.

Black West Indian parents/guardians, unsure of their own place in Canadian society, customarily defer to educational authorities vis-à-vis placement of their children. This follows a tradition of utmost respect for teachers and schools in the West Indies. In Canadian schools there is not so strong a symbiotic relationship between teachers and parents. Thus, educating blacks about Canadian education systems became an essential plank in the struggle for equality rights.

A multicultural student body presents a true challenge to an education system dominated by Eurocentric curricula. This curricula is designed, unconsciously or not, to ensure white student success. Many black students resist measuring themselves against the traditional values and goals of our public education systems because these systems do not, by and large, pertain to the "lived culture" of these students. In order for multiculturalism to work, all students must be given the opportunity to learn about the histories and cultures of races other than their own in formal academic settings. Racism, arguably, is the result of a lack of meaningful contact between racial groups. Multi-ethnic schools, therefore, have a unique opportunity to bring down the walls of ignorance and fear through meaningful contact.

Many schools attempt to do so by celebrating different cultures during religious holidays, black history month activities, and so forth. While these initiatives are good and important, they are not enough. In schools with significant concentrations of black students black history, for instance, needs to be infused throughout the curriculum. Teaching the impact of the French Revolution on St. Domingue/Haiti, Jamaica, and other Caribbean islands would be a good example of such infusion. Why should black students be particularly interested in the French Revolution if it is presented as a purely white European uprising?

The white-centred curriculum in American schools is part of that country's melting pot ideology: 'come to our shores, contribute, and be like us.' It represents an unsubtle chauvinism that many Canadians find repugnant. Canadian's have opted, quite sensibly given immigrant contributions, our on-going immigration needs, the porous nature of international borders, and the media-induced shrinking of the world, for a different model, that of a multicultural mosaic. That model is being tested daily in our schools.

West Indian students, by and large, come from countries with strict educational regimes based primarily on traditional European standards. There, teaching strategies emphasize formal discipline and the diligent learning, by rote if necessary, of correct answers. Upon arrival at Canadian schools, especially during an era of open and experimental education, these same students are faced with teaching strategies which place a premium on innovation, self-direction, and experimentation. In the comparatively unstructured environments of Canadian public schools, many West Indian students begin to "disidentify" with their school as a place of learning and "identify" with it as a community centre. In too many cases, their focus becomes extra-curricular.

The Black Education Lobby

The black education lobby has had, and is having, an enormous impact on changing Canadian education. Today, organizations like the Black Learners Advisory Committee of Nova Scotia (Executive Director, Robert Upshaw) and Toronto's Black Educators' Working Group (Co-chairs, Bev Salmon and Mac

Hunter), are largely responsible for bringing about positive change in their respective education systems. They are building on a history of black educational activism. It was, and it is, a battle for equality.

In 1988, a team of educational reformers called the Consultative Committee on the Education of Black Students in Toronto Schools submitted to the Toronto School Board a one-hundred-page report listing 45 recommendations addressing the issue of black under-achievement in Toronto schools. In a July 10, 1995 *Globe and Mail* article "Schools more attuned to race," team member Keren Brathwaite noted that the Committee's report has been sitting "on the shelf" since 1988.

> "I'm beyond frustration. I'm really scared because I don't know what's happening. If the younger kids coming up are not going to university and feeling more insecure at an earlier age, what kind of future are we going to have?"
>
> Faith Holder, University of Toronto scholarship winner, *Globe and Mail*, July 10, 1995.

Brathwaite's frustration has not led to resignation. She is currently a member of the Ontario Black Educators' Working Group and the Organization of Parents of Black Children. She and many others realize that black hopes and aspirations are inextricably tied to education.

In the area of black education, the 1994 Ontario Royal Commission Report *For the Love of Learning*, reflects, in many ways, the black education lobby's consistent message. In terms of equity perhaps its two most important recommendations are:

> 141. That in jurisdictions with large numbers of black students, school boards, academic authorities, faculties of education, and representatives of the black community collaborate to establish demonstration schools and innovative programs based on best practices in bringing about academic success for black students;
>
> 142. That whenever there are indications of collective underachievement in any particular group of students, school boards ensure that teachers and principals have the

necessary strategies and human and financial resources to help these students improve.

The Commission chose its words carefully. Lennox Farrell's thoughtful submission favouring "black focus" schools had the support of many in the community. Farrell's proposal was based partially on the success of black academies in the US. Certainly, many of these schools are achieving success, but critics point out that the inner-city school situation in America is so desperate that, in some communities, these focus schools are the only option. These critics argue that there are numerous examples of Canadian inner-city schools which cater successfully to multi-ethnic student populations, suggesting both that multiculturalism in education can work and that the American situation is not directly applicable in Canada.

The history and present controversy surrounding educational segregation inevitably comes to the fore in these discussions. Farrell, George Dei, and other advocates, maintain that black focus schools are not separatist. Rather, their purpose is to provide an education centered on black history and culture, an education in which non-black students may indeed be interested. If nothing else, this debate suggests a real determination on the part of the black community to find solutions to educational problems.

Antiracist Education:

An approach to education that integrates the perspectives of Aboriginal and racial minority groups into an educational system and its practices. The aim of antiracist education is the elimination of racism in all its forms. Antiracist education seeks to identify and change educational policies, procedures, and practices that foster racism, as well as the racist attitudes and behaviour that underlie and reinforce such policies and practices. Antiracist education provides teachers and students with the knowledge and skills to examine racism critically in order to understand how it originates and to identify and challenge it.

Ontario Ministry of Education and Training, *Antiracism and Ethnocultural Equity in School Boards: Guidelines for Policy Development and Implementation, 1993.*

Even with the advent of black focus or "demonstration schools," the system in general must meet the challenge.

The black education lobby has been instrumental in pushing Ministries of Education and school boards to move beyond the somewhat nebulous philosophy of multiculturalism, and to invoke solid anti-racist initiatives in all areas of education. The most important changes, however, must be curricular. There still exists, in some multi-ethnic high schools, the possibility of black students never being asked to read a black author. It simply makes no sense to rely entirely on Eurocentric curricula. As Stephen Lewis, in his 1992 *Report On Race Relations In Ontario,* explains:

> The students were fiercely articulate and often deeply moving. Sometimes angry. They don't understand why the schools are so slow to reflect the broader society. One bright young man in a Metro east high school said that he had reached grade thirteen, without once having a book by a black author on the curriculum. And when other students, in the large meeting of which he was a part, started to name the books they had been given to read, the titles were "Black Like Me" and "To Kill A Mockingbird" (both, incredibly enough, by white writers!). It's absurd in a world which has a positive cornucopia of magnificent literature by black authors.

Antiracist educational initiatives must be complemented by real opportunities for black students to see themselves, on a regular basis, in the curriculum. In his report, Lewis refers to students who ask, "Where are the courses in Black history?" One of the positive legacies of the US civil rights movement was the introduction of courses on black history and culture in many schools across America. Over the past few years such courses have also been introduced in dozens of schools across Canada. All indications suggest that their number will continue to grow.

Importantly, the growth of black history and culture courses has, in many instances, been student-driven. Black students in numerous schools have put the challenge directly before their teachers and administrators. More and more education systems and/or particular schools are responding positively. In 1993, for instance, sparked by a demand from students for a more inclusive curriculum which included black history and culture, the Quebec Ministry of Education, in conjunction with the Quebec Board of Black Educators, began work on a resource document to be used in high schools.

Rita Cox, *legendary black storyteller*

The result is *Some Missing Pages*. Launched in early 1996, this 187 page document details 400 years of black contributions to Canadian history. It will serve as an essential resource well into the future.

A growing number of educators understand that the real message of the black education lobby is that black students' success is inextricably tied to sustained opportunities to see themselves in positive and meaningful curricula. They understand further that offering all students a window into black history and culture improves race relations and enhances the essential narratives upon which quality education is based. To paraphrase Neil Postman (*Technopoly* (1993) and *The End of Education* (1995)), studying the "law of diversity" is fundamental to good education.

An increasing number of young black students see themselves as civil rights advocates. Black parent groups have a growing resolve to see changes implemented. An increasing number of their members are university-educated. Governments and education systems now must listen to compelling voices from without and within. In Nova Scotia in 1994, the Black

"The *BLAC Report on Education* presents a significant and vital challenge to the Department of Education and Culture and to Government. This response is not the end of the process; it is the beginning of the second stage of our journey. With the Report as our guide, we will now set in place the staff, policies, materials, and activities that will contribute to improving learning opportunities for Black Nova Scotians of all ages. More importantly, we will engage in a joint effort to address systemic issues that have disadvantaged the Black community, develop innovative approaches to creating new opportunities, and ensure that Black youth benefit from a fully supportive learning environment. I am excited to be able to work with you on these initiatives and offer you my complete support."

Honourable John MacEachern, Minister, Nova Scotia Department of Education and Culture, Conclusion, *Response to the BLAC Report on Education, June, 1995.*

Learner's Advisory Committee's three volume *Report on Education: Redressing Inequity–Empowering Black Learners* recommended sweeping changes to the education system. The fact that all its major recommendations were accepted suggests the dawning of a new era for black students in Nova Scotia.

13

To the Future

The notion of education as "liberation theology" for black people is, in our times, perhaps nowhere better illustrated than in the story of Rubin "Hurricane" Carter and Lesra Martin.

US-born Rubin Carter, once a contender for the world middleweight boxing championship, spent nearly 20 years (1966-1985) in prison for a crime he did not commit. To the New Jersey state justice system his black skin was a badge of criminality. Had reason and fairness, not racism and fear, prevailed, he would have found his place in boxing's hierarchy. He was poised, ready to assume the mantle of champion. Instead, he is remembered for an even greater triumph, achieving freedom without bitterness.

Rubin Carter lives in Toronto. How he came to reside in Canada is part of the extraordinary story related in *Lazarus and the Hurricane: The Untold Story of the Freeing of Rubin "Hurricane" Carter* (1991) by Sam Chaiton and Terry Swinton, a book which not only tells of Carter's personal odyssey, but also provides a unique perspective on human capacity. Carter entered prison an under-educated man. During his long years behind bars books became his salvation. He read voraciously. This self-education made possible *The Sixteenth Round: From Number 1 Contender to # 45472* (1991), a book he wrote while incarcerated. *The Sixteenth Round*, portions of which were scribed in the utter darkness of solitary confinement, would end up being Carter's vehicle to freedom.

"Reading and writing freed me," Carter said in a 1996 interview. "The walls were still there, but the mind was free." He paused for a moment and then continued, "Everything, every molecule, in this world is interconnected. We are all tied to one another. I look back without regret, without bitterness. I love who I am today, and who I am today was made possible by those years of physical captivity and mental liberation." His sanguineous, his perspective, his lack of grievance, his embodiment of a history both desperate and transcendent, and his determination, brings to mind Frederick Douglass:

> The frequent hearing of my mistress reading the Bible aloud…awakened my curiosity in respect to this *mystery* of reading, and roused in me the desire to learn. Up to this time I had known nothing whatever of this wonderful art, and my ignorance and inexperience of what it could do for me, as well as my confidence in my mistress, emboldened me to ask her to teach me to read…In an incredibly short time, by her kind assistance, I had mastered the alphabet and could spell words of three or four letters…[My master] forbade her to give me any further instruction…[but] the determination which he expressed to keep me in ignorance only rendered me the more resolute to seek intelligence. In learning to read, therefore, I am not sure that I do not owe quite as much to the opposition of my master as to the kindly assistance of my amiable mistress.
>
> – Frederick Douglass,
> *Life and Times of Frederick Douglass*, (1881).

It is hard to gauge what drives people like Rubin Carter. For twenty years he doggedly pursued freedom and justice, but never was his pursuit for himself alone. He fought a system designed to divide and conquer, a system based on fear, a system programmed, like the segregated schools of the US South, to keep people "separate and unequal." That he is now part of the Canadian landscape brings pride to Canadians young and old, black and white. In many respects, his story represents the very best of Canada.

Rubin Carter is a very busy man. He continues to read, to write, to speak, and to work on behalf of the wrongfully convicted. His Association In Defence of the Wrongfully Convicted has been recognized internationally for its achievements.

Lesra Martin, raised in Brooklyn, New York, grew up learning little of life outside the three-block radius of his Bushwick ghetto home. There, survival was the order of the day, and Martin was well-schooled in this form of intelligence. Pursuing other intelligences, like the educated imagination wrought by book reading, was not in the cards for Martin, or his neighbourhood friends and enemies. Many sociologists have correctly argued that such a limiting experience, especially during the formative years of youth, is a life sentence for most. The imagination becomes so circumscribed by the harsh environment of ghetto existence that thinking beyond crude survival becomes a luxury few can afford. And yet, chance and positive circumstance were to intervene in Lesra Martin's life, to present him with a new beginning, and to shatter the stereotypes of received wisdom and self-fulfilling prophecy as they apply to inner-city youth, especially inner-city black youth.

Rubin "Hurricane" Carter and Lesra Martin (Toronto, 1995).

Lesra Martin now lives in Halifax. He is completing his Ph.D. from the University of Toronto while attending law school at Dalhousie University. He has opened a cafe in Halifax called "The Hurricane." How he reached this elevated plain is part of a story no less remarkable than, and inextricably tied to, that of Rubin Carter.

Martin first came to Canada in September, 1979, to visit a group of eight white Canadians whom he had met and worked with in New York the previous summer. Most of the Canadians were in New York that summer doing research at Brooklyn's Environmental Protection Agency laboratory. The teenaged Martin was also at the lab as part of a job placement program for inner-city youth. This "chance meeting" with the Canadians would change his life.

Later on, Martin was "adopted" by the Canadians and came to live in Toronto. His education, his adopted "family" quickly realized, was sadly lacking. Martin, the product of a demoralized Brooklyn education system, had few academic skills and little general knowledge. The Canadians set about home-schooling him and, in time, Martin, like "Hurricane" Carter, became an insatiable reader. As told in *Lazarus and the Hurricane*, he too gained salvation through books:

> With the Canadians as guides, he walked through Farley Mowat's books, *The People of the Deer* and *Never Cry Wolf*; *The Heart of the Hunter* by Laurens Van Der Post; Peter Freuchen's *Book of the Eskimos*; *Lame Deer, Seeker of Visions* by John Fire/Lame Deer...He studied European history, both its accomplishments and its disgraces... Much of what Lesra studied concerned African-American history. He read *From Slavery to Freedom* by historian John Hope Franklin and *Before The Mayflower* by Lerone Bennett, Jr. Lesra desperately needed black heroes. His tutors sought out biographies of great black Americans like George Washington Carver, Harriet Tubman, Nat Turner, Dr. Daniel Drew and Robert Franklin Williams...He gobbled up the most inspiring books concerning the realities of black life in America: *The Autobiography of Malcolm X*; Richard Wright's autobiographies *Black Boy* and *American Hunger*, his novels *Native Son* and *The Longest Dream*; *Coming of Age in Mississippi* by Anne Moody; *The Street* by Ann Petry;...Carter Woodson's essay *The Miseducation of the Negro*; the poetry and short stories of Langston Hughes...

In Canada, Martin was experiencing a life and a education previously unknown to him. He was learning about possibility, about the value of a tutored mind and imagination. Growing in this way was difficult, full of inevitable setbacks and frustration. Perhaps most difficult was that it meant growing apart from what he knew, from his family and the enclosed world of the Bushwick ghetto. But Lesra Martin never really left home. Indeed, in many respects, "home" grew along with him. His families, the one he was born into and the one he was adopted by, both championed his quest and opened new doors for him. "Lesra," short for "Lazarus," derived from the biblical story of the man who rose from the dead, of the man who was twice born, had his second coming in Canada.

Martin was devouring books and the Canadians had to keep pace with his learning. One day, the Toronto Public Library system had a clearance sale. Old and tattered books were going cheap. The group went early to the sale and agreed on titles numerous enough to fill three boxes. As serendipity would have it, one of the books they purchased was *The Sixteenth Round: From Number 1 Contender to # 45472* by Rubin "Hurricane" Carter. It cost twenty-five cents.

> *...The Sixteenth Round*...appeared to strike on two themes they had been discussing: how sports is one forum in America (entertainment the other) in which blacks are allowed to succeed; and second, why it is that strong black men, black heroes like Malcolm X, can be found in the nation's prisons. What makes a man go "From Number 1 Contender to # 45472"? And what kind of fight lasts sixteen rounds when championship bouts...went fifteen?...this was the book Lesra picked to read first. From its pages Rubin Carter spoke directly to him, with power and clarity and in a voice and language that Lesra well understood. Lesra was acutely aware that Carter's was a life that just as easily could have been his own–and almost certainly would have been, had he remained in Brooklyn. From ghetto streets you matriculated to prison cells. (*Lazarus and the Hurricane.*)

Martin's reading of *The Sixteenth Round* led to an eight-year odyssey to overturn a flagrant miscarriage of justice and free Rubin Carter, an odyssey which has now touched hundreds of thousands, perhaps millions. The story was summarized, by Carter, in his 1993 Bradwin Address to Frontier College, Canada's oldest and most established literacy organization. (Frontier College runs an Each One–Teach One program, wherein successful black adults mentor black youth; prison literacy programs; and many other first-rate initiatives.) Few are as eloquent about the connection between literacy, justice, freedom, and human rights, as Rubin Carter himself.

Bradwin Address

by
Rubin "Hurricane" Carter

October 16, 1993
Good afternoon, friends of Frontier College.

Now this is the kind of company that I enjoy being in. It's truly a pleasure to be here among friends of literacy because, as Marlene mentioned, literacy–reading and writing, books and words–have had a tremendous impact on my life. There were years when books were my only friends. And because I was able to write my own book, *The Sixteenth Round*, and because Lesra, the young man who was rescued from the mean streets of Brooklyn's worst ghetto, was literate enough to read it, I was literally set free. That's the awesome power of the written word.

But I can tell you, it wasn't always easy for me to communicate in words. For the first eighteen years of my life, I had a terrible speech impediment. I couldn't talk. I stuttered–badly. And people laughed at me because of it. I tried my damnedest to speak, but I just couldn't do it. It wasn't my fault, but I didn't know that at the time. Everyone else could talk, I thought, so why couldn't I? I felt dumb, stupid. And when people would laugh at me, the only sound they'd hear in reply would be the sound of my fists whistling through the air. My fists did my talking. Now, that stopped the laughter...for a while. But it also got me into serious trouble. And it didn't solve the problem. I still couldn't speak.

Then I began to hide the fact that I stuttered: I stopped talking altogether. I was stuck in a state of silence. That frustration, that pent-up energy, that inability to communicate, was my first experience of being locked away in a prison.

You see, there are prisons and there are prisons. They may **look** different, but they're all the same. They all confine you. They all limit your freedom. They all lock you away and grind you down and take a heavy tole on your self-esteem. There are prisons made of steel, brick, and mortar. And then there are prisons without **visible** walls: the prisons of poverty, illiteracy, and racism. All too often people condemned to these metaphorical prisons (poverty, racism, and illiteracy) end up doing double time; that is, they wind up in the physical prisons as well. Our task is to recognize the interconnectedness and the sameness of all of these prisons. Because **any** kind of prison is no friend of mine. It brings out the Hurricane in me.

So what I want to do here today, is to huff and to puff (like a good Hurricane should) and blow down those prison walls of illiteracy. I'd like to read you a few pages from *Lazarus and the Hurricane*, which show how difficult it is to learn to read as an adult, but how necessary and how rewarding that struggle can be.

[Reading–an abbreviated version of pages 34–37.]

Lesra now has an Honours B.A. from the University of Toronto, a Masters Degree from Dalhousie University, and is currently back at the University of Toronto working on his Ph.D. Now, that's phenomenal! Everybody, I'd like you to meet Lesra. Lesra, will you stand up please...

But you know, today Lesra says that had he not left the Brooklyn ghetto when he did, had he not been brought to Canada and properly educated, he would have wound up either dead, on drugs, or in jail. And sadly, he is not exaggerating. Did you know that there are more black and native people in prisons in North America than there are in its universities? And most of these people can't read or write. There is a world of Lesras out there who–for whatever reason–do not have access to the kind of education that Lesra now has, and that **everyone** deserves! And those Lesras can be found not only in prison cells, but in unemployment lines, on welfare roles, and underneath park benches. Why is it that our governments seem always able to find the money to pay for prison cells, but cry "Broke!" when it comes to funding literacy programs, which would make the necessity for more prison cells obsolete? What does it say about our priorities when Hercules helicopters–weapons of destruction–are more important than books and teachers–weapons of instruction?

My guess is that old Alfred Fitzpatrick was asking the same question almost a century ago, and came up with the right answer when he pitched his first reading tent at a wilderness logging camp and founded Frontier College. And Frontier College is still giving the right answer, for which I heartily commend you. Nothing should take precedence over literacy in our society. It is the fundamental right of every citizen.

Let me leave you with one thought. No matter how difficult your challenge is–whether it's working in the field with resources stretched to the limit, or whether you're an adult struggling with self-doubt trying to learn to read–no matter how daunting your task appears to be, no matter how great the odds, you can't give up. The going may be rough. It may get you down. But take it from me, someone who faced the electric chair in 1966, someone who was told he'd never get out of prison, someone who spent almost twenty years behind bars for a crime he did not commit. Take it from me–anything is possible. You **can** win. You can do it! A day without literacy is a day without freedom. And you can take this from me, too…Freedom is where it's at.

Thank you.

Leadership comes in many forms, from many different types of people, and from many sources. Canada is blessed to have Rubin Carter and Lesra Martin within its borders. It is similarly blessed to have Louise Bennett-Coverley, and other recent black immigrants too numerous to mention. Some historians have noted that so many black achievers (like Carter and Bennett-Coverley) come from the worlds of sports and entertainment. Certainly, this is true, and because of it, separating black culture from black history denudes the narratives of both. Furthermore, to paraphrase the late great Arthur Ashe, excellence in sports, entertainment, and culture–the fields in which historically blacks were allowed to perform–did not and does not preclude excellence in other fields. Arthur Ashe himself, of course, was a Wimbledon champion and an esteemed author.

Lincoln Alexander
The first black cabinet minister in Canada, and in 1985, the first black Lieutenant-Governor (Ontario).

Jean Augustine
Educator, president of the Congress of Black Women of Canada, she was elected to the House of Commons in 1993.

The ability to traverse fields of endeavour has marked black history. In Canada, one need only to consider the lives of Emery Barnes, who graduated from an early life of Olympic high jumping and professional football, to become the longest serving member of the British Columbia legislature in history; or, Sylvia Sweeney, once one of the world's premier women basketball players, who became an acclaimed television producer. Equality of opportunity, a level playing field, has allowed these, and legions of others, to pursue excellence in new arenas, to have numerous careers and to contribute to Canadian democracy in numerous ways.

Towards Freedom concludes then with a look at issues related to black culture, media, sports, and entertainment. It does so because leadership exists in these fields, as well as in the areas of politics, social activism, and community development. It could just as easily have concluded with a look at black inventors. After all, the three-way traffic signal, gas mask, guitar, ironing board, the ice chamber and cold air ducts of refrigerators, telephone transmitter, and a host of

other devices used everyday were all invented by black people. In other words, the concluding chapter is a beginning,
not an end.

Black Cultural Expression

A community is judged and defined by its people and their
achievements. This fact was made clear at the Seoul Olympics
of 1988, when Jamaican-Canadian Ben Johnson shattered the
world 100-metre record, crossing the finish line in a lightning-
quick 9.79 seconds. Canadian pride swelled, especially since
Johnson left American Carl Lewis, that country's finest sprinter,
in his wake. All of Canada celebrated the toppling of an
American giant.

Hours later, Johnson tested positive for steroids. His fall
from grace ended the euphoria. His sprint was erased from the
record books, and the only thing left shattered was "Canadian
innocence." In time, everything about Johnson was questioned,
including his "Canadianness." Some comfort was gained by portraying his duplicitous act as somehow being more Jamaican than Canadian. (Indeed, in the minds of many "the Canadian athlete" became "the Jamaican immigrant.") Doubt was cast and, once again, blacks in Canada had to re-build.

> Each African Canadian has been able to draw sustenance and joy from a culture created over the millennia in Africa. Each generation has added to this precious cargo, which becomes richer with each river crossed–a living testament to the enduring strength of African Canadians and their culture.
>
> *Akili: The Journal of African-Canadian Studies* (March, 1995).

Historically, black Canadians have always put "a fresh spin on activities elevated and prosaic," have always rebounded, or staked out new territory. Black cultural expression, forced underground for centuries, has always survived, grown, and provided sustenance. It was, and it is, a tie that binds. Contemporary black cultural innovators are building on a storied tradition. It is a tradition created in out-of-the-way jazz venues, church basements, community centres, the Parkdale Public Library in Toronto, Nova Scotia's Black Cultural Centre, public school gymnasiums, on makeshift dance floors, late night radio, dilapidated running tracks, around family pianos, and in back rooms and secret locations across the country.

Nowhere is this more true than in the areas of sports, the arts, and media. Sammy Richardson, Herb Carnegie, Angela Issajenko, Harry Jerome, Ferguson Jenkins, Sylvia Sweeney, Grant Fuhr, Charmaine Crooks, Michael Smith and many others rose from the shadows of obscurity to the top of their respective fields of athletic endeavour. In the arts, Portia White, Oscar Peterson, Kay Livingstone, Dan Hill, Austin Clarke, and Almeta Speaks, have put black Canadian culture on the international map. Rita Cox, one of Canada's greatest storytellers, has instilled the value of black oral traditions in thousands of people, young and old, black and white.

Contemporary athletes are building on a tradition of excellence. There are linkages between George Dixon and the internationally recognized Canadian boxers of today; between Sammy Richardson, Harry Jerome, and the men of Canada's 1995 sprint relay team; between Herb Carnegie, Grant Fuhr and the growing number of black professional hockey players; and, between Sylvia Sweeney and Sue Stewart, a black who is leading Canada's national women's basketball team in pursuit of gold at the 1996 Atlanta Olympics Games.

In jazz, there are links to be drawn between the legendary Oscar Peterson, Wray Downes, Nelson Symonds, Sonny Greenwich, Archie Alleyne, the Canadian Ambassadors, and Joe Sealy, a 1995 recipient of a Canadian Black Achievement Award; in storytelling, between Rita Cox, also a 1995 CBAA winner, and children's writer and storyteller, Ricardo Keens-Douglas; in liter-

*In 1979 **Sylvia Sweeney** was named the most valuable player at the Seoul, South Korea world basketball championship. Sweeney is president of Elitha Peterson Productions Inc., an innovative television production company. Her impressive resumé includes an award-winning documentary,* In the Key of Oscar, *on Oscar Peterson (Sweeney's uncle), co-host of* POV: Women *on the Women's Television Network, director of* Hymn To Freedom: Part I, *and director of the Toronto Raptors.*

Poet and Juno Award winner, **Maestro Fresh-Wes,** *helped establish Canada's rap music scene.* Symphony In Effect, *his first album, sold more than 150,000 copies in Canada alone. Fresh-Wes was born in Toronto of Guyanese parents.*

Austin Clarke, *Canada's most widely-read black novelist, has sensitized generations of readers to the unique plight of West Indian immigrants. Born in Barbados in 1934, he emigrated as a student to Canada in 1955. Clarke's many books have won numerous awards and critical praise. His life's work is far from over, and readers are avidly awaiting his next offering.*

ature, between Austin Clarke, the other fourteen contributors to *Voices: Canadian Writers Of African Descent,* and the young black poets and story writers of *In Others Words Literary Quarterly.* Black Canadian issues and traditions inspire the rap tones and lyrics of Michie Mee, l.a.luv, the Dream Warriors, and Juno award winner Maestro Fresh-Wes. The emergent black film industry owes much to this same tradition.

Black contributions to journalism date back to 1850s newspapers, the *Voice of the Fugitive and Provincial Freeman.* It continued through *Neith, Free Lance, The Clarion, Provincial Monitor, Caribe,* and many other newspapers and periodicals across the country. Contemporary newspapers like *Share* build on this history. The CBC's Hamlin Grange, Noëlle Richardson, Ona Fletcher, and others are role models for a growing number of aspiring young black television personalities. City TV in Toronto continues to showcase black television talent in reporting and culture criticism. Media innovators Fil Fraser (Vision TV), Emmy-award winner Almeta Speaks, and many skillful black directors, recently collaborated to produce *Hymn To Freedom,* a superb four-part documentary on Canadian black history, adding to Canada's international reputation for excellence in documentary film production.

What distinguishes all of these people, along with contemporary artists and athletes like John Alleyne, Othalie

Graham, Clifton Joseph, Rosemary Sadlier, Ayanna Black, Afua Cooper, Lawrence Hill, George Elliott Clarke, Curtis Coward, and Michael Smith, is their commitment to the cause of black Canada. International recognition has not blunted their enthusiasm and energy to set things right at home. One of their chief desires is to contribute to the legacy of positive black achievement in Canada.

The Growing Black Complexion of Canadian Sport

In 1995, Oakville's Donovan Bailey assumed the title "World's Fastest Human" by winning the 100-metre sprint at the world track championships at Goteberg, Sweden. Taking silver in the same race was Montreal's Bruny Surin. Canada's position at the top of the sprint world was cemented, at the same meet, when the men's 4x100-metre relay team took gold. The legacy of Ben Johnson will follow these men to the Olympic Games, and beyond. They will have to prove themselves time and time again. Full acceptance by Canadian society waits in the balance. So, too, will acceptance of the new Canadian men's basketball team–for the first time in history, a predominantly black squad.

For some time basketball has been the icon sport for both US and Canadian urban black youth. Compared to other sports, it is inexpensive and therefore accessible to underprivileged blacks. For decades, black Canadian youth, male and

The internationally acclaimed dancer and choreographer, **John Alleyne,** *was appointed Artistic Director of the Ballet British Columbia in 1992.*

International audiences are awakening to the sound of the **Dream Warriors,** *Canada's pre-eminent rap group. Blending bhangra, calypso, reggae, jazz, ska, and rap, these innovators helped spark jazz/hip hop fusion. Winners of a Juno award for best rap recording, the band's two albums,* And Now The Legacy Begins *and* Subliminal Simulation, *make a distinctly Canadian contribution to rap music.*

*The proud legacy of Sylvia Sweeney is being carried forward by **Sue Stewart,** a rising star of Canada's women's basketball team and 1996 Olympic Games entrant.*

female, have been honing their skills at playground hoops, and on high school and league teams. However, while young black Americans looked up to "Dream Teams," National Basketball Association (NBA) superstars, and the emergent black dynamos of the US women's college game, black' ball in Canada was perceived to not fit with the national program. This was true at a time when teams of Toronto high school all-stars were regularly beating the best that the state of Michigan, a hot-bed of roundball talent, could offer!

Black Canadians now have another class of basketball players to look up to. Black youth will soon begin modelling their games on the moves of NBA players suiting up for the Toronto Raptors and Vancouver Grizzlies. Prime time has come north of the border and, as was the case with the Montreal Expos and Toronto Blue Jays, this will lead to a further "darkening complexion" of Canadian sport and society.

Golden Celebrations *The Canadian men's 4 x 100-metre relay team victory at Gotenberg (above) was followed by gold at the 1996 Atlanta Olympics and, of course, Donovan Bailey's electrifying triumph in the 100-metre final.*

No doubt, the changed policies of Canada's national program were influenced by the inclusion of Toronto and Vancouver in the NBA. Importantly, the nuts and bolts of these franchises are being run by people (Isiah Thomas, Stu Jackson, and others) who are committed to black youth and to community development in general. Over the years, thousands of black and white youth will

benefit directly from charities established by the Raptors and Grizzlies.
Canadian society has put out the
challenge to these franchises: prove
to us that you are good for Canada.
They are delivering.

Cito Gaston, winner of two
World Series' as manager of the
Toronto Blue Jays, and Felipe Alou,
the darling of Montreal baseball fans
and thought by many the finest manager and teacher in the game, have
done much to prove just how successful blacks in management positions can be. In an era when baseball
managers are subjected to revolving-
door hiring and firing practices, these
two men remain fixtures of perma-
nence.

Athletes, whether they like it or
not, are role models. Both on and off
the playing fields, they are judged by
their performances and characters.
Society imposes exacting, sometimes
unfair, standards on these men and
women. At different times in the past,
in bars, restaurants, community centres, and living rooms the dreams and
aspirations of black Canadians were
inextricably linked to athletes. World
Featherweight Champion George
Dixon became the pride of his community. So too did Sam Langford, when,
in 1906, he fought future World
Heavyweight Champion Jack Johnson
to a virtual 15-round stalemate. These
and others, have willingly accepted the
burdens of high profile performance
and the inevitable public interest in
their lives and characters.

*The Word: Toronto's Black Cultural
Magazine* summed up the feeling of
many with its August 3, 1995 head-
line: "Dreams do come true:
National Team gets Soul Power," to
explain the new black presence on
Canada's National Men's Basketball
Team.

*With rookies **Damon Stoudamire** (shown
above) and Bryant "Big Country" Reeves, the
Toronto Raptors and Vancouver Grizzlies
chose well to launch their 1995 NBA inaugur-
al seasons. Stoudamire, had a rookie-of-the-
year season.*

The Toronto Blue Jays and Montreal Expos are proud to have two of the best managers in the business, **Cito Gaston** *(shown above) and Felipe Alou.*

Overwhelmingly, black Canadian athletes have passed the test.

Sports, as shown by the cross-cultural enthuasiasm for the 1996 World Cup of Cricket, can bring people together. Tens of thousands of Canadians cheered their heroes–Brian Lara of the West Indies, India's Sachin Tendulkar, and so forth–during all night vigils around televisions from coast to coast. While allegiance to home country is strong, as in cricket clubs across Canada, respect is accorded to mastery and sportsmanship prevails. Cricket is an institution in most Commonwealth countries, and its growing popularity in Canada will no doubt result in future competitive sides and improved race relations. Historically, in sports, culture, and entertainment, there are too many examples of the principle of diversity working for all to suggest otherwise.

Passing the Test

Overcoming ingrained negative stereotypes presents black people the world over with a constant challenge. Often, they must be better than anyone else to receive positive recognition. Countless examples of the determination to do this and to "fix what's broke" in their communities mark the black struggle for acceptance in Canadian society.

In many ways *Akili: The Journal of African-Canadian Studies* symbolizes the new place of blacks in Canada. With its first issue in May, 1993, it quickly established itself as Canada's premier black academic journal. Now, with a distribution of over 3,500 across Canada and a growing list of subscribers in the US, the Caribbean, Europe, and Africa, it has become essential reading for those who want a historical perspective on black achievements and the struggle for freedom, justice, peace, and equality in Canada.

Although an academic journal, *Akili* has not strayed from its grass-roots commitment. Its mandate is to educate and to include. Its readers are as varied as high school black history enthusiasts and university scholars. It represents black Canadian historiography on the move. So too does the recently incorporated *Black Focus* quarterly out of Nova Scotia.

In 1994, the outstanding success of Toronto's Caribana festival buoyed the spirits of the organizers and the black community at large. The festival attracted some 1.2 million spectators, an estimated 350,000 of whom came from foreign countries. Black Americans, particularly, marvelled at the international flavour of Toronto and its high degree of multi-ethnic cooperation.

Roughly $250 million was pumped into the Ontario economy. Nonetheless, as of 1994 the Caribbean Cultural Committee (CCC), the group in charge of Caribana, was $260,000 in debt. While the beleaguered CCC sought more government and private sector funding, and recognition that Caribana serves as an essential broker for multicultural integration, critics pointed to internal divisions and questioned the CCC's stability and spending practices. Generally the press picked up on this negative side of the equation, deflecting attention away from the critical issue of getting those who benefit (hotels, restaurants, stores, public transit, and various levels of government) to shoulder their fair share of the costs. As Cecil Foster and others have noted, financial support for Caribana falls far short of that provided for other major cultural enterprises which, arguably, do not benefit Toronto to the same degree.

So, Caribana must prove that its house is in order. As in other matters pertaining to black life in Canada, one slip-up, one act of violence, hostility, or even airing "dirty laundry" in public, tends to negate positive accomplishments. A festival about unity cannot appear fractious and disunited. Charles Roach, chair

Caribana has deep roots. Its connection to the West Indies has been well documented. It can also be tied to the annual "Big Picnics" at Port Dalhousie, Ontario, that began in the late 1800s and continued for over fifty years.

ARTS

Austin Clarke
International acclaimed novelist, lecturer and editor

BUSINESS

Herb Phillipps, Jr.
Vice-president and chief operating officer, Royal Bank of Canada Trust, and president of the Canadian Club.

COMMUNITY ORGANIZATION

Tropicana Community Services Purveyor of essential community services daycare, education, employment, counselling and recreation.

EDUCATION

Harold Braithwaite
Director of Education, Peel Board of Education.

ENTERTAINMENT

Joe Sealy
Acclaimed entertainer, composer, musical director and award-winning jazz musician.

HISTORY

Dr. Daniel G. Hill
Sociologist, human rights advocate, author, adviser and employment equity consultant.

LAW

Honourable Judge Vibert Lampkin
Distinguished Judge in the Ontario Court of Justice.

MEDIA

Dr. Rita Shelton Deverell
Vision TV producer and host, author, arts consultant and university professor.

MEDICINE

Dr. Lanval Joseph Daly
Chief of Obstetrics and Gynaecology at The Doctor's Hospital.

POLITICS

Bev Salmon
Metro councillor for North York,
lecturer and community leader.

POSTHUMOUS

The late Eva Smith
Social worker, human rights
advocate, community-builder
and exceptional human being.

PUBLIC POLICY

Dr. Glenda Simms
President of the Canadian
Advisory Council on the Status
of Women.

COMMUNITY DEVELOPMENT

Dr. Rita Cox
Head Librarian, Parkdale Branch
of the Public Library, author and
outstanding story teller

RELIGION

Reverend Addie Aylestock
First black woman to be
ordained a BME minister.

SCIENCE

Dr. Shirley Murray
Head of the Division of Nuclear
Medicine at Women's College
Hospital, respected physician in
Nuclear Medicine and
Endocrinology.

SPORTS

Ferguson Jenkins
Chicago Cubs coach, first
Canadian inducted into the
Baseball Hall of Fame.

HALL OF FAME

Dr. John Brooks
Founder of the John Brooks
Community Foundation &
Scholarship Fund, and life-long
community advocate.

*Pride Communications
1995 Canadian Black
Achievement Awards
This group, and the
award winners of other
years, give testimony to
the fact that blacks
achieve in all walks of
life.*

of the 1966 Caribbean Centennial Committee, contends that to meet this test Caribana must return to its original mandate: to promote interest in Caribbean culture, to acquire a Caribbean Culture Centre, to give donations for charitable and educational purposes, and, in general, to secure financing and to support all aspects of black culture.

It is a tall order. In 1995, Caribana's net loss was over $400,000, leading to another dramatic rise in its accumulated debt. A revamped 1996 CCC responded with a deficit-conscious "pay for view" plan: that is, for the first time spectators will be charged a nominal fee to view the parade. Furthermore, the parade route will start and end at Exhibition Place, rather than meandering through miles of city streets. Participants are divided over these and other measures, and some are threatening to withdraw. In the end, good management, consensus, and cooperation between all those involved must win the day. The future of Caribana, Canada's largest cultural festival, rests in the balance.

Similar soul-searching and determination has infected the organizers of Montreal's Carifiesta. For almost 25 years Carifete, the city's Caribbean celebration, was the signature event for blacks from the islands. Violence during the festival in 1991 through 1993, internal disputes, security concerns, and disagreements with government led to its cancellation in 1994. Back at the drawing board, black Montrealers devised a new festival called Carifiesta. The parade of 1995 was small by past standards, and the security rather too visible, but the event ran smoothly. The first Carifiesta suggests a brighter future for black cultural events in Montreal.

Black historical societies and education groups are making their mark where it counts most, with black Canadian youth. The evolving situation in Nova Scotia being perhaps the best case in point. There, the unique Black Cultural Centre of Nova Scotia, incorporated in 1983, is busier than ever following its mandate as "keeper of the culture." Its Director and Chief Curator, Henry Bishop, notes an upsurge in interest and confidently speaks about the dawning of a new era in black Nova Scotian history. Especially noteworthy in this regard, is the near total acceptance by the Nova Scotia Department of Education and Culture of the BLAC report on education, a victory which stands as an unparalleled achievement in black Canadian educa-

To the Future 263

tional activism. The test now is to see these dramatic changes implemented in a systematic manner. Under the stewardship of Robert Upshaw (African-Canadian Education Coordinator with the Ministry), the necessary steps are being taken.

The 1994 publication *Innovations in Black Education in Canada* (National Council of Black Educators of Canada) records many other recent positive developments in black education across the country. All of this activity is part of a new awakening which augurs well for the future. Though the popular press continues to concentrate on negative stories, the long struggle for black educational equality is bearing fruit.

Black Women on the Rise

For American writer bell hooks (*Killing Rage*, 1995) and others, black civil rights movements will fall short of their goals unless black women are accorded equal status, unless these movements break with the past and allow women's voices to play an equal and determining role. Of course, black women have been on the front lines, have been equal partners in effecting change. Behind the scenes and through grass-roots initiatives, they have always been agents of reform. The brilliant documentary *Eyes On The Prize*, for instance, might not have come to fruition were it not for the local fundraising efforts of black women. Contemporary reformers are building on a storied tradition, and many are now demanding recognition.

From the young contributors of *Black Girl Talk* (Sister Vision, 1996), to Sylvia Hamilton, to bell hooks, the determination to set the record straight and to move forward fills the uncompromising voices of contemporary black women. Black racial uplift depends, to a large degree, on taking heed of voices.

> While researchers and historians have written generally about Nova Scotia's 'indigenous' Black community, they have paid little attention to the specific condition of Black women in this community. Since Black women, for the most part, have been left out of this history, it has perhaps been assumed that their status and experience were the same as that of males within this community, circumscribed only by race. While race has been a major determinant of the Black woman's status, gender also sharply

Born in Kingston, Jamaica, **Michie Mee** *moved to Toronto as a youth. By the early 1990s, she established herself as a rising star in Canadian rap music. Her album,* Jamaican Funk–Canadian Style, *was released to widespread acclaim in 1992.*

delineated her condition in Nova Scotian society. (Sylvia Hamilton, "Naming Names, Naming Ourselves: A Survey of Early Black Women in Nova Scotia" in *'We're Rooted Here and They Can't Pull Us Up,'* 1994.)

Coming to womanhood in the segregated South, I had never heard black women talk about themselves as victims. Facing hardship, the ravages of economic lack and deprivation, the cruel injustice of racial apartheid, I lived in a world where women gained strength by sharing knowledge and resources, not by bonding on the basis of being victims…We identified ourselves more by the experience of resistance and triumph than by the nature of our victimization. It was a given that life was hard, that there was suffering. It was by facing that suffering with grace and dignity that one experienced transformation. During civil rights struggle, when we joined hands to sing "we shall overcome," we were empowered by a vision of fulfillment, of victory. Much of the awareness that I brought to feminist struggle about the danger of identifying with victimhood was knowledge that came from the oppositional life practices of black folks in the segregated South. When I cautioned women involved in feminist movement to beware of embracing a victim identity, I was confident that black people active in liberation struggle already possessed this awareness. And yet by the end of the eighties black folks were more and more talking about victimhood, claiming a victim identity. (bell hooks, "Refusing To Be A Victim" in *Killing Rage*, 1995.)

Sexism, like racism, is a sturdy weed. Though legions of women in Canada have overcome this double discrimination, the battle continues. Teenage pregnancy–kids having kids–places too many high school females in the dim corners of poverty, forces too many to become old before they've had a chance to fulfil childhood dreams. The social pathology which leads teenage girls into this crap-shoot continues to befuddle teachers, parents, and guardians. What is known, however, is that, for many, having a child is a badge of honour and distinction. Feeling hopeless and desperate, they forego their own dreams to live vicariously through an innocent child.

One of the sternest tests facing Canadian society is to present these teenage girls with different options, and to engage them in the political battle to overcome the feminization of poverty. Rosemary Brown, present Chief Commissioner of the Ontario Human Rights Commission, has traversed the colour line and reached thousands of teenage women, black and white, through her uncompromising message of the value of economic independence via education in *No Way! Not Me!* Sensitive educators across Canada continue to show this timeless video. In like fashion, Almeta Speaks' *Hymn To Freedom* is changing minds and contributing directly to the black causes of freedom, justice, peace, and equality. Recent statistics indicate that such initiatives are making positive inroads. Black female self-esteem and confidence is on the rise. Black women of merit are indeed having an impact. They are overcoming a sad legacy, for blacks begun in slavery, that bound legions of young women to a subservient role.

Similarly, in the US tens of thousands of strong black women have bro-

Dionne Brand
Distinguished poet, essayist, academic, and documentary film director and writer, Dionne Brand continues to articulate, and give guidance to black Canadian women's quest for freedom and equality. In 1991, her book of poems, No Language Is Neutral, *was nominated for the Governor General's Award. Her National Film Board documentaries,* Older, Stronger, Wiser *and* Sisters in the Struggle, *resonate with audiences across Canada. (Nova Scotia's Sylvia Hamilton,* Black Mother Black Daughter *and* Speak It! From the Heart of Black Nova Scotia, *has also distinguished herself in documentary film direction.) Caribbean-born Dionne Brand lives in Toronto.*

ken through the glass ceilings of racism and sexism. They too are building on a storied tradition of determination. By successfully patterning their lives on the vigour and diligence of Sojourner Truth, Harriet Tubman, Bessie Smith, Mary McLeod Bethune, Shirley Chisholm, Maya Angelou, Toni Morrison, and scores of other role models, they have presented the African-American community with a dilemma: US black women appear to be significantly out-performing their male counterparts.

During the past ten years many stories have been written about how successful black women cannot find equally successful black men to marry and to raise a family with. These painful accounts are supported by statistics showing more black men in prison or on parole than attending college, of too many young black men imbued with "New Jack" sensibilities, romanticizing the ghetto, and/or pursuing unlikely "Hoop Dreams" of one sort or another. As a result, a growing number of black women are marrying outside of their race. Some maintain that their choices are based on free will and colour blindness; others, in moments of agonizing honesty, state that their choices are based on a scarcity of suitable and available black men. While many commentators argue that miscegenation contributes to better race relations, others suggest that this trend could signal the end of America's black community. It has become a divisive issue.

Selections from *Miscegenation Blues: Voices of Mixed Race Women* (Sister Vision, 1994) suggest that many mixed-race people suffer in ways that only the poets, story writers, and novelists can truly describe. The book's editor, Carol Camper, was born in Toronto of "Black, White and Native North American ancestry." Her own quest for identity and a sense of belonging represents one of the ultimate tests of cultural pluralism in Canada.

Though Canada has not fallen prey, to the same degree, to the politicization of race and the "race dilemmas" of the US, many critics worry that the North American Free Trade Agreement (and other examples of collapsing borders) will result in a backward slide into ethno-racial divisiveness. Avoiding this requires vigilant effort, requires a continuance of the tradition of male and female activists working in concert, requires a greater recognition of the fact that women's issues are societal issues. Unfortunately, as Canadian Human Rights

Commissioner Max Yalden maintains in his 1996 Report, racism and, especially, intolerance for ethno-racial immigrants, appears to be growing in Canada.

Always at the Crossroads

When a white man commits a criminal act, society does not generally question the white race. Blacks are not so fortunate. While interest in the Paul Bernardo trial was ghoulish, if not prurient, it has produced little, if any, soul-searching about white criminal potential. O. J. Simpson–tried first in the court of public opinion, and assumed guilty by a majority of whites–on the other hand, is held up as representative of black men, or, at the very least, the black male athlete. Black Americans are forced to say, "Yes, O. J. is one of us, but so too is Jackie Robinson, Hank Aaron, Arthur Ashe, Clyde Drexler, Walter Payton, and Jerry Rice." They are forced onto the defensive.

In the wake of O. J. Simpson's acquittal of the double murder of Nicole Simpson and Ronald Goldman and signs of worsening race relations across the US, the Nation Of Islam and its leader, Louis Farrakhan, staged the "Million Man March" on Washington. Attendance estimates varried from 400,000 to 2 million. Whatever the total numbers, it was an impressive "day of atonement" presenting black men with the challenge of redressing negative stereotypes, re-building their communities, and bringing together their families.

As was evidenced by the immediate responses to the Sir George Williams uprising, the Ben Johnson affair, Cole Harbour, Carifete, Yonge Street, the shooting death of a white woman at the hands of a black man in 1994 at Toronto's Just Desserts restaurant, or 1995 violence at high school basketball games, all blacks suffer when one or a group of their own "crosses the line." Such incidents cause many to forget or ignore black achievement, cause many to fear or distrust black people, especially black men.

As a result, race relations harden perceptively. Some whites become inured to negative stories, satisfying themselves with the belief that acts of violence and/or hostility are natural to black people. Others demand that the community get its house in order, that it learn to speak with one voice. When certain black groups protest cultural events like the 1989 Royal Ontario

Million Man March.

Though most people, black and white, reject the segregationist teachings of Louis Farrakhan, the vast majority subscribed to the messages delivered by all speakers on this day.

Museum's *Into The Heart Of Africa* exhibit, or the 1993 production of *Show Boat,* many whites, misunderstanding the poignancy of perceived misrepresentation and concerns over voice appropriation, argue that blacks will never be satisfied.

Black Canadians represent a "multicultural inflorescence" (Anderson, 1993). So do white and brown Canadians. Blacks have never, and will never, speak with one voice. Nonetheless, they have a need for cultural identity. For an increasing number of blacks that identity is secured under the umbrella term "African-Canadian," a term in keeping with their diasporic history and representative of a determination to define their own place in the Canadian mosaic.

Whither Goes the African-Canadian Community?

Many African-Canadians delight in the delicious ironies of history.

James Robinson Johnston graduated from Dalhousie Law School in 1898, becoming the first locally trained black lawyer in the Maritimes. He accomplished this feat at a time when race science was at its height and white society generally believed that blacks were uneducable. His respect in the community traversed the colour line. In 1991, the Senate of Dalhousie University passed a resolution to establish an endowed James Robinson Johnston Chair in Black Canadian Studies. The first to assume this honour and responsibility will be Esmeralda Thornhill.

In 1984, Anne Cools became the first African-Canadian appointed to the Canadian Senate. Cools, born in Barbados, was a respected social worker before entering politics. She was also one of the leaders in the 1969 protest at Sir George Williams.

On June 28, 1995, an extraordinary sporting event took place at Wimbledon in London, England. The Wimbledon Tennis Club, with its all-white dress code, its manners, its royal patrons, its Victorian era legacy of civility and exclusion, was host to a dramatic change. In the longest women's tennis match in Grand Slam history, Chanda Rubin defeated Patricia Hy-Boulais (7-6, 6-7, 17-15). Three records were broken: length of match, 3 hours and 45 minutes; most games, 58; and longest third set, 32 games. Patricia Hy-Boulais is a thirty-three-year-old Chinese-Canadian from Montreal. Chanda Rubin, following great black champions Arthur Ashe and Zina Garisson, is a seventeen-year-old African-American from Louisiana. Tennis, for centuries the sport of wealthy white classes, is experiencing a significant "darkening complexion."

These, and countless other ironic twists, speak to the notion that we must expect the unexpected. People of African descent have made a habit of rising from the ground up, of making unexpected appearances, of breaking down barriers. Edsworth Searles is a case in point. Speaking of his community's history, he said, "It wasn't always easy, but you did what you had to do...You don't have to ask what a black man did in the '40s; either you worked on the railway or as a shoe shine boy" ("From train porter to lawyer" *Toronto Star,* March 4, 1996). Searles, like his father before him, "worked on the railway." But, unlike his father, he also went to law school.

In the early 1950s, Searles' application for an articling job at a major Toronto law firm was rejected. He remembers being told: "It's nothing personal, but we can't hire you because you're black." What could be more personal than that! Undaunted, in 1858, Searles became the first black to be called to the B.C. bar. In 1959, he was called to the Ontario bar. Searles served as a distinguished lawyer in Toronto for thirty years.

African-Canadians will continue to be tested and re-tested. They will continue to be held up to standards not imposed on others. Their history in Canada dates back 400 years. For 400 years they have been presented with unique challenges, forced to overcome made-in-Canada barriers to achievement, and have experienced division and unity, ebb and flow.

Any discussion about where the African-Canadian community is going leads inevitably to black youth. Readers of Cecil Foster's *Distorted Mirror: Canada's Racist Face* (1991) understand that often black youth are forced to deal with racism at a very early age. Describing the pain of his five-year-old son, who had just encountered his first face-to-face meeting with racism, Foster writes:

> Some darling in his kindergarten class, he explained between sobs, had shattered his world by telling the class he was not welcome at her birthday party. The reason: he was Black. In confusion, my son reasoned he was different from all other children in his class. He even thought himself inferior to his older brother, who has a lighter shade of skin. He reasoned that his brother, whom he thought of at that time as white, would have been invited to the party. If he adopted the ways of his brother–sleeping in his bed, under his blanket–he too would lighten his skin by morning and get that invitation.
>
> ... Yet even with my own experiences, it was still so difficult having to explain that I was in no position to do anything about it. A child of five ought not to lose his innocence this way. A proud man ought not to be made to feel as helpless as a child of five.

The sting of discrimination falls hardest on ethno-racial youth. Many black immigrant youth identify their skin colour as a badge of inferiority only on Canadian soil. Though there is considerable enthusiasm for multicultural and anti-racist policies, Canadian society must recognize that official documents will not, in and of themselves, extinguish the pain, hurt, and shame felt by black youth who, in their confusion, attempt to bleach their skin.

The late Wilson Head, historian and sociologist, did much to uncover the realities facing black immigrants in their attempts to adapt to Canada. In his study *Adaptation of Immigrants: Perceptions of Ethnic and Racial Discrimination* (York University, 1981), he discovered that "seeking adventure" was a principal reason behind black emigration to Canada. This is undoubtedly still true today, as Canada retains a favourable international reputation. The jury is out, however, on the success of Canadian society in providing the means through which positive adventure-seekers can fulfill their dreams.

Writers and scholars such as Wilson Head, Frances Henry, Vincent D'Oyley, Carl James, Inez Elliston, George Dei, Wolseley Anderson, Elizabeth Coelho, James Walker, Agnes Calliste, Rosemary Brown, Sheldon Taylor, Patrick Solomon, Almeta Speaks, Robert Upshaw, and many others have produced excellent writings on the post-1970 black experience in Canada. This literature is growing. In it lies the historical understanding necessary for future success in race relations, integration, and positive multiculturalism. Government authorities need to listen to the emergent voices of the African-Canadian intelligentsia. There is too much at stake not to.

About the future we can only guess. Achieving freedom, justice, peace, and equality remains the cherished goal. There are positive signs across the country which suggest a brighter tomorrow. This is an educated guess based on history and on the increasing evidence of African-Canadians uniting behind common causes, if not speaking with one voice. Perhaps the most insidious aspect of systemic discrimination occurs when people come to believe in the negative stereotypes about themselves and their culture. At different times and in different ways, this phenomenon has afflicted many African-Canadians. Now, with tangible evidence of black achievement in all walks of life, this harmful legacy is in retreat. If Canadian society recognizes black achievement for what it is–success in spite of some considerable obstacles–it is unlikely to resurface.

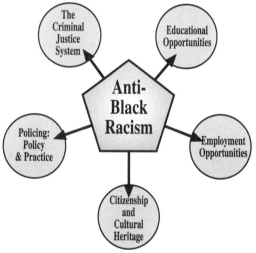

Some Critical Spheres of Anti-Black Discrimination (source: Wolseley Anderson, *Caribbean Immigrants: A Socio-Demographic Profile.)* These issues will only be dealt with successfully through the participation of concerned African-Canadians in conjunction with government authorities.

In May 1995, the *Canadian Journal of Black and African Education* was established in Montreal by the National Council of Black Educators of Canada. It focuses on innovative educational programs, human rights, lifestyle developments, conflict resolution strategies, and youth dilemmas. Its impressive editorial committee (Editor, Dr. Vincent D'Oyley) is drawn from all parts of Canada. The Journal will provide educators and government officials with essential information and opinion on the critical issues pertaining to black education in Canada.

Recognition of the fact that through hard work, dedication to family and community, and the pursuit of dreams, the silent majority of blacks–like the silent majorities of all other groups–are positively contributing to Canada will result in positive race relations. The root causes of racism are ignorance and a lack of meaningful contact between different peoples. Much has been written about how blacks and whites "view the world differently" and that there are few, if any, shared cultural reference points. Certainly there are differences, but these differences can be celebrated, can be mutually understood, can, if the principle of diversity is truly accepted, be a source of societal strength. At the same time, there are commonalities. Freedom, justice, peace, and equality are goals shared by all peoples. They far outweigh the differences.

People are people. We weave narratives to explain our histories and to shed light on our futures. Certainly, the narratives are different, and depend largely on historical circumstance. Some are exalted, ring true, and stand the test of time. Some are not and do not. But the purpose of telling these stories–to understand the world in which we live–is the same across cultures. We can all learn from the stories of others. Understanding the true value of cultural pluralism is the challenge facing Canada as it approaches the next millennium.

Chronology of Important Events in New World Black History

The following is a list of some of the important events in black history that have occurred in Canada (CAN), the United States (US), and the Caribbean (WI) over the past 500 years.

1400s   WI Settled communities throughout the Caribbean of the indigenous peoples: the Ciboney; the Taino Arawak; and the Carib, from whom the region got its name.

1492   WI Christopher Columbus lands in Cuba. This first voyage is followed by three others (1493–1504). Many Caribbean islands are "discovered," and the integration of Europe, Africa, Asia, and the Americas begins to take shape. The development of the West Indies in particular, and the Atlantic world in general, accelerates with the beginning of the trans-Atlantic slave trade. This trade is, first and foremost, an economic institution.

1500 ff.   WI After the fifteenth century black Africans constitute the major stream of immigrants to the West Indies. The term *bozales* is used to describe African-born slaves; while Caribbean-born black slaves are called *creoles*. Reports show that the Indian populations are rapidly diminishing because of wars, mistreatment, and disease.

1500 ff.   WI Spain begins to assert its control over the West Indies. Laws regulating shipping and trade are imposed. In 1508, gold is discovered in Puerto Rico, and Juan Ponce de Leon officially settles the colony. Jamaica is settled in 1509, followed by Cuba in 1511. The first sugar mills are established on Hispaniola in 1510.

1515   WI The export of gold and other precious minerals is followed by the first shipment of Caribbean sugar to Spain. Labour shortages threaten this growing trade.

1518   WI Permission is granted to import 4,000 African slaves to the Spanish Antilles. The Spanish conquest of Mexico begins with the landing of Hernan Cortes' flotilla from Cuba in 1519.

1540s   WI Spain establishes a convoy system to protect its ships from rival European powers, pirates, and renegade Spanish captains.

1565   WI / US St. Augustine, Florida is founded by Pedro Menendez. Menendez is largely responsible for the defence of Spanish America during this period.

1582   WI Island societies become increasingly multicultural. A Cuban population register lists Spanish, Hispanized Indians, mullatoes, mestizos, and free blacks all in significant numbers. In the years to come, the non-European populations greatly out-number the European populations on most islands. The social stratification of Old World cultures is imported to the New World.

1595   WI The *asiento* system — formal grants to slavers allowing them to supply African slaves to the Caribbean — is established.

1600 ff.   WI Unable to control the entire region — especially after the ascendancy of Portugal and other powers on the world scene — Spain withdraws from peripheral areas and concentrates its efforts on the mineral-rich mainland and larger Caribbean islands. This opens the door to new conquerors. The purpose of settling the islands and mainland regions moves from establishing versions of Old World cultures to economic exploitation. The exploitation of free labour in mining communities is continued and accelerated with the emergence of mono-cultural plantation economies.

1604   WI The Dutch begin developing a salt industry off the Venezuelan coast.

1604-06   CAN Mattieu da Costa, the first known black to set foot on Canadian soil, travels with the Champlain expedition to Port Royal. He is, in all probability, a free man.

1609   WI At the Truce of Antwerp Spain agrees to concessions on their Caribbean holdings. During the following fifteen years, the English and Dutch make many (some successful) attempts to establish permanent colonies. The Dutch

West India Company is formally incorporated in 1621.

1619   US Twenty Africans are deposited at Jamestown, Virginia off a Dutch ship. They are the first blacks to be forcibly settled — as indentured labourers — in North America. The notion of slavery as a permanent condition develops later.

1624-51   WI The English, Dutch, and French continue to assert their influence. The British colonize Barbados (1624), St. Kitts (1624), Nevis (1625), Antigua, Montserrat, St. Lucia (1630-1640), Suriname (1651); the Dutch settle Berbice (1624), Curacao, Saba, St. Martin, St. Eustatius (1630-1640); and the French settle Guadeloupe and Martinique. In 1648, the Dutch and French divide St. Martin.

1628   CAN Olivier Le Jeune is sold into slavery in New France. He is Canada's first officially recognized black slave.

1641   US Massachusetts becomes the first colony to officially legalize slavery.

1630-1720 WI The "Age of the Buccaneers." Some islands, like Barbados, prosper by growing sugar; others, like Jamaica and Hispaniola, prosper through piracy. Thousands opt for a life of adventure in piracy and settling land, leaving the drudgery of plantation life behind them. Until 1720, the Caribbean is divided between the planters, merchants, and slaves working sugar and other products for sale in Europe, and the buccaneers who pillage sea-lanes.

1652 ff.   WI Three Anglo-Dutch wars (1652, 1666-1667, 1672-1678) signify the importance of Caribbean holdings to European states. Prior to these wars European states had generally worked together to plunder Spanish possessions. In 1667, the Dutch acquire Suriname in exchange for their colony on Manhattan Island, New York.

1663   US The first documented slave rebellion occurs in Gloucester County, Virginia.

1685-1815 WI Britain and France fight a long series of wars to gain control of the Caribbean.

1685   WI / CAN The French slave system becomes formalized under the Code Noir. Slavery becomes legal in New France in 1709.

1688   US The first formal antislavery resolution is passed by Pennsylvania Quakers.

1713 ff.   WI The Treaty of Utrecht ends the War of the Spanish Succession and ushers in a period of relative peace in the Caribbean. Sugar becomes "king" in the eighteenth century, producing 80 to 90 percent of western Europe's total consumption. The British alone export 2,500,000 slaves to the Caribbean and Spanish America from 1690 to 1807. Triangular trade routes bring enormous wealth to European nations.

1739-63   WI A series of wars between European states. England establishes itself as the dominant power in the Caribbean. French possessions are reduced to Saint-Domingue.

1734   CAN The celebrated case of Marie-Joseph Angélique brings to the attention of many the hideous conditions of slavery in Canada. Angélique is publicly tortured and hanged for attempting to escape and, allegedly, setting fire to her mistress' home.

1720 ff.   WI Maroon communities become a concern to European colonists, who fear a domino-effect across the Caribbean resulting from Maroon uprisings. Jamaica experiences the first Maroon war in 1734.

1739   US Twenty-five whites are killed during the Cato slave revolt. The rebels are caught and more than 30 blacks are executed.

1772   WI / CAN / US Slavery is declared illegal in England by chief justice Lord Mansfield.

1775   US In Massachusetts free blacks fight with the Minutemen in the first battles of the American War of Independence.

1777   US / CAN Vermont becomes the first state to abolish slavery. Some slaves escape New France and settle in free Vermont. George Washington announces a new policy allowing for the recruitment of black soldiers, over 5,000 of whom participate in the War of Independence.

1783   CAN Over 5,000 black United Empire Loyalists (both free and enslaved) leave the US for Canada. Having sided with the British during the Revolutionary War, they are promised freedom and land. The notion of Canada as a "safe haven" for blacks gains considerable currency. Failure to keep these promises, especially in the Maritimes, leaves Canada with an embittered black population.

1787   US The Northwest Ordinance passes. It bans slavery northwest of the Ohio River.

1788   WI The "new consciousness" in France leads to the outbreak of the Revolution, Declaration of Rights of Man (1789), and the creation of the Societe des Amis des Noirs. In Saint-Domingue, France's richest colonial holding, slave revolts begin in 1791. Plantations are torched and thousands (white and black) are killed. By 1798, Toussaint L'Ouverture gains control over the ex-slaves. In 1804, Haiti is declared an independent republic, the first in the region.

1792   CAN Failed promises of land in Canada cause Maritime black Loyalists to migrate to Sierra Leone, West Africa. Eight years later, they are joined by most of the 600 Jamaican Maroons transported to Halifax in 1796.

1793   US / CAN The US Congress passes the first Fugitive Slave Act. Upper Canada (under the leadership of John Graves Simcoe) passes a law forbidding the importation of slaves. Though the provisions of this legislation do not abolish slavery, Upper Canada becomes the first British territory to enact anti-slavery legislation.

1804   US The Ohio legislature passes an early version of segregation laws restricting the legal rights of "free" blacks.

1808 ff.   WI / CAN / US Great Britain and the US abolish the slave trade. Though laws go into effect, they are largely circumvented. Britain gives teeth to the legislation in 1811 by making slave trading a felony. In 1827, it becomes a felony punishable by death.

1812   CAN Blacks play critical roles during the War of 1812. Approximately 2,000 migrate from the US to the Maritimes during the war.

1815   WI / US The end of the Napoleonic wars (1815) solidifies Britain's position.

1800-60   US / CAN During the early-to-mid 1800s tens of thousands black Americans escape slavery via the Underground Railroad and come to Canada. In 1849, Harriet Tubman escapes from slavery. From her base in St. Catharines, Ontario, the "Moses of her people" makes 20 trips into the US to help 300 slaves escape. The second Fugitive Slave Act (1850) dramatically increases the flow. Canada refuses to extradite fugitive slaves. By 1860, there are at least 40,000 blacks in Ontario.

1820-40   US The divided nature of US society is made plain through a series of slave revolts (e.g. the Denmark Vesey conspiracy, Nat Turner), David Walker's *Appeal to the Coloured People of the World*, and the successful Supreme Court ruling in favour of black slaves who gained their freedom by overtaking a Spanish ship and sailing it to New York.

1825   US / WI Both the US and the West Indies had African populations of about two million. However, up to 1810 roughly 3,500,000 slaves had been transported to the islands and only 375,000 to British North America. Simply put, black life in the Caribbean was expendable. War, disease, and sugar plantations were killing machines.

1833   WI / CAN / US The Emancipation Act is passed by the British Parliament. In 1834, slavery comes to an end in all British territories.

1837   CAN Blacks form their own militia units and are recruited by the government to help defend Upper Canada during the Mackenzie Rebellion of 1837. Josiah Henson fights on the side of the government.

1850   CAN / US The Common Schools Act is passed in Ontario, legalizing segregation in schooling. Later, a riot breaks out in Hamilton as black parents insist that their children attend white schools. The US passes the second Fugitive Slave Act.

1850s CAN Canada's black population continues to grow. Thousands come from the US via the UGR. This decade represents the high-point of black achievement in pre-Confederation Canada. Many black settlements from coast to coast flourish. The Anti-Slavery Society of Canada is established in Toronto. Black newspapers, *Voice of the Fugitive* and *Provincial Freeman*, are founded. Mary Ann Shadd becomes the first woman editor of a newspaper in North America (1853).

1857 US The infamous Dred Scott decision of the Supreme Court rejects the notion of black citizenship. It also denies Congress the power to restrict slavery in federal territories.

1858 CAN / US Approximately 800 blacks from California migrate to Vancouver Island. They come at the invitation of Governor Douglas, who is concerned about American encroachment on Canadian soil during the gold rush days. The blacks from the Zion Church of San Francisco help safeguard B. C. Blacks outnumber whites on Vancouver Island. In 1860, the all-black Victoria Pioneer Rifle Company is formed to defend Victoria. Mifflin Gibbs later plays a key role convincing B. C. to join Confederation.

1859 CAN Abraham Shadd is the first black Canadian elected to public office. He sits on the town council in Raleigh, Ontario.

1862 US / CAN The US Congress allows blacks to be enlisted in the Union Army. Over 186,000 blacks participate; 40,000 dying in service. Black Canadians join the Civil War effort in large numbers, beginning the depopulation of their community which continues for roughly 50 years. Anderson Ruffin, a Canadian-trained black doctor, serves as a surgeon for the Union Army.

1863 US The Emancipation Proclamation frees slaves in the rebel states. This is followed by the 13th Amendment to the Constitution (1865), outlawing slavery throughout the US.

1860s WI The 1860s proves to be a turbulent decade. Santo Domingo is made a province of Spain, and then declares its independence; riots break out as a result of escalating food prices and food shortages; Holland finally abolishes slavery in 1863; Jamaica is rocked by the Morant Bay revolt, led by Paul Bogle; the Ten Years' War in Cuba begins; and Puerto Rico becomes a Spanish province.

1865-77 US The Reconstruction period brings many reforms and positive changes. Dozens of black universities are founded in the South and thousands of schools built. In the 50 year period following the Civil War the black literacy rate doubles. Thousands of black Canadians head south to take advantage of new opportunities. In 1868, the South Carolina legislature boasts a black majority (87 blacks to 40 whites); and the 14th Amendment is ratified, giving citizenship rights to all persons born or naturalized in the US. In 1870, the 15th Amendment, which secures voting rights for all male US citizens, becomes law. In 1875, Congress' civil rights bill bans discrimination in places of public accommodation.

1872 CAN / US Elijah McCoy, born in Colchester, Ontario, invents the lubricating cup (used on trains and in factories). Ten years later, John Ware moves from Texas to Alberta, bringing longhorn cattle to Canada and pioneering the development of the rodeo. Blacks go on to invent numerous devices used in everyday life.

1875 ff. CAN / US / WI Race science impacts negatively on legislation. Images comparing blacks to apes proliferate. Canada, Confederated in 1867, adopts measures to "keep blacks out or in their place." Many US Reconstruction reforms are overturned, and the seeds of officially sanctioned segregation are planted. In 1896, in a decision that has a dramatic impact on schooling, the Supreme Court's ruling in *Plessy vs. Ferguson* affirms the notion of "separate but equal" public facilities. The West Indies becomes increasingly stratified along colour lines.

1886   WI Cuba, the last hold-out, finally abolishes slavery.

1900 ff.   WI Hurricanes of the natural and political kind sweep through the Caribbean. The transition from colonialism and authoritarian rule to independence and democracy is rocky and fraught with instability. Riots and US intervention mark the period, but so too does the determination for reform. In 1902, the Republic of Cuba is established, but the US retains the right to intervene; a volcanic eruption in Martinique kills 40,000; and, Montego Bay, Jamaica and Port of Spain, Trinidad experience major urban riots. Similar riots occur in British Guiana (1905); St. Lucia (1908); Cuba (3,000 blacks killed), Kingston, Jamaica, and the Dominican Republic (1912); Haiti (1915); Belize, British Honduras, and San Fernando, Trinidad (1919); Barbados and Trinidad (1937). In 1937, the authoritarian ruler Trujillo massacres 20,000 Haitian sugar-cane workers in the Dominican Republic. In 1938, riots in Jamaica help lead to the establishment of political parties. In 1900, Puerto Rico becomes a US territory. The US intervenes in the Dominican Republic (1905) and Cuba (1906); occupies Haiti (1915-1934) and the Dominican Republic (1916-1924). From 1926-35, hurricanes hit the Caribbean. Local economies suffer dramatic losses, and the region becomes more reliant on international aid. Across the Caribbean, black upward mobility is restricted by colour-line politics.

1900 ff.   CAN The activities of the Coloured Women's Club of Montreal bring into sharp focus the determination of black women to provide essential services for their community.

1905   CAN / US W.E.B. Du Bois meets with other American civil rights activists in Fort Erie, Ontario. The Niagara Movement (precursor to the NAACP) is founded.

1909   CAN / US While Canada is passing restrictive immigration policies to keep black Oklahomans from settling the Prairies, Matthew Henson co-discovers the North Pole.

1914-18   CAN / US Black Canadians and Americans refuse to accept that WW I is "a white man's war." In Canada, black soldiers fight the enemy on the battlefield and racism within their combat units. The all-black Nova Scotia No. 2 Construction Battalion is established. Though a compromise, it is an important step in the struggle for equality.

1915   US Billie Holiday, the great blues and jazz singer, is born. Carter G. Woodson, author of the influential essay *The Miseducation of the Negro*, establishes the Association for the Study of Negro Life and History. Woodson and his Association later sponsor Negro History Week, now Black History Month.

1914 ff.   US / CAN / WI Marcus Garvey of Jamaica establishes chapters of the Universal Negro Improvement Association, emphasizing black pride and world black consciousness. The UNIA becomes highly influential in the US and Canada. By the early 1920s it is the voice of protest in Nova Scotia and Quebec.

1920s   US / CAN Black literature and art reach a new pinnacle during the Harlem Renaissance. Political and cultural black consciousness spreads. In 1925, A. Philip Randolph organizes the Brotherhood of Sleeping Car Porters, marking an important turning point in black union activity. Canadian porters soon establish their own union. Also in the 1920s, American born Charles Drew studies medicine at McGill University in Montreal. He becomes a distinguished surgeon.

1936   US / CAN At the Berlin Olympics, American runner Jesse Owens shatters the notion of white supremacy by collecting four gold medals. Canadian sprinter Sammy Richardson wins silver in the two-hundred metres.

1940-52   WI Universal suffrage is extended to most Caribbean islands.

1939-45   US / CAN During WW II authorities again attempt to limit black involvement in the armed forces. Once again, blacks on both sides of the border persevere. In Canada, they eventually join all services. In the US, Benjamin O. Davis, Sr. becomes the first black general in the army.

1946 CAN Through *The Clarion* and later *The Negro Citizen*, Nova Scotian writer and historian Carrie Best brings the discrimination facing blacks in her province to Canada's attention.

1940 ff. CAN Successful civil rights lobbying results in most Canadian provinces passing significant anti-discrimination legislation.

1946 CAN The Nova Scotia Association for the Advancement of Coloured People support Viola Desmond in her case against a New Glasgow theatre which refused to allow her to sit in the white section.

1947 US / CAN Jackie Robinson breaks baseball's colour barrier with the Brooklyn Dodgers. He plays for the Montreal Royals in 1946, and is warmly received.

1948-62 WI Over 300,000 West Indians emigrate to Britain. After 1962, Britain "closes the door" and Canada becomes a preferred destination.

1950 US On September 22, Ralph J. Bunche becomes the first black to win the Nobel Peace Prize for mediating the end of the Arab-Israeli War. The poet, Gwendolyn Brooks, is the first black woman to win the Pulitzer Prize for literature.

1951-76 CAN The Canadian Negro Women's Association is founded by Kay Livingstone and others in Toronto (1951). It, and its offshoots (e.g. the National Congress of Black Women of Canada), contribute directly to racial uplift, civil rights, and community development.

1953 US / CAN Charlie "Bird" Parker plays with great black Canadian jazz musicians in Montreal (Jazz Workshop) and Toronto (Massey Hall).

1954 US Racial segregation in public schools is ruled unconstitutional in the *Brown vs. Board of Education of Topeka, Kansas* Supreme Court decision. Segregated school legislation remains on the books in some Canadian provinces.

1954 ff. CAN The Negro Citizenship Association (NCA) goes to Ottawa (1954) to press for an end to racist immigration policies. They ask government officials to "bring down this Jim Crow Iron Curtain." In 1955, Canada initiates the West Indian Domestic Scheme. This restrictive entry policy is offensive to many, especially the NCA and newly politicized black women. The NCA had stressed Canada's Commonwealth commitments. Later, under Prime Minister John Diefenbaker, Canada moved to isolate South Africa and, because of its Apartheid policies, have it expelled from the Commonwealth.

1955 US The Montgomery, Alabama bus boycott is launched after Rosa Parks was arrested for refusing to give up her seat to a white person. Non-violent civil disobedience (sit-ins, freedom rides, marches, voter registration drives) becomes the key strategy in the civil rights movement. The Voting Rights Bill is passed in 1957.

1956 WI Eric Williams forms the People's National Movement in Trinidad. His book, *Capitalism and Slavery*, is first published in 1964.

1950 ff. CAN More anti-discrimination laws, including provincial Bill of Rights,' are passed. Immigration policies are liberalized and large numbers of blacks, especially from the Caribbean, enter Canada.

1959 WI Fidel Castro comes to power in Cuba.

1960s CAN The proud residents of Africville, Nova Scotia, having had their community fall to the wrecking ball, fight for reasonable reparations and relocation opportunities. They are largely frustrated in the efforts.

1962 ff. WI / CAN The struggle for independence is being won. Jamaica and Trinidad and Tobago become independent. They are followed by Barbados and Guyana (1966); Bahamas (1973); Grenada (1974); Suriname (1975); St. Lucia (1977); Dominica (1978); St. Vincent and the Grenadines (1979); Belize,

Antigua and Barbuda (1981); and, St. Kitts-Nevis (1983). In 1974, the Caribbean Community and Common Market (CARICOM) is established. In 1962, Canadian immigration policy changes. New regulations emphasize education and skills, and result (in 1967) in the "points system." Thousands of meritorious West Indians take advantage of this opening.

1963 ff.   US The August 28 March on Washington attracts 250,000 people. Martin Luther King, Jr. delivers the "I Have a Dream" speech. Unity proves to be an elusive goal, however, as American cities experience successive waves of riots and demonstrations, and black leaders (including King in 1968, and Malcolm X in 1965) are gunned down.

1963   CAN Leonard Braithwaite becomes the first black to serve in a provincial legislature (Ontario).

1966   US The Black Panther Party is founded in Oakland, California by Huey Newton and Bobby Seale. The Panther's platform ("Guns and Breakfasts") attracts interest across the continent. Their militancy is symbolized at the 1968 Mexico City Olympics by medal winning athletes using the "Black Power" salute.

1967   US Thurgood Marshall, brilliant lawyer for the NAACP, becomes the first black judge appointed to the Supreme Court.

1972   CAN Emery Barnes and Rosemary Brown (the first black woman elected to a provincial legislature) are voted into office in British Columbia.

1974   US Henry Aaron launches his 715th home run, breaking Babe Ruth's long-standing record. For his efforts, Aaron receives both adulation and a flood of hate mail.

1974   CAN / WI The largest number (27,915) of West Indian immigrants arrive in Canada. Many groups representing immigrants from specific Caribbean islands are established during the late 1960s and early 1970s.

1975   CAN Wilson Head establishes the Urban Alliance on Race Relations. It quickly becomes one of Canada's most effective lobby groups. Fifteen hundred Haitians

are deported after immigration authorities reject their claims for refugee status.

1976   CAN Meritorious blacks continue to make inroads. Jean Alfred becomes a Minister in the Quebec legislature for the Parti Quebecois, and Stanley Grizzle is named Canada's first black citizenship court judge.

1979   CAN As Minister of Labour for the federal government, Hamilton, Ontario's Lincoln Alexander becomes the first black cabinet minister. He later serves as the Lieutenant-Governor of Ontario. Sylvia Sweeney is named most valuable player at the Seoul, South Korea Women's World Basketball Championship.

1980   WI / US The Mariel boat lift brings 125,000 Cuban refugees to the US.

1980s   CAN /WI Jean-Bertrand Aristide, who later became the President of Haiti, studies at the University of Montreal. His tenure as President is cut short by a military coup.

1983   US / CAN The last racial discrimination law — the state legislature of Louisiana reserving the right to classify as black any person with 1/32nd Negro blood — is finally repealed. The Garvey Institute, a private school for blacks, is founded in Montreal.

1984-88   CAN Daurene Lewis, the first black woman elected mayor of a Canadian city, serves for five years in Annapolis Royal, Nova Scotia.

1986   WI Jean-Claude Duvalier is overthrown in Haiti.

1987   CAN Nova Scotian historian Calvin Ruck's book, *Canada's Black Battalion No. 2 Construction 1916–1929*, is released. It helps set the record straight on black participation in WW I, and is part of an important drive to have blacks represented in Canadian history books. The Consultative Committee on the Education of Black Students in Toronto Schools presents its excellent Report to school board and government officials.

1988   US / CAN All charges against Rubin "Hurricane" Carter are dismissed. Carter, once a contender for the middleweight boxing championship, had spent nearly 20 years in prison for a crime he did not commit. Largely speaking, he owes his freedom to Lesra Martin (a Brooklyn ghetto youth) and a group of white Canadians who took up his cause.

1988   US Jesse Jackson receives over 1,200 delegate votes at the Democratic National Convention. He loses his bid to Michael Dukakis who receives 2,082 votes.

1989   US General Colin L. Powell becomes Chair of the US Joint Chiefs of Staff. He is praised for his leadership during the US-Iraq war, and appears to a large cross-section of Americans as "presidential material." In 1995, after being wooed by both Republicans and Democrats, he chooses not run for the Oval Office.

1980s ff.   WI / CAN Canadian audiences are exposed to the high art and clever brilliance of Caribbean storytelling by Louise Bennett-Coverley, Rita Cox, and Ricardo Keens-Douglas.

1990s   CAN / US With the publication of *The Bell Curve* (US) and the widely publicized and circulated work of Philipe Rushton (Canada), race science theories gain renewed credibility. Once again, blacks are forced to refute this damaging brand of racism.

1991   CAN / WI Julius Alexander Issac, born in Grenada, is named Chief Justice of the Federal Court of Canada.

1992   CAN Civil rights activist Burnley "Rocky" Jones (once dubbed "Canada's Stokely Carmichael") graduates from law school at Dalhousie University. He becomes a lawyer at the Dalhousie Legal Aid Service.

1992-93   WI / US Derek Walcott from St. Lucia is the first Caribbean-born writer to win the Nobel Prize for literature (1992). American writer Toni Morrison becomes the first black woman to win the same prize (1993).

1993   CAN *The Black Experience in Manitoba: A Collection of Memories* is published. It stands as a model of educational excellence in Canada.

1994   CAN Austin Clarke furthers his reputation as Canada's pre-eminent black man of letters with the release of *The Prime Minister* and *A Passage Back Home.*

1995   CAN Nova Scotia responds positively to the Black Learners Advisory Committee's *Report on Education.* Comprehensive and realistic, the *Report* could serve as a basis for Canadian educational initiatives.

1995   US Louis Farrakhan and the Nation of Islam stage the "Million Man March."

1995-96   CAN In Toronto, debate swirls over "black focus" schools as one such school opens. In general, a renewed commitment to self-help permeates black consciousness as government budgets are slashed.

1996   AFR Though the transition to true democracy continues to be relatively smooth in South Africa, blacks encounter staunch resistance in attempting to integrate white schools.

1996   CAN Lincoln Alexander becomes the first chairperson of the Canadian Race Relations Foundation, a centre of excellence to study and defeat racism. Donovan Bailey (100 metres) and the men's 4 x 100 metre relay team win Olympic gold at Atanta.

1996-97   US Controversy erupts over an Oakland (Cal.) school board decision to use ebonics – from *ebony* and *phonics* – as a teaching strategy for black students "disidentifying" with school.

1997   WI / CAN Millions mourn the deaths of leaders Michael Manley (Jamaica) and Cheddi Jagan (Guyana). Canadian Heritage and the Canadian Alliance of Black Educators launch "The Griots Tour Across Canada." Featuring Austin Clarke, Dionne Brand, Cecil Foster, and Mairuth Sarsfield, the Tour clearly marks a renaissance in black Canadian writing. George Elliott Clarke's *Eyeing The North Star: Directions in African Canadian Literature*, Dorothy Williams' *The Road To Now: A History Of Blacks In Montreal*, the reissue of Robin Winks' *The Blacks In Canada*, Bruce Shepard's *Deemed Unsuitable*, and other notable recent works suggest that this burst of great writing on the black experience stretches across Canada.

A Selected Guide to History Books on the Black Experience

We, the authors of *Towards Freedom*, have compiled this bibliography as a selected guide, not an authoritative list. Apart from a few notable exceptions, space prevents us from suggesting titles from the vast reserve of great literature by black authors. For those interested, we suggest *An Open Book: A Listing of Books, Films and Stories About People of Colour (For concerned teachers, parents and for the children of Canada)*. It is available through The Equatoria Collection, P.O. Box 52132, 41 York Street, Ottawa, Ontario, K1N 5S0. A listing of important articles and academic papers can be found in *The Colour of Democracy: Racism in Canadian Society* by Frances Henry, et al.

Though Neil Postman is an American education and culture critic, his books have had a most definite impact on us as teachers and writers. They have international relevance and we highly recommend them. Finally, for high school audiences we recommend the video series' *Eyes On The Prize* (US civil rights movement), *Hymn To Freedom* (Canadian black history), *Black on White* (adapted for film from *The Story Of English*), and the many documentaries featuring Basil Davidson on African history.

Abernathy, Ralph, D. *And The Walls Came Tumbling Down*. New York: Harper & Row, 1989.

Abrahams, Roger D. *Singing the Master: The Emergence of African-American Culture in the Plantation South*. Toronto: Penguin Books, 1992.

Adams, Emile L. *Understanding Jamaican Patois: An Introduction to Afro-Jamaican Grammar*. Kingston, Jamaica: Kingston Publishers Limited, 1992.

Anderson, Wolseley. *Caribbean Immigrants: A Socio-Demographic Profile*. Toronto: Canadian Scholars' Press Inc., 1993.

Asante, Molefi K. and Asante, Kariamu W. *African Culture: The Rhythms Of Unity*. Trenton, N.J.: Africa World Press, Inc., 1990.

Ashe, Jr., Arthur R. *A Hard Road To Glory: The African-American Athlete In Baseball*, (Also: *Basketball, Football, Boxing, Track*). New York: Amistad Press, 1993.

Baldwin, James. *The Fire Next Time*. New York: Dial Press, 1963.

Beckles, Dr. Hilary and Shepherd, Verene. *Caribbean Slave Society and Economy*. New York: The New Press, 1991.

Bennett, Jr., Lerone. *Before The Mayflower: A History Of Black America*. New York: Penguin Books, 1984.

Bertley, Leo. *Canada and Its People of African Descent*. Pierrefonds, 1977.

Best, Carrie. *That Lonesome Road: The Autobiography of Carrie M. Best*. New Glasgow, N.S.: Clarion Publishing, 1977.

Birbalsingh, Frank. *Indo Caribbean Resistance*. Toronto: TSAR Publications, 1993.

Black, Ayanna. *Voices: Canadian Writers of African Descent*. Toronto: Harper Collins Publishers Ltd., 1992.

black girls, the. *Black Girl Talk*. Toronto: Sister Vision, 1995.

Bogle, Donald. *Blacks in American Films and Television: An Illustrated Encyclopedia*. Toronto: Simon & Schuster, 1989.

Boyd, Frank S. *A Brief History of the Coloured Baptists of Nova Scotia*. Halifax: Afro Nova Scotia Enterprises, 1976.

Boyd, Herb and Allen, Robert. *Brotherman: The Odyssey of Black Men In America–An Anthology*. New York: Ballantine Books, 1996.

Boyd, Herb. *Down The Glory Road: Contributions of African Americans in United States History and Culture*. New York: Avon Books, 1995.

Braithwaite, Daniel. *The Banning of the Book "Little Black Sambo" From the Toronto Public Schools 1956*. Toronto: Overnight Typing and Copy Co., 1978.

Bramble, Linda. *Black Fugitive Slaves In Early Canada*. St. Catharines: Vanwell Publishing Limited, 1988.

Bristow, Peggy, et al. *'We're Rooted Here and They Can't Pull Us Up:' Essays in African Canadian Women's History*. Toronto: University of Toronto Press, 1994.

Brown, Rosemary. *Being Brown: A Very Public Life*. Toronto, Random House, 1989.

Camper, Carol. *Miscegenation Blues: Voices of Mixed Race Women*. Toronto: Sister Vision, 1994.

Carew, Jan. *The Fulcrums of Change: Origins of Racism in the Americas and Other Essays.* Trenton, N.J.: Africa World Press, 1988.

Carson, Clayborne, et al. *The Eyes On The Prize Civil Rights Reader.* New York: Penguin Books, 1991.

Carter, E.H. *History of the West Indian Peoples (Vol. 1-4).* Surrey, Eng.: Nelson Caribbean, 1967.

Carter, Rubin "Hurricane". *The 16th Round: From Number 1 Contender To Number 45472.* Toronto: Penguin Books, 1991.

Carter, Velma and Carter, Levero. *The Black Canadians: Their History and Contributions.* Edmonton: Reidmore Books Inc., 1989.

Chaiton, Sam and Swinton, Terry. *Lazarus and the Hurricane: The Untold Story of the Freeing of Rubin "Hurricane" Carter.* Toronto: Penguin Books, 1991.

Clairmont, Donald, et al. *The Spirit of Africville.* Halifax: Formac Publishing Company Limited, 1992.

Clarke, Austin. *Public Enemies: Police Violence and Black Youth.* Toronto: Harper Collins Publishers Ltd., 1992.

Coelho, Elizabeth. *Caribbean Students in Canadian Schools.* Toronto: Carib-Can Publishers, 1988.

Connah, Graham. *African Civilizations: Precolonial cities and states in tropical Africa: an archaeological perspective.* New York: Cambridge University Press, 1991.

Cornelius, Janet Duitsman. *When I Can Read My Title Clear: Literacy, Slavery, and Religion in the Antebellum South.* South Carolina: University of South Carolina Press, 1992.

D'Oyley, Vincent. *Innovations in Black Education in Canada.* Toronto: Umbrella Press, 1994.

Davidson, Basil. *Africa in History.* New York: Macmillan Publishing Company, 1991.

Davidson, Basil. *The African Slave Trade.* Toronto: Little Brown and Company, 1980.

Davis, Francis. *The History Of The Blues: The Roots, The Music, The People From Charley Patton to Robert Cray.* New York: Hyperion, 1995.

Davis, Miles with Troupe, Quincy. *Miles: The Autobiography.* Toronto: Simon & Schuster, 1990.

Davis, Thulani. *Malcolm X: The Great Photographs.* New York: Stewart, Tabori & Chang, 1992.

Epps, Archie. *Malcolm X: Speeches At Harvard.* New York: Paragon House, 1991.

Fernando, Jr., S.H. *The New Beats: Exploring the Music, Culture, and Attitudes of Hip-Hop.* Toronto: Anchor Books, Doubleday, 1994.

Fliegel, Seymour and MacGuire, James. *Miracle In East Harlem: The Fight For Choice In Public Education.* New York: Random House, 1993.

Foster, Cecil. *Distorted Mirror: Canada's Racist Face.* Toronto: Harper Collins Publishers Ltd., 1991.

Franklin, John H. *From Slavery to Freedom: A History of Negro Americans.* New York: Alfred A. Knopf, 1967.

Gairey, Harry. *A Black Man's Toronto 1914-1980: The Reminiscences of Harry Gairey.* Toronto: The Multicultural History Society of Ontario, 1981.

George, Nelson. *Elevating The Game: The History & Aesthetics of Black Men in Basketball.* Toronto: Simon & Schuster, 1992.

George, Nelson. *The Death of Rhythm & Blues.* Markham, Ont.: Penguin Books, 1988.

Giddings, Paula. *When and Where I Enter: The Impact of Black Women on Race and Sex in America.* New York: William Morrow, 1984.

Goss, Linda and Barnes, Marian E. *Talk That Talk: An Anthology of African-American Storytelling.* Toronto: Simon & Schuster, 1989.

Govia, Francine. *Blacks in Canada: In Search of the Promise* (A Bibliographical guide to the history of Blacks in Canada). Edmonton: Harambee Centres Canada, 1988.

Graham, Pat and Stevenson, Darryl. *The Black Experience in Manitoba: A Collection of Memories.* Winnipeg: The Winnipeg School Division No. 1, 1993.

Griffiths, John. *The Caribbean.* East Sussex: Wayland Publishers Limited, 1989.

Haley, Alex. *Roots: The Saga of an American Family.* New York: Doubleday, 1974.

Haley, Alex. *The Autobiography of Malcolm X.* New York: Ballantine Books, 1973.

Hampton, Henry and Fayer, Steve. *Voices Of Freedom: An Oral History of the Civil Rights*

Movement from the 1950s through the 1980s. Toronto: Bantam Books, 1990.

Hazzard-Gordon, Katrina. *Jookin': The Rise of Social Dance Formations in African-American Culture*. Philadelphia: Temple University Press, 1990.

Head, Wilson and Lee, E. *The Black Presence in the Canadian Mosaic*. Toronto: Ontario Human Rights Commission, 1975.

Hebdige, Dick. *Cut 'N' Mix: Culture, Identity and Caribbean Music*. New York: Routledge, 1987.

Henry, Frances. *Forgotten Canadians: The Blacks of Nova Scotia*. Don Mills, Ont.: Longman, 1973.

Henry, Frances. *The Caribbean Diaspora in Toronto: Learning to Live with Racism*. Toronto: University of Toronto Press, 1994.

Henry, Frances, et al. *The Colour of Democracy: Racism in Canadian Society*. Toronto: Harcourt Brace & Company, Canada, 1995.

Henson, Josiah. *The Life of Josiah Henson: Formerly a Slave, Now an Inhabitant of Canada*. Dresden, Ont.: Uncle Tom's Cabin Museum, 1984.

Hill, Daniel G. *The Freedom Seekers: Blacks in Early Canada*. Agincourt: Book Society of Canada Limited, 1981.

Hill, Lawrence. *Women of Vision: The Story of the Canadian Negro Women's Association 1951–1976*. Toronto: Umbrella Press, 1996.

Hill, Lawrence. *Trials And Triumphs: The Story of African-Canadians*. Toronto: Umbrella Press, 1993.

hooks, bell. *Black Looks: Race and Representation*. Toronto: Between the Lines, 1992.

hooks, bell. *Killing Rage–Ending Racism*. New York: Henry Holt And Company, 1995.

James, Carl and Shadd, Adrienne. *Talking About Difference: Encounters in Culture, Language, and Identity*. Toronto: Between The Lines, 1994.

Katz, William L. *Black Indians: A Hidden Heritage*. New York: Atheneum, 1986.

Killian, Crawford. *Go Do Some Great Thing: The Black Pioneers of British Columbia*. Vancouver: Douglas & McIntyre, 1978.

Knight, Franklin W. *The Caribbean (Second Edition): The Genesis of a Fragmented Nationalism*. New York: Oxford University Press, 1990.

Leab, Daniel J. *From Sambo to Superspade: The Black Experience in Motion Pictures*. Boston: Houghton Mifflin Company, 1975.

Lerner, Gerda. *Black Women in White America: A Documentary History*. New York: Vintage Books, 1973.

Lowenthal, D. *West Indian Societies*. London: Oxford University Press, 1972.

MacEwan, Grant. *John Ware's Cow Country*. Saskatoon: Western Producer Prairie Books, 1973.

Major, Clarence. *Juba to Jive: A Dictionary of African-American Slang*. New York: Penguin Books, 1994.

Marable, Manning. *How Capitalism Underdeveloped Black America*. Boston: South End Press, 1983.

Matas, David. *No More: The Battle Against Human Rights Violations*. Toronto: Dundurn Press, 1994.

McCrum, Robert, et al. *The Story Of English*. Boston: faber and faber, 1987.

McKague, Ormond. *Racism in Canada*. Saskatoon: Fifth House Publishers, 1991.

McKissack, Patricia and Fredrick. *The Royal Kingdoms of Ghana, Mali, and Songhay: Life in Medieval Africa*. New York: Henry Holt And Company, 1994.

McMillan, Terry, et al. *The Films Of Spike Lee: Five for Five*. New York: Stewart, Tabori & Chang, 1991.

Miller, Mark. *Boogie, Pete & The Senator: Canadian Musicians in Jazz: The Eighties*. Toronto: Nightwood Editions, 1987.

Miller, Mark. *Jazz In Canada: Fourteen Lives*. Toronto: University of Toronto Press, 1982.

Miller, Mark. *Cool Blues: Charlie Parker in Canada 1953*. London, Ont.: Nightwood Editions, 1989.

Moore, Donald. *Don Moore: An Autobiography*. Toronto: Williams-Wallace, 1985.

Murray, Jocelyn. *Cultural Atlas Of Africa*. New York: An Equinox Book, 1993.

Nederveen Pieterse, Jan. *White on Black: Images of Africa and Blacks in Western Popular*

Culture. New Haven: Yale University Press, 1992.

Oakley, Giles. *The Devil's Music: A History of the Blues*. New York: Harcourt Brace Jovanovich, 1976.

Oliver, Roland and Atmore, Anthony. *Africa Since 1800*. Cambridge: Cambridge University Press, 1994.

Oliver, Roland. *The African Experience*. London: Pimlico, 1993.

Pachai, Bridglal. *Beneath the Clouds of the Promised Land: The Survival of Nova Scotia's Blacks*. Halifax: The Black Educators Association of Nova Scotia, 1990.

Pachai, Bridglal. *Peoples of the Maritimes: Blacks*. Tantallon: Four East Publications, 1993.

Peterson, Robert. *Only the Ball Was White*. New York: McGraw-Hill, 1970.

Rogozinski, Jan. *A Brief History Of The Caribbean: From the Arawak and the Carib to the Present*. New York: Meridian, 1992.

Rohr, Janelle. *Problems of Africa — Opposing Viewpoints Series*. San Diego: Greenhaven Press, 1986.

Rose, Tricia. *Black Noise: Rap Music and Black Culture in Contemporary America*. Hanover: University Press of New England, 1994.

Ruck, Calvin. *Canada's Black Battalion No. 2 Construction 1916–1920*. Halifax, N.S.: Nimbus, 1987.

Sadlier, Rosemary. *Mary Ann Shadd: Publisher, Editor, Teacher, Lawyer, Suffragette*. Toronto: Umbrella Press, 1995.

Salley, Columbus. *The Black 100: A Ranking of the Most Influential African-Americans Past and Present*. New York: A Citadel Press Book, 1993.

Saunders, Charles R. *Sweat and Soul: The Saga of Black Boxers From the Halifax Forum to Caesar's Palace*. Westphal and Hantsport, Nova Scotia, 1990.

Shapson, Stan and D'Oyley, Vincent. *Bilingual and Multicultural Education: Canadian Perspectives*. Clevedon, England: Multilingual Matters Ltd., 1984.

Shepard, R. Bruce. *Deemed Unsuitable*. Toronto: Umbrella Press, 1996.

Smith, Jessie C. *Black Firsts: 2,000 Years of Extraordinary Achievement*. Detroit: Visible Ink Press, 1994.

Smith, Jessie C. *Notable Black American Women*. Detroit: Gale Research, 1992.

Solomon, R. Patrick. *Black Resistance in High School: Forging a Separatist Culture*. Albany: State University of New York Press, 1992.

Spray, W.A. *The Blacks in New Brunswick*. Fredericton: Brunswick Press, 1972.

Susman, Warren I. *Culture as History: The Transformation of American Society in the Twentieth Century*. New York: Pantheon, 1984.

Talbot, Carol. *Growing Up Black in Canada*. Toronto: Williams-Wallace, 1984.

Ullman, Victor. *Look to the North Star: A Life of William King*. Toronto: Umbrella Press, 1969 rev. ed. 1994.

Walker, James. *The Black Loyalists: The Search for a Promised Land*. New York: Africana Publishing Company, 1976.

Walker, James. *Racial Discrimination In Canada: The Black Experience*. Ottawa: Canadian Historical Association, 1985.

Walker, James. *The West Indians In Canada*. Ottawa: Canadian Historical Association, 1984.

Wallace, Michele. *Black Popular Culture*. Seattle: Bay Press, 1992.

West, Cornel. *Race Matters*. New York: Vintage Books, 1994.

Williams, Eric. *Capitalism and Slavery*. London: Andre Deutsch Limited, 1993.

Williams, Eric. *From Columbus to Castro: The History of the Caribbean*. New York: Vintage Books, 1984.

Williams, Juan. *Eyes on the Prize: America's Civil Rights Years, 1954-1965*. New York: Vinking, 1987.

Winks, Robin. *The Blacks in Canada: A History*. Montreal: McGill-Queens University Press, 1971.

Woodson, Carter G. *The Mis-Education of the Negro*. 1933. Reprint. Trenton, N.J.: African World Press, Inc., 1990.

Credits

Grateful acknowledgement is made for the kind permission to include the illustrations in the book.

13 Canapress Photo Service / H. Deryk; 14 Canapress Photo Service / Dan Callis; 21 Mike Sturk / *Calgary Herald*; 23 UPI / Bettman 25 Pierre Verhoeff Fotographie; 28 Don Rooke; 35 Urban Alliance on Race Relations; 39 McCord Museum of Canadian History; 40 LEFT, North American Black Historical Museum; right, Ontario Black History Society (OBHS); 45 Hulton Deutsch; 47 National Gallery of Canada, Ottawa; 48 Mary Evans Picture Gallery; 49 The Black Cultural Centre for Nova Scotia; 52 OBHS; 60 OBHS; 61 TOP, OBHS; BOTTOM OBHS; 63 Public Archives of Canada; 64 OBHS; 65 TOP LEFT, OBHS; TOP RIGHT, OBHS; BOTTOM OBHS; 66 Raleigh Township Centennial Museum; 67 OBHS; 68 Raleigh Township Centennial Museum; 71 Metropolitan Toronto Library Board; 73 Metropolitan Toronto Library Board; 74 OBHS; 75 OBHS; 79 Metropolitan Toronto Library Board; 84 Pierre Verhoeff Fotographie; 87 Corbis - Bettman; 89 OBHS; 94 The Beaton Institute / University College of Cape Breton; 96 Dalhousie University; 97 Glenbow Archives; 99 Photographs and Prints Division, Schomberg Center for Research in Black Culture, The New York Public Library, Astor, Lenox and Tilden Foundations; 101 Corbis - Bettman; 104 Oklahoma Historical Society; 111 Provincial Archives of British Columbia, HP 72553; 113 Glenbow Archives; 114 E. Lockhart Hemmings; 118 The Winnipeg School Division No. 1; 121 The Black Cultural Centre for Nova Scotia; 122 Public Archives of Nova Scotia, Bob Brooks; 125 TOP, OBHS; BOTTOM, The Black Cultural Centre for Nova Scotia; 128 Schomberg Center for Research in Black Culture, The New York Public Library; 136 The Black Cultural Centre of Nova Scotia; 139 The Black Cultural Centre of Nova Scotia; 140 OBHS;

146 The Archie Alleyne Collection; 147 Canapress Photo Service; 149 Share newspaper; 152 Daniel G. Hill; 155 BOTH, The Black Cultural Centre of Nova Scotia; 156 OBHS; 157 BOTH, William Humber; 159 Photograph by Harris & Ewing, Collection of the Supreme Court of the United States; Canapress Photo Service; 160-62 Conversation among Rosa Parks, Martin Luther King, Jr., and E.D. Nixon from *Eyes On The Prize*, video; 163 Printed by permission of the Norman Rockwell Family Trust Copyright © 1964 the Norman Rockwell Family Trust; 165 Canapress Photo Service; 166 Canapress Photo Service; 167 OBHS; 168 OBHS; 169 The Archie Alleyne Collection; 170 Sheldon Taylor; 174 LEFT, Al Gilbert, FRPS, and Regal Recordings Limited; RIGHT, Public Archives of Nova Scotia; 175 Mrs. Donald Moore; 177 OBHS; 192 OBHS; 196 L. Braithwaite; 197 High Commission for South Africa; 198 Howard McCurdy; 199 Ontario Ministry of Tourism; 200 Schomberg Center for Research in Black Culture, The New York Public Library; 204 AP / Wide World Photos; 209 Canapress Photo Service; 219 UPI / Bettman; 221 Anne Cools; 224 Jules Elder; 227 LEFT Rosemary Brown; RIGHT, Emery Barnes; 229 Mrs. W. Head; 231 Carrie Best; 234 Canapress Photo Service / Remiorz; 241 Rita Cox; 245 Rubin Carter; 251 LEFT, Lincoln Alexander / Peter Caton, Gerald Campbell Studios; RIGHT, Jean Augustine; 253 Sylvia Sweeney; 254 TOP, Attic Records; BOTTOM, Penguin Books, Canada; 255 TOP, Ballet British Columbia / Cylla von Tiedmann; BOTTOM, Patrick A. Nichols / EMI; 256 TOP, Basketball Canada; BOTTOM, Reuters / Wolfgang Rattay / Archive Photos; 257 Toronto Raptors Basketball Club; Toronto Blue Jays Baseball Club; 261-62 Photos courtesy of Pride Newspaper; 264 Atlantic Records; 265 National Film Board of Canada; 268 Canapress Photo Service / Steve Halber.